This book provides the first full account of the Italian nobility in the post-unification era, from the height of the Risorgimento to the period following World War I. It challenges recent scholarship which has stressed the rapid fusion of old and new elites in Italy, and the marginality of the nobility after 1861. Instead it highlights the continuing economic strength, social power, and political influence of Italy's most prominent regional aristocracy.

In Piedmont the nobles developed more indirect forms of influence that reflected not only their wealth and prestige, but also a hunger for leadership based on something older than constitutions or electoral politics. They remain a largely separate group within local society, distinguished by their attachment to the values of lineage, military service, landownership, and social exclusivity. This aristocratic exclusivity and influence survived the agricultural depression of the nineteenth century before succumbing finally to the devastating effects of World War I. After 1918, the surviving noble families abandoned finally their old way of life and merged with Italy's industrial elites.

CAMBRIDGE STUDIES IN ITALIAN HISTORY AND CULTURE

ARISTOCRATS IN BOURGEOIS ITALY

CAMBRIDGE STUDIES IN ITALIAN HISTORY AND CULTURE

———

Edited by GIGLIOLA FRAGNITO, Università degli Studi, Parma
CESARE MOZZARELLI, Università Cattolica del Sacro Cuore, Milan
ROBERT ORESKO, Institute of Historical Research, University of London
and GEOFFREY SYMCOX, University of California, Los Angeles

This series comprises monographs and a variety of collaborative volumes, including translated works, which concentrate on the period of Italian history from late medieval times up to the Risorgimento. The editors aim to stimulate scholarly debate over a range of issues which have not hitherto received, in English, the attention they deserve. As it develops, the series will emphasize the interest and vigour of current international debates on this central period of Italian history and the persistent influence of Italian culture on the rest of Europe.

For a list of titles in the series, see end of book

ARISTOCRATS IN BOURGEOIS ITALY

ITALY

THE PIEDMONTESE NOBILITY, 1861–1930

ANTHONY L. CARDOZA

Loyola University of Chicago

CAMBRIDGE
UNIVERSITY PRESS

PUBLISHED BY THE PRESS SYNDICATE OF THE UNIVERSITY OF CAMBRIDGE
The Pitt Building, Trumpington Street, Cambridge, United Kingdom

CAMBRIDGE UNIVERSITY PRESS
The Edinburgh Building, Cambridge CB2 2RU, UK
40 West 20th Street, New York NY 10011–4211, USA
477 Williamstown Road, Port Melbourne, VIC 3207, Australia
Ruiz de Alarcón 13, 28014 Madrid, Spain
Dock House, The Waterfront, Cape Town 8001, South Africa

http://www.cambridge.org

First published 1997
First paperback edition 2002

Typeface Bembo 10/11½ pt.

A catalogue record for this book is available from the British Library

Library of Congress Cataloguing in Publication data
Cardoza, Anthony L., 1947–
Aristocrats in Bourgeois Italy: the Piedmontese nobility, 1861–1930 / Anthony L. Cardoza /
p.   cm. – (Cambridge studies in Italian history and culture)
Includes bibliographical references and index.
ISBN 0 521 59303 4
1. Nobility – Italy – Piemonte – History.
2. Piemonte (Italy) – History.   3. Nobility – Italy – Piemonte – Political activity.
4. Nobility – Italy – Piemonte – Economic conditions.
5. Elite (Social sciences) – Italy – Piemonte.
I. Title.   II. Series.
HT653.I8C35   1997
305.5′223′09451–dc21   97-1848   CIP

ISBN 0 521 59303 4 hardback
ISBN 0 521 52229 3 paperback

FOR CATHERINE AND MICHAEL

CONTENTS

TABLES

ACKNOWLEDGMENTS

A great many individuals and institutions helped me in the preparation of this book. A special thanks goes to Arno J. Mayer of Princeton University. The questions he posed in his own scholarship helped inspire me to study the role of aristocrats in modern Italy, while his unstinting interest and encouragement of my work have helped to sustain me over the long years of research and writing.

Most of the research for this book was carried out in Turin, Italy, between 1987 and 1989. During my frequent visits to that city, I benefited immensely from the exceptional hospitality and generosity of Giovanni Levi and his wife Luisa Accati, whose beautiful house in the foothills of Turin became my home away from home. Professor Levi not only provided me with an invaluable introduction to the academic and research institutions of the city, but also made critical suggestions that fundamentally shaped the trajectory of my research. Outside Turin, I have profited greatly from the friendship and stimulating discussions with Raffaele Romanelli of the European University Institute in Florence and Alberto Banti of the University of Pisa. In addition, my warmest thanks are due to Professor Mayer, Alexander DeGrand of North Carolina State University, Marion Miller of the University of Illinois Chicago, Geoffrey Symcox of the University of California at Los Angeles, and Cesare Mozzarelli of the Università Cattolica del Sacro Cuore of Milan who read earlier drafts of the manuscript.

A number of institutions have been most cooperative. First and foremost, I must express my gratitude to Dr. Isabella Massabò Ricci and her staff at the Archivio di Stato di Torino for their knowledge, patience, and assistance in the face of my relentless quest for documents. Dr. Barbara Bertini, in particular, greatly facilitated my research in the largely unexplored probate records of Turin. My thanks are also due to Dr. Guido Gentile of the Sovraintendenza Archivistica and to the staffs of the Archivio Comunale di Torino, the Biblioteca Nazionale di

Torino, the Biblioteca Comunale, the Biblioteca Provinciale, and the Biblioteca Reale. Closer to home, I must record my gratitude to Loyola University of Chicago for the paid leaves of absence in 1987 and 1991 that allowed me to do much of the research and initial writing on this book.

Both my time and my research were enriched by the friendship and assistance of a few old-line Piedmontese families who took an interest in my work. Especially helpful were Lodovico and Gabriella Salvi del Pero and Gregorio and Nicoletta De Siebert who took me into their homes and provided me with invaluable insights and introductions. Filippo Beraudo di Pralormo, Admiral Ernesto Balbo Bertone di Sambuy, and Maria Balbiano di Aramengo kindly permitted me to consult their family papers, while Gustavo Figarolo di Gropello, Emilio Avogadro di Cerrione, and Maria Beraudo di Pralormo (née Incisa della Rocchetta) allowed me to see unpublished memoirs from their families' archives.

A final word of appreciation goes to my wife Catherine Mardikes and our son Michael who have enormously enriched my life during the period of writing. This book is dedicated to them.

INTRODUCTION

This study examines the evolution of aristocratic identities and roles in an ostensibly post-aristocratic society, namely that of Italy from the middle of the nineteenth century to the decade following World War I. As such, it aspires to contribute not only to our understanding of traditional elites, but also to the ongoing scholarly discussion of the social contours and characteristics of the Italian bourgeoisie at its upper reaches. The changing relations between old aristocratic and new bourgeois elites has long been viewed as one of the central themes in the larger processes of modernization in Europe. Indeed, historians have used this relationship to explain England's extraordinary political stability (and more recently its industrial decline), Germany's authoritarian path to modernity, the failure of liberal polity in Italy, and the crisis of the late Czarist regime in Russia.

Most scholars would agree that at some time between the early nineteenth century and the end of World War II the aristocracies and upper middle classes of Europe became so intertwined and intermarried that they no longer functioned as separate groups and effectively merged into a single upper class. There has been considerably less agreement, however, on the pace, mechanisms, terms, and consequences of this fusion of aristocracy and bourgeoisie. Older approaches strongly influenced by the French revolutionary experience have either stressed the overwhelming political triumph of the capitalist bourgeoisie or else argued that the old nobility lost its distinctiveness and disappeared into the ranks of a new class of propertied notables in the course of the nineteenth century. Developments in central Europe have shaped a second approach that emphasizes the relative weakness of the middle classes and the resilience of aristocratic elements who blocked or distorted democratic advances by dominating both politics and society into the twentieth century. The English experience has suggested a third vision of aristocratic–bourgeois relations as a mutually beneficial compromise or what Perry Anderson has called a "deliberate, systematized symbiosis" in which the landed elite remained the senior partner.

Despite the interpretive weight that has been attached to relations between new and old elites, until quite recently European nobilities, with the exceptions of the English and Russians, have remained relatively uncharted territory in the modern era.[1] Both Marxist and liberal historiographical traditions as well as newer theories of modernization led historians to focus on the great agents of change in the nineteenth century. Accordingly, the rise of the factory system, the growth of cities, the formation of the working class, and middle-class triumphs provided the main themes of scholarly research and debate. Nor did the explosion of social historical research initially alter this picture, since it was devoted chiefly to illuminating the lives of the lower classes.

As Arno Mayer argued in his *Persistence of the Old Regime*, however, concentration on the agents of modernization results in a neglect of those forces of tradition and continuity that, in his view, continued to shape and condition all aspects of European society at least until World War I.[2] Such neglect has been strikingly evident in the case of the nobility in Italy. While the past decade and a half have seen a number of new works on the Italian middle classes in the nineteenth century, virtually all studies of the local nobilities have stopped with the French Revolution.[3] Aristocrats appear in the historical literature on Italy after 1815, but chiefly as exceptional individuals in an essentially bourgeois drama. As a social group, the old titled elites have been left largely to genealogists, novelists, and the society pages of the popular press.

What little work has been done on the role of noble groups in Italian

---

[1] On the limits of the work done on the European nobility, Dominic Lieven has observed that "many German historians and social scientists share with some of their European and more of their North American peers the conviction that in the modern world aristocracy is an irrelevant and politically suspect area of study, to which only scholars tainted by social snobbery and attracted by a love for superficial glitter will dedicate themselves." See *The Aristocracy in Europe*, pp. xix–xx. For the most recent work on the British aristocracy, see Cannadine, *The Decline and Fall of the British Aristocracy*. On the Russian case, see Manning, *The Crisis of the Old Order in Russia*, Hamburg, *Politics of the Russian Nobility*, and Becker, *Nobility and Privilege in Late Imperial Russia*.

[2] Mayer, *The Persistence of the Old Regime*.

[3] Romanelli, "Political Debate, Social History, and the Italian *Borghesia*," pp. 717–39 provides the most recent survey of the work done on the Italian middle classes. For the most recent and most complete study of Italy's middle classes in the nineteenth century, see Banti's *Storia della borghesia italiana*. For the literature on the Italian nobility in the early modern period, see Visceglia (ed.), *Signori, patrizi, cavalieri nell'età moderna*, pp. v–xxxiii. The paucity of scholarship on the Italian nobility in the nineteenth century is clearly evident in Petersen's survey "Der italienische Adel von 1861 bis 1946."

society has grown out of the lively debate on the supposed weaknesses and peculiarities of Italy's bourgeoisie. Older Marxist approaches closely associated with the writings of Antonio Gramsci and Emilio Sereni underscore both the backwardness of the middle classes and their predisposition to compromise with "semi-feudal" aristocratic and landowning elements during the Risorgimento. The result, in their view, was a socially conservative power bloc that promoted parliamentary transformism, economic protection, and increasingly authoritarian domestic policies which paved the way to Fascism.[4]

Recently, this interpretation has come under heavy attack on both theoretical and empirical grounds. Raffaele Romanelli, for one, has argued that the concept of feudal vestiges is a holdover from political and ideological debates of the nineteenth century and rests upon German sociological models that simply do not fit the Italian situation.[5] At the same time, a new body of revisionist scholarship has challenged the picture of bourgeois subordination in favor of one that emphasizes the vitality of the middle classes and the corresponding marginality and decorative impotence of old aristocratic groups. According to this view, the varied and checkered nobilities in Italy lacked the necessary monarchical, caste, and landed traditions of their German and British counterparts to survive for long as autonomous and influential forces in the new nation state that emerged after 1861. Once legal distinctions between the nobility and commoners had disappeared, nobles suffered a crisis of identity and either declined rapidly or else fused into a larger and more heterogeneous class of landed proprietors. The results of this revisionist scholarship have led to the conclusion that although aristocratic values continued to model the path of upward mobility for the middle classes, "nobility as such did *not* play an important role in the Italian nineteenth century social structure, because it did not constitute a well-defined group in itself, due to its regional more than national status."[6]

---

[4] See Sereni, *Il capitalismo nelle campagne (1860–1900)* and *La questione agraria*; for Gramsci's views, see Quintin Hoare and Geoffrey Nowell Smith (eds.), *Selections from the Prison Notebooks of Antonio Gramsci* (New York 1971).

[5] Romanelli, "Political Debate, Social History, and the Italian *Borghesia*," pp. 717–721.

[6] Romanelli, "In search of an Italian bourgeoisie: trends in social history," paper presented to Round Table n. 1 "The Bourgeoisie. Structures and Cultures in 19th Century Europe" of the 18th International Congress of Historical Sciences, Montreal, September 1995, p. 9. The principal revisionist works are Rumi, "La politica nobiliare del Regno d'Italia 1861–1946", Banti, "Note sulle nobiltà nell'Italia dell'Ottocento"; Di Gregorio, "Nobiltà e nobilitazione in Sicilia"; Jocteau, "Un censimento della nobiltà italiana", Romanelli, "La nobiltà nella costituzione dell'Italia contemporanea."

The fate of traditional elites has been attributed in part to the characteristics they inherited from the past. Various scholars have stressed, for instance, how important segments of the Italian nobility were, in fact, patrician aristocrats with strong urban, commercial, and republican rather than feudal, monarchical traditions. Even before the French Revolution, these patriciates defined themselves less in legal than economic terms, and were largely open to the more successful members of the propertied middle classes.[7] The political and legal reforms of the Napoleonic Era greatly accelerated the processes of social osmosis, especially in the south where the abolition of feudal entails greatly accelerated the decline of the old Neapolitan nobility and its coalescing with a new class of bourgeois *galantuomini*.[8]

Amalgamation continued apace in the decades after 1815 as the growth of a wealthy bourgeois propertied class and the resultant lure of large dowries and financial assistance led increasing numbers of nobles into marriages with non-noble families. Politically, aristocratic–bourgeois fusion found its highest expression in the middle decades of the century in the moderate liberal party that guided the campaign for national unification and then forged a new governmental order based on property rather than birth or privilege. The story of aristocratic decline and fusion typically concludes with the exodus of the old elites from both public life and the countryside in the wake of electoral reforms and agricultural depression in the last decades of the nineteenth century. As a separate and distinct component of the Italian upper classes, the nobility disappears completely from the historical literature on the period after the 1880s.[9]

While these revisionist historians have greatly enriched our understanding of Italy's middle classes, in their treatment of the old nobilities, they have relied largely on legalistic and positional notions of social formation and political power. As a result, they have tended to underestimate the role of cultural values, symbolic practices, and more specifically those informal mechanisms of prestige and influence that

---

[7] See Meriggi, "La borghesia italiana," pp. 180–182; Romanelli, "Political Debate, Social History, and the Italian *Borghesia*," pp. 726–727. For a regional case in point, see Giacomelli, "La dinamica della nobiltà bolognese," pp. 55–112.

[8] Pasquale Villani has written that with the elimination of "baronial privileges and feudal bonds, there was no real difference between nobility and haute bourgeoisie and the two classes tended to merge." See Villani, "Ricerche sulla proprietà fondiaria," pp. 240–241, as well as Lyttelton, "Landlords, Peasants, and the Limits of Liberalism," pp. 120–121; Davis, "The Napoleonic Era in Southern Italy," pp. 133–148; Barbagli, *Sotto lo stesso tetto*, p. 514. For a general discussion of the French Revolution's impact on the Italian peninsula, see Capra, "Nobili, notabili, elites," pp. 12–42.

[9] Banti, "I proprietari terrieri nell'Italia centro-settentrionale," pp. 45–103.

serve to perpetuate consensual hierarchies and inequalities. In the process, they wind up resuscitating, at least implicitly, an old-fashioned and rather teleological vision of nineteenth-century developments as the inexorable triumph of the bourgeoisie and decline of the aristocracy.

Most of the arguments for the fusion of old and new elites, in fact, focus on four major developments: the juridical reforms that eliminated the legally privileged status of old nobles, the growth of non-noble land-ownership, the new forms of political collaboration based on propertied status and gradual change, and the shrinking numbers of nobles within the political institutions of the new national state.[10] As John Davis has observed, however, one should not infer changes in cultural and social values and practices from changes in economic behavior and political organization. Paolo Macry's study of Neapolitan patrician families, for instance, shows how old elites could come to terms with economic changes without losing their sense of caste or their aristocratic preten-sions.[11] Even the most outspoken proponents of aristocratic marginality concede that "the actual paths of this process of osmosis remain to be investigated in depth at the level of matrimonial alliances, social net-works, and elite associational life."[12]

It is in this context that my work addresses a number of basic ques-tions: What did it mean to be a noble in the nineteenth century and did individual nobles continue to constitute a distinctive and self-conscious nobility? To what extent and in what ways did they remain a ruling status group exercising social, cultural, and political sway on the society as a whole? More specifically, to what degree and at what levels did nobles continue to share a common moral ethos? What was the fre-quency and nature of social contacts and relationships within the nobility? In what settings and how often did aristocrats interact with new men from commerce, finance, and industry? How successful were nobles in adapting to an increasingly industrialized society and demo-cratic polity, and what did they sacrifice in the process? In order to provide answers to these questions, I have explored changes and conti-nuities in political roles, wealth, economic behavior, educational and professional preferences, residential and marriage patterns, and processes

---

[10] The principal exception to this generalization is the recent work on elite associational life. See, for example, the issue of *Quaderni Storici* devoted to the theme of "Elites e associazioni nell'Italia dell'Ottocento," 77: n. 2 (August 1991), and Meriggi, *Milano borghese.*

[11] Macry, *Ottocento.* For Davis's comments, see his essay, "Remapping Italy's Path," p. 301.

[12] Banti, "I proprietari terrieri," pp. 56–57. For Banti's most recent views on the role of the nobility in Liberal Italy, see his "Note sulle nobiltà," pp. 13–27.

of social assimilation and exclusion within a prominent regional aristocracy over the course of the nineteenth and early twentieth centuries.

A regional study offers both advantages and limitations as an approach
to the issues of aristocratic survival and influence in the Italian setting.
On the one hand, it provides a social group that is sufficiently circum-
scribed geographically and numerically to allow the type of comprehensive treatment that would be inconceivable at the national level. The
tangled history of the Italian peninsula greatly accentuates the difficulties
inherent in a national study. At the end of the eighteenth century there
really was no cohesive Italian nobility. The geography, history, and the
economic features of the various states produced a number of nobilities
that "differed from one another in organization, in custom and taste, in
the wealth they possessed, and in the power they exercised."[13] On the
other hand, this enormous variety of circumstances necessarily limits the
scope of the generalizations that can be made on the basis of a single
region. Indeed, quite different conclusions can be drawn from the study
of different regional nobilities.[14]

Thus, I have chosen to focus on the Piedmontese nobility not because
they were somehow typical or representative of all titled elites on the
peninsula, but rather because of the prominent and influential role they
played in the life of the country in the nineteenth century. The region of
Piedmont, situated in the northwest corner of Italy, lends itself to a local
study of aristocracy for a variety of reasons. Over the centuries, the nobility's close association with the ruling House of Savoy and their strong
martial traditions gave them a high degree of cohesion and continuity
that helped them adjust to the loss of privileged status and enhanced
their role in the unification of the Italian peninsula in the middle of the
nineteenth century. Headed by Count Camillo Benso di Cavour, they
contributed key ideas, models, and leadership to the campaign that successfully brought the new national state into existence in 1861. After
unification the Piedmontese nobles continued to account for more
parliamentary deputies, senators, statesmen, and army officers than any
of the other old titled elites. At the same time, Turin, the capital city of
Piedmont, began to emerge as one of the most dynamic business centers
of Italy at the end of the nineteenth century. As a result, the city offers
an ideal setting for exploring the impact of industrial development and
urbanization on aristocratic status, comportment, and values.

---

[13] Roberts, "Lombardy," p. 60.
[14] On the difficulties of making national generalizations on the basis of regional experiences, see Romanelli, "La nobiltà nella costituzione dell'Italia contemporanea,"
pp. 11–12, paper delivered to the conference, Anciennes et nouvelles aristocraties,
de 1880 à nos jours, Toulouse, France, September 21–24, 1994.

In my examination of the Piedmontese nobility, I have attempted to avoid the limitations of much of the literature on elites in Italy which has either adopted ideal types that tend to mask the complexity of social identities or else generalized on the basis of the experiences of a single prominent, but exceptional individual or family.[15] Accordingly, I have utilized both quantitative and qualitative source materials to examine the attitudes and practices of a comparatively large body of aristocratic families. This book rests, first and foremost, on an exhaustive exploration of all surviving probate records in Turin from unification to World War I. These records have yielded an abundance of information not only on the changing structure and distribution of aristocratic and large bourgeois fortunes, but also on family networks, inheritance strategies, patterns of landownership, and investment practices. Probate materials have been supplemented by a wide range of other primary sources that include genealogies, luxury tax records, electoral and urban property owners' rolls, private school class rosters, as well as the membership lists of corporate boards, professional societies, civic, cultural, and charitable organizations, and local gentlemen's clubs. With the assistance of the state archivists in Turin and a few of the surviving old-line families, I have also consulted a large number of family archives. In addition to legal and financial records, these archives include some private correspondence that illuminate more intimate aspects of aristocratic family life and values.

The predominantly quantitative approach I have taken in this book has been largely dictated by the taciturn character of the Piedmontese nobility. Unlike their French or British counterparts, they left virtually no published memoirs or diaries that might have shed light on how they saw themselves or experienced the great challenges and problems that confronted them in the post-1861 era. The very few memoirs that I did locate were private documents written for the immediate family. In the absence of an impressionistic literature, I have tried to interpret values and attitudes from the collective practices and actions of large numbers of aristocratic families.

As Dominic Lieven has recently written, "blurred definitions and

---

[15] For an example of the former, see Sereni, *La questione agraria*, pp. 76–99. There have been a number of excellent studies of individual aristocratic families. See, for instance, Romeo, *Cavour e il suo tempo*; Pescosolido, *Terra e nobiltà*; Biagioli, "Vicende e fortuna di Ricasoli imprenditore," pp. 77–102; Girelli, *Le terre dei Chigi*; Coppini, "Aristocrazia e finanza in Toscana," pp. 297–332; Petrusewicz, *Latifondo*; Massa Piergiovanni, *I Duchi di Galliera*; Romanelli, "Famiglia e patrimonio nei comportamenti della nobiltà borghese dell'Ottocento," 9–27. The new book by Montroni, *Gli uomini del Re*; attempts to provide a broader treatment of the nobility, but much of its argument rests on examples drawn from only a few families.

unclear dividing lines" are inevitable in virtually any study of Europe's aristocracies.[16] The case of Piedmont is certainly no exception. Here a wide range of groups could advance some legal claim to noble status in the nineteenth century. Moreover, there was no necessary correspondence between titles and wealth or status in Piedmont, since some of the oldest, richest, and most prestigious families could be found in the ranks of the lesser titles. Consequently, I have not attempted to provide a formal legalistic definition of nobility. Instead I have relied on a more fluid sociological concept that involves not only the possession of hereditary titles, but also a set of social and economic values and practices that collectively distinguished aristocratic families from other segments of the Piedmontese propertied classes.

In a similar vein, the terms aristocratic, noble, blue blood, old-line, and titled have been used interchangeably for stylistic variety to describe the subjects of this book. I have given the most attention to a core group of families who already possessed titles and fiefs and played leading roles in the Savoyard state and army in the seventeenth and eighteenth centuries. I have done so because it was these families who continued to enjoy the greatest wealth, prestige, and influence after 1848 and who set the standards and tone for the nobility as a whole up to the Great War. As a group, this titled elite conformed to Benedict Anderson's description of traditional aristocracies as pre-bourgeois social formations whose concrete, rather than imagined, solidarities were the products of kinship, friendship, and personal acquaintance.[17]

The portrait of the Piedmontese aristocracy that emerges from my study challenges those interpretations that have stressed the rapid fusion of old and new elites and the resultant marginal importance of nobilities in Liberal Italy. In the case of Piedmont, the pace of aristocratic decline was slower and the extent of fusion with newer business, professional, and bureaucratic elites less complete than recent scholarship has suggested. Here dominance was followed not so much by decadence and disappearance as by the development of more indirect forms of aristocratic influence that exploited a hunger for leadership based on something older and deeper than abstract principles or electoral politics. The enduring importance of a nobility of pedigree and patent in public life resulted less from social accommodation with new elites than from the appropriation of new economic arrangements and ostensibly bourgeois forms of sociability based on statutory institutions and voluntary access to bolster their wealth as well as their traditional way of life. Far from

---

[16] Lieven, *The Aristocracy in Europe*, p. xiv.
[17] Anderson, *Imagined Communities*, pp. 76–77.

fusing with other elements of the propertied classes, Piedmontese nobles remained a largely separate and distinct group within local upper-class society at least up to World War I, distinguished by their attachment to the values of lineage, military service, landownership, endogamy, patriarchy, and social exclusivity. Distinctive patterns of investment, marriage, profession, residence, and life-style demonstrate that the social gulf separating old-line aristocrats from other segments of the propertied classes in Piedmont remained pronounced, and may well have actually widened in the decades prior to 1914.

In this respect, the case of aristocratic persistence in Piedmont also diverges from Arno Mayer's model of *ancien régime* elites who diversified their presence, modernized their influence, and spread their cultural model by selectively coopting and assimilating new men from the worlds of finance, industry, and the professions. Piedmont's old-line titled families responded to the challenges of civil equality and parliamentary politics by closing ranks socially; they showed relatively little interest in absorbing elements of the bourgeoisie or winning their support for an aristocratic forms of behavior. For their part, Turin's business elites showed less and less of an inclination to imitate aristocratic values, let alone assimilate into or seek the social acceptance of the aristocracy in the last decades preceding World War I. While a few prominent industrial and banking families continued to pursue hereditary titles of nobility, most wealthy non-nobles seemed increasingly content to remain within their own social circles and to follow a "bourgeois" way of life. This situation suggests an alternative vision of upper-class relations to the view that in Italy there existed a contrast between those regions with a strong aristocracy and a subordinate bourgeoisie and those where the bourgeoisie emancipated itself. In Piedmont aristocratic prestige co-existed with bourgeois autonomy so that upper-class social relations, much as in pre-war Germany, were characterized by the presence of two parallel but separate elites before 1914.[18]

The experience of the aristocracy in the heartland of the "industrial triangle" before World War I certainly lends credence to the view that a status system distrustful of private enterprise and based less on wealth than older forms of social distinction may well have continued to exercise a powerful and widespread hold on Italian society into the early twentieth century.[19] In this context, enduring aristocratic exclusivity

---

[18] Lyttelton, "The middle classes in Liberal Italy," p. 231. On the issue of "bourgeois autonomy" in Germany, see Kaelble, "Borghesia francese e borghesia tedesca. 1870–1914," pp. 127–160 and Augustine-Perez, "Very wealthy businessmen in imperial Germany," pp. 299–321.

[19] Lyttelton, "The middle classes in Liberal Italy," pp. 227–228.

and influence both reflected and helped to perpetuate a more diffuse culture of deference, traditional patronage, and territorial parochialism, a culture that still conditioned in subtle but significant ways social relations and political allegiances in pre-war Piedmont.

At the same time, a set of special circumstances contributed to the capacity of Piedmontese aristocratic families to resist social fusion. To begin with, they had constituted Italy's only feudal, martial, service nobility, which imbued them with a stronger set of pre-bourgeois values and traditions than most of their counterparts on the peninsula. Accordingly, the cultural ideal of the proud and aloof "cavalier and man of honor," who disdains commerce and trade, flourished among them, buttressing their strong sense of hierarchy and separateness from the rest of society. Piedmontese nobles, much like the Prussian Junkers, also benefited from the capitalist transformation of their country estates, which ironically made it easier for them to perpetuate a view of society based on status and obligation. Most titled families continued to enjoy a level of wealth sufficient to sustain a dignified, if not opulent, standard of living without recourse to intermarriage with the new rich or demeaning involvement in trade and industry.

The longstanding ties of the nobility in Piedmont to the House of Savoy and the state apparatus of the Kingdom of Sardinia further paralleled the situation of the Prussian Junkers, providing local titled families with a host of advantages not shared by other aristocratic groups on the Italian peninsula. From the outset, the allegiance and service of Piedmontese nobles to a single dynastic family, for instance, gave them a degree of continuity and cohesion as well as a tradition of exercising state power that contrasted sharply with the more polyglot noble groups in Lombardy and the Kingdom of Naples which were the accretions of successive waves of foreign rulers. More importantly, their special relationship with the dynasty that unified Italy and became the national monarchy after 1861 assured the old titled elite of Piedmont a secure place in the army and civil service of the new state and thus another way of perpetuating caste traditions. These conditions were largely absent in the case of other regional nobilities who either lacked a state of their own or, worse yet, had supported regimes and dynasties that opposed unification and had fallen from power between 1859 and 1870.[20] The enduring prominence and active presence of the royal family in Piedmontese society helped mightily to legitimize and perpe-

---

[20] On the weaknesses and shortcomings of the regional nobilities in the nineteenth century, see Meriggi, "La borghesia italiana," pp. 167–168.

tuate traditional social hierarchies in which old-line aristocrats still occupied a preeminent position of leadership and prestige.

Such advantages, however, should not lead automatically to the conclusion that the experience of Piedmontese nobility is simply the exception that proves the rule of aristocratic marginality in nineteenth-century Italy. On the contrary, new work on southern titled elites suggests that many attitudes and practices of Piedmontese aristocratic families were echoed elsewhere on the Italian peninsula. In Naples, for instance, nobles remained far and away the wealthiest social group prior to the Great War, while in certain provinces of the south a shrinking group of titled families actually increased their share of the wealth in the late nineteenth century. Moreover, much like their Piedmontese counterparts, Neapolitan nobles displayed a pattern of increasing social rigidification and exclusivity after 1860 that found expression in high levels of endogamy, separate forms of sociability, and life styles. Their wealth and distinctive identity permitted southern nobles to conserve a notable prestige and influence in public life into the new century.[21]

Finally, the experience of Piedmontese aristocrats underscores the importance of World War I as the great watershed in the history of Italy's traditional elites. Pierre Bourdieu has observed how strategies of reconversion designed to safeguard or improve family or individual positions in social space become especially important "at a stage in the evolution of class societies in which one can conserve only by changing – to change so as to conserve."[22] For the old titled families of Piedmont, World War I and its aftermath constituted just such a stage. Indeed, the war proved to be a considerably more pivotal event than the agricultural depression of the late nineteenth century in the transformation of the local aristocracy. Its consequences posed formidable new problems and challenges that few old families were able to surmount without substantial changes in attitude and behavior. In this regard, the very practices that contributed so much to the cohesion and prestige of aristocrats in Piedmont before 1914 – reliance on caste-like exclusivity, landownership, and military service, together with a decided reluctance to enter the board rooms of industry and high finance – proved to be handicaps after 1918 as they delayed social accommodation with new entrepreneurial elites and thus limited the role of noble families in the greatly transformed society that emerged from the Great War. Much as elsewhere in Europe, the war and its aftermath seriously eroded the material foundations of the old aristocratic way of life at the same time

[21] For these arguments, see Montroni, *Gli uomini del Re.*
[22] Bourdieu, *Distinction*, p. 157.

that they undermined the prestige and glamour associated with the officers' corps and military service. As a result, when the economic pressures for adaptation greatly intensified in the inter-war decades,
accommodation tended to take place in Piedmont on terms that were
relatively unfavorable to titled families. Those nobles, who avoided
decline and disappearance by entering the worlds of business and
finance, did so rather late and thus wound up less as partners and equals
than as employees of the new industrial dynasties. And even that modest
success came at a high price, namely the abandonment of most of the
customs and traditions that had defined and distinguished the Piedmontese nobility.

CHAPTER I

THE MAKING OF THE PIEDMONTESE NOBILITY: 1600–1848

A remarkably consistent image of Piedmont's titled nobility emerges from contemporary accounts of both the eighteenth and nineteenth centuries, an image which suggests they were respected, but seldom loved. Observers invariably commented on the arrogance, bigotry, narrow-mindedness, and self-satisfaction of the second estate. In the 1760s, for instance, Giuseppe Baretti noted an "excessive pride of birth" among Piedmontese aristocrats, the majority of whom "disdain any familiarity" with persons of less exalted lineage. On those rare occasions when they agreed to speak to outsiders, Baretti claimed that "their kindness is such a bizarre mixture of courtesy and haughtiness that it is impossible for a man of substance not to be offended."[1] Nearly a century later, Vincenzo Gioberti observed in the 1840s how "the concept of their own superiority is inborn in the Piedmontese aristocrats; they make you feel it although they are courteous; they dominate while they bow; they show that they are your masters while professing themselves your servants."[2] In the 1860s, one of the nobility's most distinguished figures, Massimo d'Azeglio, provided a striking confirmation of these outsiders' impressions:

> My dear reader, I feel sure that more than once it has fallen to your lot to have to do with someone who, in his attitude towards you, failed in nothing due to courtesy, who uttered no word to which you could object without being ridiculous or absurdly punctilious, and yet at the same time gave forth from his whole person such a clear "keep your distance," such an obvious "I'm what I am and you don't count," that, as there was reason to get angry and no possibility of putting up with it, one simply longed to get out of range, and, if possible, never let oneself

---

[1] Giuseppe Baretti, *Gli italiani*, as cited in Bianchi, *Storia della monarchia piemontese*, vol. I, p. 111.

[2] Vincenzo Gioberti, *Introduzione allo studio della filosofia*, as cited in Cognasso, *Life and Culture in Piedmont*, p. 298.

be caught again. Such was the effect produced by the Piedmontese nobility . . .[3]

At the same time, most observers recognized that the subalpine nobility was not without its virtues. The Piedmontese aristocrat was supposed to have a resolute character, an unswerving devotion to duty, and a rare energy that clearly distinguished him from his purportedly effete and decadent counterparts elsewhere on the Italian peninsula. According to Cristina Morozzo della Rocca, the mother of d'Azeglio, the nobility of her youth in the late eighteenth century displayed "a sense of honor, based on faith in God and loyalty to King, probity and loftiness of soul."[4] Even a much less sympathetic commentator like Baretti conceded that the Piedmontese aristocrats had the qualities of character that gave them an exceptional "martial spirit" and assured their "great military superiority."[5] These images of aristocratic virtues continued to inform historical and popular accounts throughout the nineteenth century. Historians like Cibrario and Manno wrote admiringly of the nobility's dedication to state service, their tenacity, and their willingness to sacrifice themselves for the sake of the country. Likewise, Leandro Carpi, in his survey of Italian elites in the late 1870s, still spoke of the Piedmontese aristocrat's "courage, loyalty, unselfishness, sincerity, and deep sense of honor."[6]

Of course, the stereotype of the honorable but arrogant nobleman concealed considerably more complex legal and social realities. At one level, the nobility was a body with a legally defined composition, privileges, and obligations prior to the nineteenth century. In the *ancien régime*, a wide range of groups had some claim to noble status in Piedmont; they included holders of fiefs, members of ancient consortia or factions of nobles, descendants of certain urban patriciates, men who belonged to knightly military orders, designated office holders, and those families who had customarily enjoyed noble status and maintained a *vita more nobilium*.[7] The members of this large and amorphous estate, which may have numbered as many as 5,000 families in the early eighteenth century, claimed a special status, but they certainly did not constitute a single, homogeneous social formation. Much like the privileged estates elsewhere in Europe, the structure of the nobility in Piedmont resembled more a pyramid, with descending levels of wealth,

---

[3] D'Azeglio, *Things I Remember*, pp. 6–7.   [4] *Ibid.*, p. 6.

[5] See Bianchi, *Storia della monarchia piemontese*, vol. I, p. 391.

[6] Carpi, *L'Italia vivente*, p. 149. See Genta, *Senato e senatori*, pp. 98–99, for a discussion of the judgments of nineteenth-century historians.

[7] See Cibrario, *Notizie genealogiche di famiglie nobili*, p. 57. On the difficulties of defining the nobility, see Genta, "Il concetto di nobiltà."

power, and influence, as well as sizeable differences in lineage, custom, taste, values, and prestige.[8]

In the broadest terms, the Piedmontese nobility could be divided into a *noblesse d'épée* and a *noblesse de robe*. A proud old feudal aristocracy provided the central core of the former; this group consisted of probably no more than 100 families by the seventeenth century who maintained strong military traditions and close ties to court. These families accounted for most of the great landowners of the realm and set the tone for those members of the nobility who fulfilled military functions or whose status had a military provenance. With their pride of caste, warrior virtues, and chivalric code of honor, they also conformed most closely to the popular image of the Piedmontese nobleman. Predictably, they played a dominant role in the army, diplomatic corps, and the court. Alongside of the old feudal-military aristocracy was a second group of nobles whose status came originally from tenure of office rather than patent or prescription. These titled officials supposedly represented a culture that glorified the values of service, professional competence, and merit. Their strongholds within the Savoyard state tended to be in the administration of justice and finance. In theory, if not always in practice, these office holders were of more recent origins, less haughty, and more educated than their military counterparts.[9]

On the whole, the Piedmontese nobility differed in important respects from the other privileged elites on the Italian peninsula. To begin with, they never constituted an independent ruling class of merchant origins with a monopoly of political power like the relatively closed patrician oligarchies that dominated Milan, Venice, Genoa, and Florence until the end of the eighteenth century. Although some families came from the urban nobilities of Turin and other provincial cities, the bulk of the old aristocracy was feudal in origin. As a result, they were more open to the effects of social mobility and constant renewal than their northern counterparts.[10] At the same time, the subalpine nobles differed in their privileges, relations to royal authority, and military traditions from the feudal baronages of Naples and Sicily.

[8] On the size of the Piedmontese nobility, see Stumpo, "I ceti dirigenti in Italia nell'età moderna," p. 194.

[9] Carpi, *L'Italia vivente*, pp. 149–151 provides a discussion of the differences between the two sectors of the nobility in Piedmont. On the size of the old feudal aristocracy in the seventeenth century, see Stumpo , "I ceti dirigenti in Italia," p. 168. For the culture of the service nobility, see Ricuperati, *I volti della pubblica felicità*, p. 242. Rosso, *Una burocrazia di antico regime* provides a detailed examination of one group of civil servants.

[10] See Stumpo, "I ceti dirigenti in Italia" for an illuminating comparison of the Piedmontese nobility and the Florentine patricians.

Unlike their southern counterparts, they enjoyed neither vast landholdings and sizeable feudal revenues nor a prolonged period of weak
central government in the late middle ages that might have accustomed
them to direct political power.

These circumstances helped to give the Piedmontese their striking
distinctiveness in the Italian setting: a feudal baronage that embraced
service to the state as its principal vocation and as the defining ingredient of its status.[11] Not surprisingly, the transformation of their feudal
ethos into a military-bureaucratic ethos of army and state service was
inseparably linked to the ambitions and policies of the ruling dynasty of
the area, the House of Savoy. Indeed, the growth of the absolute monarchy played a decisive role in shaping the composition and mentality of
the Piedmontese nobility in the two centuries preceding the French
Revolution.

FROM FEUDAL ARISTOCRACY TO SERVICE NOBILITY: 1600–1790

Much like hereditary elites elsewhere in Europe at the end of the *ancien
régime*, most Piedmontese nobles in the 1790s were relatively recent
creations, the beneficiaries of an enormous expansion of the ruling class
that had taken place during the seventeenth and eighteenth centuries. It
has been estimated that the ranks of vassals rose from roughly 1,800 in
the era of Emanuele Filiberto (1559–1586) to between 5,000 and 5,800
two centuries later. The old feudal aristocracy continued to enjoy great
prestige and, in many cases, substantial wealth, but they clearly constituted a small minority within this much more heterogeneous hereditary
noble estate. By the late 1770s, there were only four families whose
titles went back to the tenth century; no more than fifty could trace
their noble status to the eleventh and twelfth centuries.[12] The bulk of
families owed their position to less distant ancestors – bankers, mer-

[11] I am grateful to Professor Geoffrey Symcox of the University of California at Los
Angeles for sharing these insights with me. Astarita, *The Continuity of Feudal Power*,
pp. 1–18 provides a useful summary of the situation in the south. For more general
comparative treatments of the Italian nobilities in the seventeenth and eighteenth
centuries, see Roberts, "Lombardy," pp. 60–61; Borelli, "Il problema della
nobiltà," 486–503; Ricuperati and Carpenetti, *Italy in the Age of Reason*, pp. 54–74;
Donati, *L'idea di nobiltà*.

[12] Cibrario, *Notizie genealogiche di famiglie nobili* as cited in Bianchi, *Storia della monarchia
piemontese*, vol. I, p. 352. For general developments in Europe, see Blum, *The End of
the Old Order*, pp. 15–16. Woolf, "Studi sulla nobiltà piemontese," p. 137 and
Stumpo, *Finanza e stato moderno*, p. 278 provide estimates on the size of the nobility;
for the lower figure of 5,000, see note 40.

chants, officials, and free professionals who had gained their titles through their offices, royal favor, or the purchase of fiefs.

These drastic changes in the size and social composition of the second estate appear to have generated surprisingly little friction and did not give rise to sharp internal distinctions or divisions. The fusion of old and new families took place quickly in one or two generations through intermarriage and the adoption of common values and prejudices. The relative cohesiveness of the nobility stemmed from a number of factors: the absence of extreme disparities between rich and poor titled families, a unifying commitment to state service, and a shared sense of loyalty to the dynasty. Rapid fusion was more difficult in the eighteenth century, however, when established families closed ranks against a flood of newcomers.[13]

The extraordinary growth in the size of the titled nobility coincided with the development of a centralized absolutist monarchy in the territories ruled by the Dukes of Savoy. The old feudal aristocracy, which had monopolized office holding prior to 1559, saw its commanding role in the Savoyard state shrink steadily during the following two centuries. Beginning with the reign of Carlo Emanuele I, the Dukes of Savoy pursued with varying success a strategy designed to enhance their own authority by weakening the privileged orders.[14] Accordingly, the feudal nobility were gradually ousted from much of the state administration and replaced by able and ambitious new men in the course of the seventeenth century. Between 1600 and 1648, the middle classes accounted for more than three-quarters of the purchasers of state financial, judicial, and administrative offices. By the beginning of the next century, nearly 90 percent of the central and local offices were in the hands of nonnobles.[15]

These changes in personnel, however, did not mean that the bourgeoisie controlled the Savoyard state system. While feudal aristocrats gradually, and often reluctantly, accepted the dominance of the state, they remained the core of the highest order in Piedmontese society, a wealthy and powerful elite that still dominated the army, diplomatic corps, church hierarchy, and high court posts. Great "thoroughbred"

---

[13] Woolf, "Studi sulla nobiltà piemontese," pp. 137–138; Stumpo, "I ceti dirigenti in Italia," pp. 163–169. The vision of rapid fusion advanced by Woolf has been challenged recently by Rosso, who has found that a small percentage of his ostensibly noble *segretari di stato* ever acquired the feudal status, let alone access to the titled nobility. See Rosso, *Una burocrazia di antico regime*, pp. 213–223.

[14] See Quazza, *Le riforme in Piemonte*, p. 93.

[15] On the purchase of state offices, see statistics provided by Stumpo, *Finanza e stato moderno*, pp. 230–233; percentages for the early eighteenth century are from Quazza, *Le riforme in Piemonte*, pp. 93–95.

families like the Cacherano di Bricherasio, Costa della Trinità, Ferrero della Marmora, and Valperga di Masino continued to provide the commanding officers of the cavalry and infantry, generals, provincial governors, and viceroys. The same families also furnished every archbishop of Turin from 1632 to 1814.[16] Above all, the officers' corps became the principal means of reinforcing the collective identity of the traditional nobility. The old families began to compensate in part for the gradual loss of direct political power in the seventeenth century by monopolizing the command structure of the army which they transformed into an institution that reaffirmed their exclusivity and distinguished the "authentic" nobility from the newly ennobled.[17]

At the same time, the eagerness of new men to seek noble status and imitate aristocratic behavior helped to preserve the social power of the old families. Two groups in particular furnished the bulk of the recently ennobled: a wealthy urban economic elite and a much larger bloc of state officials. Of the eighty-six merchants and bankers in Turin in 1625, thirty-six attained noble status in the course of their careers. Most of them followed a similar path, one that entailed loans to the Dukes of Savoy in times of war, followed by substantial investment in land and castles that carried with them titles and feudal prerogatives.[18] The House of Savoy opened a second path into the aristocracy through the rapid expansion of state office holding which created a kind of *noblesse de robe* of magistrates and upper-level bureaucrats who accounted for most of the other newly titled families in this period. Their ranks included the Beraudo di Pralormo, Nicolis di Robilant, Coardi di Carpeneto, and Gabaleone di Salmour – all families that would play leading roles in Piedmontese society and politics by the nineteenth century. The growing identification of noble rank with state service helps to explain, in turn, the ability of these new families to merge with and become virtually indistinguishable from the old feudal nobility.[19]

As the experiences of the Perrone di San Martino, Turinetti di Priero, and Nicolis di Robilant suggest, great wealth, state service, intermarriage, demographic good fortune, and the adoption of a mili-

---

[16] Stumpo, *I ceti dirigenti in Italia*, p. 168; Rosso, *Una burocrazia di antico regime*, pp. 222–223. For a complete list of the archbishops of Turin, see Chevallard and Frova, *Cronaca di Torino*, pp. 5–7, 16.

[17] Barberis, *Le armi del Principe*, pp. 103–106.

[18] Stumpo, *Finanze e stato moderno*, pp. 300–301.

[19] Rosso's recent work suggests that the process of fusion was considerably more difficult than Woolf suggests. See in particular his discussion of the top families who provided *segretari di stato*, the Carron, Pasero, and Claretti in Rosso, *Una burocrazia di antico regime*, pp. 282–301.

tary-aristocratic way of life all contributed to this process.[20] The tendency of these three families to conform to a traditional aristocratic code of behavior appears to have been typical of the newly ennobled in the seventeenth century. The very fact that the middle classes continued to dominate financial and judicial administration in the Savoyard state strongly suggests that as new families moved into the nobility they were quick to abandon these less socially prestigious offices.[21]

The Savoyard rulers launched a more formidable assault on the privileged position of the nobility in the first half of the eighteenth century. In particular, the great financial reforms of Vittorio Amedeo II in the 1720s and 1730s confronted the old families with an unprecedented challenge to their wealth. Upon becoming king in 1713, the Duke of Savoy embarked on an aggressive campaign to recapture lands and revenues that his predecessors had alienated in the past. This campaign culminated in two key measures: the confiscation of about 800 "illegally" granted fiefs in 1720 and the introduction of a new land measurement in 1731, the *perequazione*, which sought to eliminate many of the tax exemptions of the privileged orders.[22] Among those hardest hit by the edict revoking the fiefs were some of the oldest and wealthiest families of the realm, while the nobility lost nearly a third of their fiscal immunities as a result of the *perequazione*.[23]

Affluent and socially ambitious commoners were the chief beneficiaries of the reforms. Nearly two-thirds of the initial buyers of fiefs between 1722 and 1725 were *parvenu* vassals, lawyers, merchants, and bankers; a pattern that became even more pronounced in the years that followed. In little more than seventy years, Vittorio Amedeo II, and his successors Carlo Emanuele III and Vittorio Amedeo III, sold approximately 1,300 patents of nobility to a horde of eager supplicants.[24]

---

[20] For genealogical information on the Perrone di San Martino and Nicolis di Robilant families, see Manno, "Il patriziato subalpino." See also Dagna, "Un diplomatico ed economista del Settecento," pp. 9–11. On the triumphant social ascension of the Turinetti di Priero, see Stumpo, "I ceti dirigenti in Italia," pp. 163–165.

[21] See Stumpo, *Finanza e stato moderno*, pp. 299–305, for a discussion of bourgeois aspirations in the seventeenth century.

[22] For a general treatment of these developments, see Symcox, *Victor Amadeus II*, pp. 190–225.

[23] Among the families hit by the edict were the Avogadro, Arborio, Dal Pozzo, Falletti di Barolo, Morozzo, San Martino d'Aglié, and Valperga di Masino, *ibid.*, p. 203. For the fullest treatment of the confiscations, see Quazza, *Le riforme in Piemonte*, pp. 164–171. On the damage done to certain families by the *perequazione*, see Woolf, "Economic Problems of the Nobility," pp. 274–275.

[24] See Bianchi, *Storia della monarchia piemontese*, p. 353; Quazza, *Le riforme in Piemonte*, p. 173. According to Quazza, 61 percent of the buyers in the first three years were new men. Of the thirty-six individuals who purchased fiefs between 1725 and 1728,

Ironically, the legal intervention of the state in the affairs of the nobility that resulted in the creation of so many new titled families also led to the demotion and decline of the old, but untitled "generic" nobility whose claims to special status had rested upon custom and a distinctive way of life.[25]

Possession of a fief and title, however, did not translate automatically into immediate or enduring social benefits. On the contrary, the "nobility of '22", the disparaging label attached to the new families, found the path to full social acceptance somewhat more difficult than their seventeenth-century predecessors. Although they were noble in juridical terms, they received a predictably hostile reception from the established aristocratic families who snubbed and ridiculed them at court and in high society.[26] As late as the 1780s, the virtual absence of the newly ennobled from the list of the 200 cavaliers who belonged to the exclusive Patriotica Nobile Società del Casino attested to the persistence of an unofficial hierarchy within the second estate that ascribed a subordinate status to the post-1722 nobility.[27] Even when a recently ennobled family did win acceptance from the old elite, the prestige expenditures that accompanied the acquisition of a fief and titled status could lead to financial ruin.[28]

More importantly, the reform initiatives of the Savoyard rulers did not permanently weaken the aristocracy or result in any sweeping embourgeoisement of the second estate. On the contrary, the trials and tribulations of the first half of the eighteenth century actually revitalized the nobility with new wealth and talent, and enhanced aristocratic power and prestige within both the state and society, precisely at a time when the urban patriciates elsewhere in northern Italy were heading toward political and demographic decline. Above all, the reluctance of

---

only two were old nobles. For the estimate on the total number of titles sold during the century, see Davico, *"Peuple et notables" (1750–1816)*, pp. 51–52.

[25] See Genta, *Senato e senatori*, pp. 94–100.

[26] *Ibid.*, p. 93 and Quazza, *Le riforme in Piemonte*, vol. III, p. 343.

[27] Founded in 1784 by a group of Turin's foremost aristocrats, who saw the need for a locale where "our large and flourishing nobility" could gather, the Casino was intended to provide an elegant setting for "conversation, gaming, and dancing." In fact, the statutes of the Casino explicitly restricted daily access to the small and select circle of old-line aristocrats who were members; the rest of the nobility could enter its rooms only on two designated days each week. For more information on the origins, structure, membership, and policies of the Casino, see Archivio di Stato di Torino (hereafter cited as AST), Sezione Riunite, Archivio privato Villa di Villastellone, busta 15, "Carte e sottoscrizioni originali relative alla formazione ed al regolamento della Patriottica Nobile Società del Casino," April 17, 1784.

[28] See, for example, Giovanni Levi's detailed study of the Sibaldi, a patrician family from Alessandria in "Strutture famigliari e rapporti sociali," pp. 617–630.

the Savoyard rulers to abolish privilege altogether, allowed Piedmont's titled elite to still possess disproportionate economic weight, enjoy some fiscal immunity, control local administration, and dominate the officer class of the army and diplomatic corps in the last quarter of the century.[29]

As the wave of royal reforming zeal receded in the latter half of the eighteenth century, the second estate in Piedmont still found itself headed by a small elite of no more than 100 prominent old families. These families had weathered the crises occasioned by the confiscation of the fiefs and the *perequazione* with limited damage. With few exceptions, they had sufficient liquid assets and alternative sources of income needed to buy back their possessions and fiefs in the 1720s. In fact, they went on to monopolize purchases of the largest and most valuable fiefs in the ensuing decades. Likewise, the loss of some fiscal exemptions in the 1730s had less of an impact on the wealthier families than aggregate statistics might indicate, since the *perequazione* did not alter the distribution of propertied wealth or eliminate seigneurial rights over the land and labor.[30]

Family strategies clearly contributed to the enduring economic primacy of the old titled elite throughout the century. While the leading titled families did expand their landed properties through new acquisitions, they also relied increasingly on such traditional devices as strict legal ties and intermarriage to maintain and consolidate their landed estates. By the late eighteenth century, most patrimonies were effectively tied up in primogeniture and trust deeds (*fidecommessi*) that prohibited alienation. In this fashion, possessions previously in the hands of collateral branches of the families were consolidated, the rights of younger sons nearly eliminated, and inheritances concentrated in the hands of the first sons, who were obligated, in turn, to transfer to their first born male heirs the entire estate they had received. Such legal devices, combined with astute marriage alliances, appear to have worked very effectively for families like the Falletti di Barolo who tripled their landed possessions in the two centuries after 1550.[31]

---

[29] Serfdom in Savoy had to be abolished, but it did not operate in Piedmont. See, for instance, Woolf, "Economic Problems of the Nobility," p. 283; Symcox, *Victor Amadeus II*, p. 207; Quazza, *Le riforme in Piemonte*, vol. II, pp. 341–346. On the dominant role played by the nobility in Savoyard diplomacy, see Frigo, *Principe, ambasciatori e "jus gentium,"* pp. 119–166.

[30] For a list of fiefs purchased between 1722 and 1797, their prices, and their buyers, see Manno, *Il patriziato subalpino*, vol. I, pp. 3–72. Symcox, *Victor Amadeus II*, p. 203 provides a brief discussion of the limited impact of the *perequazione*.

[31] Woolf, "Economic Problems of the Nobility," p. 277 and "Studi sulla nobiltà piemontese," pp. 25–50.

Aristocratic landowners not only consolidated and expanded their properties; they also found various ways to increase their profitability, and thereby compensate themselves for the loss of their old fiscal exemptions. Initially, their response took the form of a feudal reaction entailing intensified exploitation of the peasant labor force. In the wake of the *perequazione*, they raised rents, revived seigneurial dues, shortened leases, and appropriated large tracts of common lands.[32] In the second half of the century, however, many aristocratic landowners were also taking steps to increase the efficiency of their estates in order to exploit the growing European demand for cereal products. The great landed grandees of the eastern plains, in particular, were in the forefront of agricultural modernization in Piedmont, replacing the old sharecropping system with more lucrative, large-scale lease holding contracts, investing in land reclamation and the development of canals and irrigation networks, introducing new livestock breeds and methods of farming, and expanding the lucrative cultivation of rice.[33] The nobility's interest in development of their land also found additional expression in the leadership they provided to the Royal Academy of Agriculture, founded in the 1780s to encourage scientific research and promote improved methods of farming.[34]

In an era of prolonged peace and stability, such initiatives made most of the old landed aristocratic families considerably wealthier than they had been a century earlier. In the province of Vercelli, for instance, the territory devoted to rice cultivation quadrupled over the course of the century, lease rates nearly tripled in the same period, while prices rose 70 percent after 1750.[35] Not surprisingly, the scions of the most illustrious feudal families monopolized a list of the richest men in the realm compiled at the end of the century by the French authorities. With the exception of the Turinetti di Priero and the Coardi di Carpeneto who were ennobled in the seventeenth century, those on the list with estates valued at over L. 1 million all belonged to families whose roots lay in the medieval period, with the Falletti di Barolo, Solaro del Borgo, and Valperga di Masino at the top.[36]

The same great old families also belonged to a legal estate that con-

---

[32] See Symcox, *Victor Amadeus II*, pp. 203–205; Woolf, "Studi sulla nobiltà piemontese," pp. 169–170.

[33] See Pugliese, *Due secoli di vita agricola*. For statistics on the stockpiles of rice in the city of Vercelli, see Davico, *"Peuple et notables 1750–1816,"* pp. 112–113.

[34] See Donna d'Oldenico, *L'Accademia di Agricoltura di Torino*, pp. 15–18, 36–37; Woolf, "Studi sulla nobiltà piemontese," pp. 169–170; Marchisio, "Ideologia e problemi dell'economia familiare," 98–101.

[35] See Pugliese, "Produzione, salari e redditi," pp. 21–88.

[36] Bulferetti, "I piemontesi più ricchi," pp. 77–79.

tinued to enjoy a range of exclusive rights and privileges. The reforms of Vittorio Amedeo II effectively destroyed any lingering pretensions of the nobility to independent political power, but they did not eliminate all their fiscal exemptions; in fact, the nobility and clergy still owned more than a fifth of the land in Piedmont taxfree after 1731. Moreover, in many areas of Piedmont, titled landowners were able to maintain some of their judicial and chancellory powers, their old monopolies of milling and ovens, their authority to collect tolls and feudal dues, and their exclusive hunting, fishing, and water rights. Similarly, only nobles were permitted to establish primogenitures and *fidecommessi*.[37] The nobility benefited as well from the outward symbols of their superior status. Only titled gentlemen were admitted to a court, displayed coats of arms, and used special seals. They and their wives alone held boxes at the Teatro Regio in Turin and sat in the places of honor at church services. Even at balls attended by the general public, the nobility danced and socialized separately from the rest of the guests.[38]

Like aristocratic elites elsewhere, the dominant position of the old families in late eighteenth century Piedmont also rested on their ability to dictate the values and patterns of behavior that defined the terms of social acceptance or exclusion of new men. In the case of Piedmontese society, the extraordinary prestige associated with service in the officer class of the army and observance of a feudal-chivalric code of comportment testified most eloquently to the abiding preeminence of the traditional aristocracy.

The reliance of the old families on the military and diplomatic corps as measures of social distinction became even more accentuated in the eighteenth century when the crown seemed to be selling fiefs and titles to the highest bidders and opening court to all nobles irrespective of their social origins or pedigree. In a context where titles no longer provided an accurate measure of status, the army afforded a clear system of precedence to help allay the anxieties of the old established families and give focus to the newly ennobled's mania for emulation.[39] Service in the military – particularly as a cavalry or infantry officer – became virtually *de rigueur* for Piedmontese aristocrats in the eighteenth century, since it represented, in

---

[37] Bianchi, *Storia della monarchia piemontese*, vol. I, pp. 113–119, and Prato, *La vita economica in Piemonte*, pp. 407–413. On the fiscal exemptions enjoyed by the nobility, see Symcox, *Victor Amadeus II*, p. 203.

[38] Carutti, *Storia della diplomazia*, vol. IV, pp. 513–514; Bianchi, *Storia della monarchia piemontese*, vol. I, pp. 358–403.

[39] See Barberis, *Le armi del Principe*, pp. 170–187; Loriga, "L'identità militare," 447–449. On the social role of the diplomatic corps, see Frigo, *Principe, ambasciatori e "jus gentium,"* pp. 119–123.

the words of Count Corrado Alfieri, the only option "by which a person, who is well-born, educated, and connected, can succeed in all sorts of positions."[40] The distribution of noble officers within the armed forces reflected their underlying social values. While the nobility accounted for nearly two-thirds of the entire corps in 1769, they provided over 90 percent of the cavalry officers and nearly three-quarters of the infantry, but little more than a quarter of the artillery and engineers, the less prestigious branches of the army.[41] Aristocratic officers, especially those from the old families, also dominated the most important posts at court.[42] In this fashion, the integration of new and old nobles continued to take place within an institutional and ideological framework largely dictated by the more traditional elements of the aristocracy.[43]

Such a strong feudal-military ideology had its costs. For one thing, it encouraged a certain reluctance on the part of the nobility to accept new cultural and commercial developments in the last decades of the eighteenth century. Thus, the vision of the military life as the highest expression of aristocratic values, prestige, and power led the blue-blooded top commanders and the bulk of the officer class to prefer the virtues of ignorance and high birth over those of merit and work, and to oppose the introduction of scientific innovations and a more modern technical training into the army as threats to their supremacy and traditions.[44] Intellectual life and specialized professional training, in general, continued to enjoy little status among the great majority of titled families. Although the aristocratic presence within the student population at the University of Turin more than doubled in the six decades from 1729 to 1789, no more than twenty young noblemen ever enrolled in any given year.[45]

---

[40] See Loriga, "L'identità militare," 457. In 1776 there were 5,000 aristocratic males between the ages of 15 and 60 in Piedmont, 3,000 of whom served the state in some capacity while another 1,000 either were in training for it or had retired from it. The overwhelming majority of these titled servants of the state – some 2,500 – were enrolled in the army. They included 87 generals of various grade, 86 governors or commandants of forts, and 225 other high-ranking officers. See Bianchi, *Storia della monarchia piemontese*, I, p. 431.

[41] See Loriga, "L'identità militare," 445.

[42] See Barberis, *Le armi del principe*, pp. 188–190. For a more general statistical analysis of the military courtiers, see Loriga, "L'identità militare," 457.

[43] See Barberis, "Continuità aristocratica e tradizione militare," pp. 588–589.

[44] For a fuller treatment of the aristocratic resistance to late-eighteenth-century military reforms, see Barberis, *Le armi del principe*, pp. 170–205, "Continuità aristocratica e tradizione militare," pp. 581–589, "La nobiltà militare sabauda fra corti e accademie scientifiche," pp. 559–569; Pinelli, *Storia militare del Piemonte*, vol. I, pp. 33–41; Ferrone, "L'apparato militare sabaudo," pp. 177–185.

[45] Balani, Carpanetto, and Turletti, "La popolazione dell'Università di Torino,"

The same feudal-military ideology also tended to accentuate traditional aristocratic prejudices against manufacturing and commerce. The Savoyard rulers effectively recognized the strength of these prejudices by their frequent efforts to combat and overcome them.[46] Such royal initiatives appear to have had only limited success. On the whole, the investments of aristocratic families in industry or commerce were quite marginal, especially given the economic importance of the nobility in the kingdom.[47]

Yet resistance to intellectual and economic innovation did not weaken or threaten the position of the Piedmontese nobility in the short run. The leading old families, in particular, emerged at the end of the eighteenth century with their political, social, and economic power essentially undiminished and perhaps even enhanced, in contrast to their urban patrician counterparts elsewhere on the peninsula. Their landholdings were relatively modest when compared to those of the Roman or Neapolitan aristocracy, but they were sufficient to make them the unchallenged wealthy elite in the Kingdom of Sardinia.[48] These families also continued to dominate local administration and to control the highest and most prestigious offices at court and in the army, diplomatic corps, and church. At the same time, successful commoners effectively recognized the social supremacy of the nobility through their pursuit of fiefs and titles and their emulation of aristocratic values and comportment. The anti-aristocratic reforms of Vittorio Amedeo II contributed in no small way to this state of affairs by leaving the nobility's privileged status largely intact, by leavening their ranks with fresh wealth and talent, and by forcing them to employ more efficient methods of estate management. In the late eighteenth century, the position of the Piedmontese nobility may well have been comparable to that of the Junkers, the dominant element in the militaristic and bureaucratic society of Brandenburg-Prussia.[49]

pp. 84–5, 104–5, 120–1. This is not to say that the Piedmontese nobility did not produce any intellectuals. See Bianchi, *Storia della monarchia piemontese*, vol. I, pp. 433–434 for some of the patrician academicians and savants.

[46] See Prato, *La vita economica in Piemonte*, p. 269.

[47] See *ibid.*, pp. 269–270; Woolf, "Economic Problems of the Nobility," 280–281, and "Studi sulla nobiltà piemontese," pp. 12–13; Bianchi, *Storia della monarchia piemontese*, vol. I, pp. 410, 432–433.

[48] For a comparative analysis of landholding on the Italian peninsula at the end of the eighteenth century, see Zangheri, "La proprietà in Italia," pp. 9–16. On the difficulties experienced by the patriciates of Venice, Milan, and Florence, see Davis, "The Decline of the Venetian Nobility," pp. 34–125; Roberts, "Lombardy," pp. 60–83; Stumpo, "I ceti dirigenti in Italia," pp. 191–197; Bulferetti, "I piemontesi più ricchi," pp. 57–83.

[49] Woolf, "Economic Problems of the Nobility," p. 283.

SURVIVAL AND ADAPTATION IN THE FRENCH REVOLUTIONARY
ERA

The situation of Piedmontese aristocrats, however, differed from that of their Prussian counterparts in at least two key respects: first, in the limited power they exercised over their peasants and, second, in their geographical and cultural proximity to France. To begin with, the sub-alpine nobility lacked the strong tradition of private and personal domi-nation on their estates that was so vital to the Junkers' sense of superiority and notions of authority.[50] For their part, Piedmontese aris-tocrats grew up in a bilingual society bordering on France which made them more cosmopolitan than the East Elbian nobility, but which also exposed them much more directly and intensely to French political and cultural developments. The importance of these differences became especially pronounced in the turbulent era after 1789.

The old view that the French Revolution swept away the last rem-nants of feudalism and produced a decisive victory of the capitalist bour-geoisie over the landed aristocracy not only in France, but also in much of Western Europe no longer enjoys much credibility. It now appears that shared incomes, interests, and styles of life linked the nobles and upper bourgeois in France both before and after 1789. Revolution resulted less in a victory of either one or the other than in a compromise in which the nobility absorbed the bourgeoisie into a new and broader ruling class of conservative landed notables in the early nineteenth century.[51]

In the case of northern Italy, in general, and Piedmont in particular, underlying social and economic continuities were even more pro-nounced than on the other side of the Alps. Here the nobility suffered less than their French counterparts from the social upheavals of the revolution. No great transfers of land took place in Italy; whatever gains non-nobles made came at the expense of the church. As a result, the leading aristocratic families were better able to maintain their position as a dominant group in society.[52]

Still, such continuities should not obscure the extent to which the revolutionary war and the ensuing Napoleonic occupation disrupted

---

[50] See Berdahl, *The Politics of the Prussian Nobility*.

[51] See, for instance, Cobban, *The Social Interpretation of the French Revolution*; Lucas, "Nobles, Bourgeois, and the Origins of the French Revolution," pp. 84–126; Furet, *Interpreting the French Revolution*; Chaussinand-Nogaret, *Une histoire des élites, 1700–1848*.

[52] For a summary of the arguments and evidence, see Capra, "Nobili, notabili, elites," pp. 12–42.

the Piedmontese nobility's collective confidence and sense of security. In rapid succession titled families experienced military defeat, the loss of their monarchy, economic deprivation, petty humiliations, and in some cases exile. More importantly, the French regime introduced egalitarian legal reforms that undermined the privileged status of the nobility. The resulting combination of lost prerogatives and newly acquired opportunities weakened in turn the cohesion of the old nobility by accentuating economic and ideological divisions within its ranks.

A combination of circumstances in the 1790s made the Savoyard state particularly vulnerable to the repercussions of the French Revolution. The years from 1791 to 1797 saw mounting discontent in the countryside brought on by a combination of long-term structural changes in the agricultural economy and short-term price and wage movements. Rural folk reacted to the crisis by attacking both new commercial leasing contracts and traditional feudal rights and prerogatives.[53] At the same time, the nobility became the favorite targets of propaganda spread by a nascent Jacobin movement drawing support from the middle classes and poor clergy in the towns and cities.[54] While these developments, in themselves, did not constitute a serious challenge to the established order in Piedmont, they did demoralize the monarchy and weaken its will to resist the invading French armies.

From its beginning in September 1792, the intermittent war with the French went badly for the Piedmontese army. Almost immediately, Vittorio Amedeo III's forces had to abandon Nice and Savoy, where revolutionary assemblies denounced the claims of the House of Savoy and abolished the titled hierarchy.[55] While the next major confrontation did not take place until the spring of 1796, it also ended quickly in a devastating defeat for the Piedmontese army. In April Vittorio Amedeo surrendered and accepted a humiliating separate peace with General Bonaparte at Cherasco that ensured French primacy in Piedmont.[56]

---

[53] Prato, *L'evoluzione agricola nel secolo XVIII*, p. 41; Davico, "*Peuple et notables (1750–1816)*," pp. 96–113.

[54] See Bianchi, *Storia della monarchia piemontese*, vol. II, pp. 538–584, Carutti, *Storia della Corte di Savoia*, vol. I, pp. 269–285, and Davico, "*Peuple et notables (1750–1816)*," pp. 68–71. Romeo, *Cavour e il suo tempo*, vol. I, pp. 17–18 provides a good portrait of the prevailing mood of Piedmontese aristocrats in these years.

[55] On the French occupation of Nice and Savoy and its impact on aristocratic fortunes in these provinces, see Romeo, *Cavour e il suo tempo*, vol. I, p. 16; Carutti, *Storia della Corte di Savoia*, vol. I, pp. 194–211; Bianchi, *Storia della monarchia piemontese*, vol. II, pp. 1–52.

[56] See Ferrero, *The Gamble: Bonaparte in Italy*, pp. 1–28; Bianchi, *Storia della monarchia piemontese*, vol. II, pp. 115–167, 190–213, 269–300, provides a detailed account of the course of the war.

The nobility, which had borne the brunt of defeats on the battlefield as the officer class of the Savoyard army, also suffered sizeable losses in the ensuing peace. Under pressure from the French authorities and their radical supporters within Piedmont, the new king, Carlo Emanuele IV, eliminated the last vestiges of aristocratic privilege. On July 27, 1797, a royal decree made all feudal lands allodial and free of all bonds, abolished most feudal rights and prerogatives, and prohibited the creation of primogenitures and *fidecommessi*.[57]

These difficulties paled, however, in comparison to the indignities endured by virtually all strata of the subalpine nobility after the resumption of warfare in the summer of 1798, and the subsequent abdication of Carlo Emanuele, and French military occupation in December of that year. The winter of 1798/9 marked the nadir of aristocratic fortunes during the entire era of French domination. Two days after the king had gone into exile, the provisional government abolished all noble titles and distinctions, and prohibited the use of livery, weapons, or coats of arms.[58] Additional decrees ordered the complete elimination of any remaining feudal privileges, rights, and monopolies regardless of their origins or legal status, canceled all ongoing litigation, and denied title holders the right to compensation or even payment of back taxes and dues. Those families who possessed feudal titles and deeds were required to turn them over immediately to local authorities.[59]

Persecution of ex-nobles in the winter of 1798/9 assumed a variety of other forms as well. In several communes, officials newly appointed by the French army seized a number of castles, mills, and farms, claiming that they had been illegally usurped by the nobility.[60] Military authorities and the republican provisional government also made sure that they shouldered the heaviest burden of taxes and military exactions.[61] Some aristocrats were not only deprived of wealth, but also of their freedom. The provisional government arrested Marchese Solaro del Borgo,

---

[57] See Arnone, *Diritto nobiliare italiano*, pp. 63–64. On the political and social climate in Piedmont during this period, see Bianchi, *Storia della monarchia piemontese*, vol. II, pp. 585–628. For some titled families, the abolition of feudal privileges translated into substantial economic sacrifices. For the case of the Benso di Cavour family, see Romeo, *Cavour e il suo tempo*, vol. I, pp. 21–22.

[58] Decrees of December 10 and December 17, 1798, cited in Bianchi, *Storia della monarchia piemontese*, vol. III, p. 61.

[59] Decree of March 2, 1799, cited in *ibid.*, p. 61; on the destruction of the feudal documents, see pp. 134–139.

[60] See *ibid.*, pp. 185–186; Nada, *Roberto d'Azeglio*, vol. I, p. 36; and Romeo, *Cavour e il suo tempo*, vol. I, p. 22.

[61] See, for instance, the Decree of December 23, 1798, cited in Bianchi, *Storia della monarchia piemontese*, vol. III, p. 186.

Marchesa Asinari di San Marzano, and Marchese Mazzetti di Frinco on charges that they had been the chief instigators of anti-French insurrections; eventually all three were found innocent. The same winter French military authorities took as hostages an additional eighty-six prominent aristocrats, many of whom had been members of the old government, and deported them to Grenoble.[62] The nobles who remained in Piedmont had to endure public ridicule and insults. This abuse became so excessive that the French commander in Turin intervened in early January, warning that "aristocrats, when they respect the law, must be respected in turn, and therefore mockery and insults against them in the theaters are forbidden."[63]

A new Austro-Russian offensive brought to a close this traumatic period for the nobility, but it did not result in a return to the status quo ante. In May 1799, the French were expelled from Turin and the short-lived Piedmontese Jacobin republic collapsed. But the continued presence of foreign troops on Piedmont's soil translated into new financial impositions and other inconveniences for noble landowners. For their part, the Savoyard ruling family showed little regard or consideration for its most loyal and devoted aristocratic supporters during the brief interregnum before the return of the French in the summer of 1800.[64] After Napoleon's decisive victory at Marengo in June 1800 and the French reoccupation of northern Italy, many of Piedmont's most distinguished aristocrats chose to go into voluntary exile in Tuscany or at least sent their children there in order to escape the ravages of war and foreign occupation.[65]

The abolition of feudal privilege, recurrent warfare, and Jacobin persecution may have caused the nobility a great deal of discomfort and humiliation, but they did not destroy overnight century-old positions of wealth and prestige. Indeed, most of the old titled families managed to hold on to the lion's share of their landed wealth, while even at the height of the anti-aristocratic campaign, the middle classes continued in their private dealings with ex-nobles to treat them deferentially and to

---

[62] See *ibid.*, pp. 183–189.

[63] Order of the Day, January 5, 1799, cited in *ibid.*, p. 184.

[64] In regard to the continued economic difficulties, see, for example, the situation on the estates of the d'Azeglio family in the winter of 1799–1800, as reported in Nada, *Roberto d'Azeglio*, vol. I, pp. 36–37n. The attitude of the royal family and the discontent it aroused within aristocratic circles is explored in Vaccarino, "La classe politica piemontese," p. 37; Bianchi, *Storia della monarchia piemontese*, vol. II, pp. 531–534; Perrero, *I Reali di Savoia*, pp. 37–99; and Romeo, *Cavour e il suo tempo*, vol. I, p. 42.

[65] Between 1799 and 1806, forty-nine boys from old titled families enrolled in the prestigious Collegio Tolomei in Siena. See Lovera and Rinieri, *Clemente Solaro della Margarita*, vol. I, pp. 24–25, and Nada, *Roberto d'Azeglio*, vol. I, pp. 42–49.

address them by their old titles.[66] As a result, the nobility were well situated to take advantage of the more favorable situation that emerged after the return of Piedmont to the French Empire in 1802.

With the appointment of General Menou as the first consul in Turin in 1803, the French authorities pursued policies that clearly favored the conservative propertied classes and the old nobility in particular. Leading aristocrats received preferential treatment in the distribution of the lucrative new public offices, posts at court, and titular honors created by Napoleon. Such treatment also extended to their sons, who were given prestigious appointments as cadets to the French military school of Saint-Cyr, auditors to the Council of State, or pages at the court of Prince Camillo Borghese, the French governor of Piedmont, Parma, and Liguria. In this fashion, nobles who transferred their loyalties from the House of Savoy to the French emperor soon found themselves in a position to regain much of their old social and political influence.[67]

The Napoleonic regime's blend of rewards and threats eventually persuaded many prominent aristocrats to put aside their old Savoyard loyalties and assume important offices in the Napoleonic state.[68] These men were rewarded in turn with the most prestigious positions in the new social hierarchy which Napoleon attempted to forge after 1808. French authorities made certain that representatives of the old aristocracy accounted for a disproportionately large share of imperial nobility and members of Napoleonic knightly orders created between 1808 and 1814.[69]

At the same time, the Napoleonic regime gave enterprising Piedmontese nobles, and the major landed grandees in particular, extraordinary opportunities not only to recoup financial losses suffered during the brief Jacobin interlude, but also to increase their wealth and property holdings. Many of them took advantage of the new land market created by the partial expropriation of the property of the Roman Catholic Church. In aggregate terms, the nobility's presence in the sales was comparatively modest, especially in relation to their

[66] Bianchi, *Storia della monarchia piemontese*, vol. III, pp. 181–182.

[67] *Ibid.*, vol. IV, pp. 7–8; Romeo, *Cavour e il suo tempo*, vol. I, p. 44; Nada, *Roberto d'Azeglio*, vol. I, pp. 56–58.

[68] See Bianchi, *Storia della monarchia piemontese*, vol. IV, pp. 368–374; Nada, *Roberto d'Azeglio*, vol. I, pp. 56–66; Romeo, *Cavour e il suo tempo*, vol. I, p. 50. For an account of those nobles who emigrated with their Savoyard sovereign to the island of Sardegna, see Perrero, vol. I, *Reali di Savoia*, pp. 202–253.

[69] For the names of Piedmontese inducted into the new Imperial Order, see Bianchi, *Storia della monarchia piemontese*, vol. IV, pp. 366–367; Manno provides a complete list of all those individuals who received hereditary imperial titles in *Il patriziato subalpino*, vol. I, pp. 107–113.

economic weight in the society.[70] There were significant variations in the amount of land acquired by aristocratic buyers, however, variations that perhaps reflected the growing gap between rich and poor within the former privileged estate. A small group of twenty-five old landed families, or 6 percent of all titled buyers, accounted for 55 percent of the total acreage acquired by the nobility in these years. The six biggest buyers alone took over a quarter of this acreage.[71] The experience of the Avogadro di Casanova family provides a classic illustration of how the sale of church properties could help the old rich get richer in Napoleonic Piedmont. Already the largest landed family in their ex-fief of Casanova, they purchased an additional 211 hectares in the commune in 1806 that had been seized from the Order of Malta. This purchase, when added to their former feudal estates, gave the Avogadro di Casanova ownership of 75 percent of all the land in the commune by 1812.[72]

Many of the same families also took advantage of the profitable investment opportunities that emerged after 1800. For families like the Benso di Cavour, whose economic situation had been severely shaken during the late 1790s, these investments proved a godsend, elevating them in a brief span of years to the ranks of the wealthiest elite in Piedmont.[73] In a similar fashion, the abolition of restrictions on crop cultivation and the elimination of overseas competition by the Continental System ushered in a golden age for great aristocratic landowners of the eastern plains who were already among the leading rice growers of northern Italy. These men, who had converted thousands of hectares to rice production during the previous half century, were uniquely well placed to benefit from the dramatic rise in the price of their chief crop, especially after 1802.[74]

---

[70] Some 388 ex-nobles purchased over 4,000 hectares of land and 63 urban properties seized from the church and auctioned off by French authorities between 1800 and 1814. They represented 17 percent of the buyers, but purchased a mere 14 percent of the acreage sold, a state of affairs that has been ascribed to their enduring religious loyalties and their lack of liquid assets. See Notario, *La vendita dei beni nazionali in Piemonte*, pp. 255–257, 265–267.

[71] The Magnacavallo di Varengo, Falletti di Barolo, Colli di Felizzano, Luserna di Rorà, Arborio di Gattinara, and Avogadro di Casanova families purchased 1,093 of the 4,243 hectares sold to the nobility between 1800 and 1814. *Ibid.*, pp. 317–583, provides a virtually complete listing of all properties sold, the names of the buyers, and the prices they paid.

[72] In 1812, the Avogadro di Casanova owned 1,102 of the 1,472 hectares of land in the commune of Casanova. See *AST*, Sez. Riunite, "Catasto Francese," Mandamento di San Germano, Commune of Casanova, f. 448.

[73] See Romeo, *Cavour e il sus tempo*, vol. I, pp. 47–52.

[74] See Davico, "*Peuple et notables*," pp. 112–113, 139. On the dramatic expansion of

The results of the land survey carried out by the French in 1812 graphically testify to the continued economic predominance of these old titled families in a society in which land remained the chief form of wealth. Analysis of data drawn from sixty-eight communes in the plains of Vercelli and Cuneo reveals a virtual aristocratic monopoly of large-scale landholdings. Nobles accounted for the five biggest estates in Vercelli, each measuring over 1,000 hectares, as well as sixteen of the twenty estates that exceeded 200 hectares. A similar pattern prevailed in the province of Cuneo. Although their properties did not measure up to those of their Vercellese counterparts, titled families owned all fourteen of the estates over 200 hectares and three-quarters of those over 100 hectares in twenty-one communes of the Cunese plains. New men clearly took advantage of the opening of the land market and the sale of church properties to become landowners in the years after 1800, but their possessions still paled in comparison to the estates of the old feudal nobility.[75]

Despite the wealth, power, and prestige the great aristocratic families continued to enjoy under the Napoleonic regime, their positions now rested upon new circumstances that were antithetical to the old institutional status of the nobility. First and foremost, their role as a separate and privileged hereditary estate with special juridical rights and prerogatives had been seriously eroded, both in eyes of the law and in the opinion of important segments of the middle-class public. With their emphasis on efficiency, personal achievement, and equality, agents of the French Revolution embodied values that were inimical to traditional forms of aristocratic power based on birth, rank, privilege, and ascriptive status. Thus, while the Revolution did not abolish the aristocracy, it had fundamentally altered the legal and social framework within which nobles operated.

This new framework not only lowered some of the barriers separating aristocrats from bourgeois; it also accentuated economic and ideological divisions within the nobility. The elimination of the old mechanisms that protected their estates, for instance, left less enterprising titled families far more exposed to the risks and uncertainties of a market economy, in which they now had to compete on more equal terms

---

rice cultivation in Vercelli, see Pugliese, *Due secoli di vita agricola*, p. 156, and Bullio, "Problemi e geografia della risicoltura," pp. 54–58.

[75] The five biggest landowners in the province of Vercelli were the Falletti di Barolo, Dal Pozzo della Cisterna, Avogadro di Casanova, Valperga di Masino, and Mossi di Moirano. Some of the major landed families in the Cunese included the Costa della Trinità, Seyssel d'Aix, and Oreglia di Novello. For data on landownership, I have consulted AST, Sez. Riunite, "Catasto Francese," provinces of Vercelli and Cuneo.

with non-nobles. At the same time, the French occupation introduced new ideological divisions, pitting diehard aristocrats who remained tenaciously loyal to the Savoyard royal family against those who came to terms with the new Napoleonic order. Such divisions prefigured, in turn, a growing polarization of attitudes on how the nobility should respond to the challenges posed by the new egalitarianism.

THE INDIAN SUMMER OF ARISTOCRATIC PRIMACY: 1815–1848

Compromise with egalitarian ideas did not figure prominently on the monarchical agenda in Piedmont after the collapse of the Napoleonic Regime in 1814. While collaboration with the French temporarily tarnished the reputation of certain families, the position of the nobility as a whole was enhanced in the political climate of the Restoration. The composition of the provisional government appointed by the victorious powers to administer the country prior to the return of the king provided a clear indication of things to come. It was headed by one of the most distinguished figures of the nobility, Marchese Filippo Asinari di San Marzano, and consisted exclusively of well-known titled gentlemen.[76]

The resurrection of monarchical absolutism and aristocratic influence was strikingly evident in both the form and content of the new Savoyard regime that supplanted the regency council in the late spring. When Vittorio Emanuele I made his triumphant reentry into the city of Turin on May 20, 1814, even his physical appearance betokened a return to the good old days for the more tradition-minded nobility. He and his entourage, recalled Massimo d'Azeglio who stood in Piazza Castello that day, "were all dressed in antiquated style, with powdered hair in pigtails, and eighteenth-century tricorn hats à la Frederick II."[77] His first royal edict, issued the following day, aimed to turn the clock back, abrogating all legislation and legal codes introduced by the French and restoring the Royal Constitutions of 1770 and any subsequent revisions and additions decreed by his predecessors prior to June 1800. As a result, the legal equality of all citizens was abolished, while distinctions based on social condition and religious faith were reestablished.[78]

The mechanisms governing the political and administrative order that emerged in the restored Kingdom of Sardinia ensured the dominance of high office by the aristocracy. Although Vittorio Emanuele I and his

---

[76] See Brofferio, *Storia del Piemonte*, p. 10.
[77] D'Azeglio, *Things I Remember*, p. 70.
[78] See Astuti, "Gli ordinamenti giuridici degli stati sabaudi," pp. 538–539.

inner circle of titled advisors did not go so far as to restore feudal bonds, they did reinstate the aristocratic primogenitures and *fidecommessi* as well as pursuing policies that openly favored the nobility in the selection and promotion of public officials. Their special status received official recognition in the royal edict of November, 1817 which designated the nobility as "the order which by its very nature is closer to the throne."[79] The status of the nobility as a separate order received additional confirmation five years later when Carlo Felice took his brother's place on the throne. Among his first acts, the new king called upon all his nobles to take a special oath of loyalty as members of a body that was legally distinct from the rest of Piedmontese society.[80]

In theory, the Restoration regime maintained the Napoleonic principle of equal access of all classes to state offices, but in practice a general clause, concerning the wealth and "civilized" condition of the applicant's family, served to give preference to the nobility. Not surprisingly, personal influence and aristocratic family connections proved essential to advancement in the decades after 1814. In his memoirs, Count Lodovico Sauli d'Igliano recalled that it was "known to everyone how among the noble and powerful of Turin every other factor has to lower humbly the flag in the presence of family considerations."[81] Aristocratic status and kinship were especially useful for advancement within the military hierarchy. Thus, Massimo Taparelli d'Azeglio attributed his own appointment as a cavalry officer in 1816 to the historical circumstance that "in 1240 or '60 or '80 . . . a certain man-at-arms of the family of Brenier Capel happened to take a wife from Savigliano and had the good fortune to be the actual progenitor of that long line of Taparellis, of which I have the honor to be the last but one."[82]

At the local level, the nobility enjoyed once again official corporative representation after 1814. Turin's municipal administration was put back into the hands of the General Council of sixty decurions who were chosen for life; the decurions were divided into two categories, with the first coming from the nobility and the second from the other

---

[79] For a complete version of the edict, see *Raccolta di Regi Editti, Manifesti, ed altre provvidenze*, vol. VIII (Turin, 1817), pp. 164ff as cited in Genta, "Eclettismo della Restaurazione," p. 358.

[80] See Genta, "Eclettismo giuridico della Restaurazione," pp. 352–356.

[81] Sauli d'Igliano, *Reminiscenze della propria vita*, vol. I, p. 361. On the mechanisms of preferment and the nobility, see Cognasso, "Nobiltà e borghesia," pp. 228–229. On the family connections of Count Clemente Solaro della Margarita and his rapid rise within the Ministry of Foreign Affairs after 1814, for instance, see Lovera and Rinieri, *Clemente Solaro della Margarita*, vol. I, p. 48. For Solaro's support of d'Azeglio, see Nada, *Roberto d'Azeglio*, vol. I, p. 259.

[82] D'Azeglio, *Things I Remember*, p. 83.

classes of citizens. While the offices were supposed to be divided equally between the two, in reality a majority of the decurions came from the ranks of the aristocracy.[83]

Analysis of the social origins of high office holders in the Kingdom of Sardinia between 1814 and 1847 reveals the extent to which these arrangements insured aristocratic dominance. In the absence of any representative institutions, all power rested in the royal family and the central administration.[84] Predictably, members of the old feudal nobility maintained a stranglehold on all offices at court and in the royal household from the lord chamberlain and grand master to the gentlemen-in-waiting and major-domos, some 152 positions in all that gave them privileged access to the king. In the case of Count Filiberto Avogadro di Collobiano, a military officer and close confidante of Carlo Felice, such access translated into an influence that surpassed even that of the top government ministers.[85]

The same families also provided the great majority of men who conducted the business of government at the highest levels of the state. At the apex of the administrative hierarchy were the ministers of state and first secretaries who oversaw the chief branches of government. Although the number of ministers of state rose from nine in 1820 to seventeen by 1845, these top posts remained the exclusive preserve of titled aristocrats such as Marchese Filippo Asinari di San Marzano, Ottavio Thaon di Revel, Luigi Provana di Collegno, and Venceslao Arborio Gattinara di Breme, all men with strong connections at court as well. Indeed, only two outsiders – Giuseppe Barbaroux and Stefano Gallina – achieved ministerial rank prior to 1848, and both of them did so only after they had been ennobled and absorbed into the titled nobility. After 1831, a new body, the state-council, became the center of all important discussions, but it too remained a patrician stronghold; in 1836, for instance, fourteen of the nineteen councilors were nobles.[86]

---

[83] On the structure of the municipal council, see Raumer, *Italy and the Italians*, p. 241 and Cognasso, *Storia di Torino*, p. 245.

[84] As Count Carlo Ilarione Petitti di Roreto noted in the 1831, "the influence of the court is total in the current government, since the primary management of things receives impetus from it alone." See Petitti di Roreto, *Opere scelte*, p. 143.

[85] The radical journalist, Angelo Brofferio went so far as to claim that Avogadro di Collobiano actually "ruled over Piedmont while Charles Felix lived, and continued after his death to rule over Maria Cristina." See Brofferio, *Storia del Piemonte*, p. 107.

[86] Barbaroux received the title of count in 1815 and his son married into one of the old noble families, Baudi di Selve. Gallina was ennobled in 1834; both his daughters married noblemen in the 1870s. See Manno, *Il patriziato subalpino*, vols. II and XII. For a complete listing of office holders in the Kingdom of Sardinia, see AST, Prima Sezione, the annual Palma Verde for the years 1815 to 1824, and the Calendario Generale del Regno from 1825 to 1847.

The aristocracy also continued to account for most of the provincial governors, top diplomats, and military commanders throughout the Restoration.[87]

The nobility once again enjoyed a dominant place within the army officer corps after 1814 as well. In his description of the Piedmontese military in the earlier years of the Restoration, Ferdinando Pinelli noted that the highest ranks were occupied by "haughty generals, all of noble birth, who . . . presumed to have the right to their celebrity because their grandfather or great-grandfather had served with honor beside his sovereign."[88] The published *Elenco Militare, 1818* reflected a command structure within the army that remained firmly in the hands of men from a few old-line families, who simultaneously occupied powerful positions in the civilian administration and at court. More importantly, 90 percent of the new generation of future officers admitted to the Royal Military Academy of Turin in the first years of the Restoration came from the titled nobility. Once they were admitted to the Academy, young nobles enjoyed a much greater chance of being commissioned than non-nobles. Between 1835 and 1844, 96 percent of all noble cadets who entered received their officer's bars as opposed to 65 percent of their untitled colleagues. While pressures to enlarge and professionalize the army brought about gradual changes in the social composition of the Military Academy, the aristocracy continued to account for a majority of all the newly commissioned officers prior to 1848.[89] And those officers of middle-class origins who did manage to reach the higher levels of the military hierarchy were often ennobled by the king; 46 men attained titled status in this fashion between 1815 and 1847.[90]

Many of the great aristocratic families who occupied the commanding heights of the Piedmontese state also played a prominent role in

---

[87] As late as 1845, all four governors – the officials in whose hands rested the full power of government at the provincial level in Piedmont – came from the old-line patrician families. The same year the titled nobility was still furnishing the entire corps of Savoyard ambassadors, special envoys, and ministers plenipotentiary to the other Italian states, the rest of Europe, the Middle East, and the Americas. See the *Calendario Generale del Regno 1845*.

[88] Pinelli, *Storia militare del Piemonte*, vol. II, as cited in Gerbore, *Dame e cavalieri del Re*, p. 23.

[89] According to Del Negro, *Esercito, stato, società*, pp. 61–4, the nobility accounted for 66 percent of the commissioned officers from the Academy in the 1830s and 55 percent in the 1840s. On the aristocratic presence within the Academy in 1816, see Rogier, *La R. Accademia Militare di Torino*, vol. II, pp. 1–19. For an analysis of the command structure in the army, see Barberis, "La nobiltà militare sabauda," pp. 561–62.

[90] For a list of the men ennobled in this period, see Manno, *Il patriziato subalpino*, vol. I, pp. 75–93.

local administration, especially in the major urban centers of the kingdom. Although representation was supposed to be divided equally between the nobility and the other classes of citizens, the former typically accounted for thirty-nine to forty-six of the sixty decurions and the majority of important committee posts in the city of Turin throughout the first half of the nineteenth century. Similarly, both of the *sindaci*, the chief municipal officials, were often titled aristocrats.[91] Even these figures do not fully measure the extent of aristocratic influence in Turin, since many of the most important bourgeois decurions such as Barbaroux, Rignon, Ricciolio, Pansoya, Borbonese, and Nigra had themselves already embarked on a path that would lead to their ennoblement and eventual absorption into the old titled elite.[92]

Such political dominance helped aristocratic families in turn to reassert their social identity as a separate and superior caste in Piedmont in the decades after 1815. While the French occupation eliminated the last vestiges of feudalism in most of the Kingdom of Sardinia, it hardly destroyed the caste consciousness of the Piedmont's titled nobility. On the contrary, the loss of juridical privileges accentuated the social prejudices and pretensions of old families who now tended to treat the middle classes with even greater condescension.

Contemporary observers in the first half of the century commented frequently on the persistence of old social barriers which they attributed to aristocratic arrogance and snobbery. Writing in the 1830s, for instance, Niccolò Tommaseo accused the Piedmontese nobility of being "stubbornly resistant to any innovation." Gioberti came to a similar conclusion a decade later, charging that "the tyranny and arrogance of the nobility have enslaved and humiliated the bourgeoisie and the people . . . "[93] These views were echoed in the reports of foreign diplomats stationed in Turin in these years. The British ambassador

---

[91] In 1835, for example, Count Pallio di Rincio and Baron Martin di S. Martino occupied these posts, while five years later, it became the turn of Count Pochettini di Serravalle and Count Marchetti Melina; Pochettini di Serravalle continued to occupy the same office in 1845 alongside of Count Bosco di Ruffino.

[92] For the role of the nobility in the administration of Turin, I have relied on data drawn from the Archivio Comunale di Torino (hereafter cited as ACT), Amministrazione, b.2, Decurioni e Uffici decurionali, for the years 1820, 1825, 1830, 1835, 1840, and 1845. A similar pattern prevailed in the main provincial centers. As late as 1845, aristocrats still headed the municipal administrations in Biella, Ivrea, Cuneo, Mondovi, Saluzzo, Alessandria, Acqui, Casale, and Vercelli. Nor was it uncommon for big titled landowners to be the mayors of the villages that were tied to their estates. See *Calendario Generale del Regno, 1845*, pp. 480ff. for lists of mayors in the provincial capitals and the rural communes of Piedmont.

[93] For the critical judgments of Tommaseo and Gioberti, see Niccolò Tommaseo, *Dell'Italia* (1833), ed. G. Balsamo Crivelli (Turin, 1921), vol. II, p. 166 and letter of

underscored aristocratic resistance to the notion of allowing "people not belonging to the nobility to share in the royal favors." In somewhat stronger terms, the Neapolitan ambassador claimed that the aristocracy took "no account" of the bourgeoisie and "kept themselves entirely separated from the [bourgeoisie], from whom they are distinguished . . . by their way of speaking."[94] Even a prominent local aristocrat like Count Ruggero Gabaleone di Salmour conceded the social gulf separating the nobility from the bourgeoisie in Piedmont, which he attributed to the importance attached to the fact that "the one has a more or less old parchment . . . [and] the other does not."[95]

The House of Savoy reinforced such aristocratic caste-consciousness in the opening decades of the Restoration. Its highly traditional court once again provided both a focal point and an exclusive setting for much of the nobility's social activities. Indeed, the rigid etiquette observed at the courts of Vittorio Emanuele I and Carlo Felice ensured that titled status remained a virtual prerequisite for admission to royal festivities. Years later, Count Charles Arrivabene claimed that the Sardinian court was so strict in these matters that "no one would have been admitted to the balls of the Court, had he not been able to show at least two centuries of nobility."[96] In a similar vein, Luigi Des Ambrois recollected how in Turin "the Court represented a sort of caste, which had the privilege of approaching the sovereign, and which formed, at least in appearance, a barrier between him and the mass of subjects."[97]

The aristocratic social order that prevailed in these years was most clearly represented in the Teatro Regio. Much like the Teatro San Carlo in Naples, the Regio was built adjacent to the royal palace and was dominated the presence of the king, whose central box was surrounded by those of the nobility.[98] Distribution of boxes, especially during *carnevale*, the high point of Turin's social season, reflected the aristocracy's supremacy and exclusivity. A strict, hierarchical formula governed the seating arrangements, with status measured by one's relative proximity to the royal box. Accordingly, the most important government ministers and military officers, the chief foreign ambassa-

Vincenzo Gioberti to Vieusseux in F. Orlando, *Carteggi italiani* (Florence, 1896), vol. III, p. 63 as cited in Rodolico, *Carlo Alberto negli anni 1843–1849*, p. 10.

[94] See *ibid.*, pp. 7–8.   [95] Gabaleone di Salmour, *Le riforme e il patriziato*, p. 17.

[96] Arrivabene, *Italy under Victor Emanuel*, vol. I, p. 20. For additional descriptions of Sardinian court life in this period, see Gerbore, *Dame e cavalieri del Re*, pp. 16–25, 29–32, 34–44; Falletti, *Saggi*, pp. 176–177.

[97] L. Des Ambrois, *Notes et souvenirs* (Bologna, 1901) p. 52, as cited in Rodolico, *Carlo Alberto negli anni, 1843–1849*, p. 11.

[98] On the San Carlo, see Robinson, *Naples and the Neapolitan Opera*. For a general discussion of the social role of opera, see McDonogh, *Good Families of Barcelona*.

dors, and top court officials, or more commonly their wives, occupied the stalls in the second tier on either side of boxes of the members of the royal family as well as those on the tiers immediately above and below. Each fall the king and his Grand Chamberlain personally oversaw the assignment of the keys to the remaining boxes, a process in which other high state officials and the wives or widows of "cavaliers of the knightly orders, grandees of the crown [and] ministers of state" were given the highest priority.[99] These criteria, which emphasized lineage and service rather than wealth, ensured that participation in the social rituals of the Teatro Regio remained the virtually exclusive preserve of the older titled families, especially in the first two decades of the Restoration. Caste barriers appear to have softened somewhat by the late 1830s and 1840s when the newly ennobled and bourgeois notables managed to occupy a number of boxes. But even then their inferior status continued to be marked by the size, number of occupants, and location of their boxes. They were invariably the smallest, most crowded, and furthest removed from the royal box in the highest and most remote tiers of the theater.[100]

There appears to have been equally little informal mingling between the aristocracy and other social groups in the decades after 1815. As the French ambassador reported in the 1820s, between nobles and the non-nobles "the separation that defines social customs is complete, profound, and without exception."[101] In her memoirs of her childhood in Restoration Turin, Baroness Olimpia Savio recalled that the "only point of contact allowed then between one class and the other" came on Sundays and holidays when the nobles and "those who were among the better sort in the city touched elbows" as they promenaded under the arcades near the royal palace. As late as 1840, Cavour lamented how just the idea of "mixed balls, half noble, half bourgeois" created a scandal in aristocratic circles. Still, even politically liberal nobles like

[99] When the number of former key holders exceeded the available supply of boxes in the winter of 1825/6, for instance, the Grand Chamberlain at the time, Marchese Carlo Emanuele Alfieri di Sostegno, recommended that preference be given to certain women because of "the prominent positions of their husbands and their seniority in the assignment of stalls." See AST, Prima Sez., Archivio Alfieri di Sostegno, b. 31, "Carte relative alla destinazione dei palchi nel Teatro Regio (1814–1841)," f. 1, 1825–26.

[100] In the winter of 1840/1, women from newly ennobled or bourgeois families occupied 24 of the 137 boxes in the theater. All 24 were located in the fifth tier. That tier contained 30 boxes as compared to the second tier which had only 22 More-over, boxes on the fifth tier were shared by 4 people, those on the second by 1 or 2. See ibid., "Distribuzione de' Palchi del R. Teatro fatta d'ordine di S. M. pel Carnevale 1840–41" for list of boxes and their occupants.

[101] Quoted in Gerbore, Dame e cavalieri del Re, pp. 31–32.

Cavour were not exempt from caste prejudices in their social relations.[102]

As in the previous century, the monarchy continued to allow certain "new" families an entrée into this aristocratic social hierarchy through the mechanism of ennoblement. In fact, the House of Savoy granted some 400 hereditary titles in the years from 1814 to 1861.[103] During the Restoration, however, access to the ranks of the titular nobility became much more tightly regulated and restrictive than in the past. The simple buying of noble titles, a widespread practice in the eighteenth century when a lively market in feudal jurisdictions existed, became virtually impossible in the decades after 1814.

This did not mean that enormous wealth was an obstacle to ennoblement.[104] As a rule, court officials considered a sizeable personal fortune "sufficient to sustain the dignity of the noble position with a sumptuous life style" as an essential asset for those seeking elevation. By the 1830s, patrimonial requirements for each rank existed, ranging from L. 100,000 for the simple title of *nobile* to L. 300,000 for that of count, largely to ensure that the throne did not "bestow titles on so many poor families." In fact, insufficient resources proved to be a fatal obstacle to a number of aspirants to titled status.[105]

Nevertheless, the House of Savoy placed greater emphasis on the

---

[102] For more on Cavour's aristocratic sensibilities, see *ibid.*, p. 73 and Mack Smith, *Cavour*, pp. 193–194. For Savio's comments, see Ricci (ed.), *Memorie della Baronessa Olimpia Savio*, vol. I, p. 11. On the question of mixed balls, see sources cited in Romeo, *Cavour e il suo tempo*, vol. I, pp. 791–792.

[103] See Carpi, *L'Italia vivente*, pp. 75–77 for statistics on the number of hereditary titles.

[104] Stefano Gazzaniga is a clear case in point. Officials estimated Gazzaniga's personal fortune to be more than L. 9 million. In supporting Gazzaniga's appeal for the title, Count of Pirocco, the procurate generale claimed that while hereditary titles ought to be limited to those who had performed exceptional services to the state, such criteria should not "preclude in fact the path to it for those who possessed extraordinary riches, provided of course that they sufficient civility of birth and comportment that conforms to the rank to which they want to be elevated . . ." Gazzaniga appears to have encountered few difficulties. See AST, Prima Sez., "Titoli di Nobiltà," b. 9, Reports dated July 7 and 22, and September 18, 1831.

[105] Domenico Barile, for instance, saw his hopes for elevation to the status of *nobile* in 1836 dashed as a result of debts on his estate that reduced it to a level insufficient "to sustain with the necessary decorum the implored title of nobiltà." Similarly, a major in the cavalry, Carlo Giovanni Alberti, had his petition for a baronial title rejected in 1840 due to "the insufficiency of his material resources," which were "a long way" from the L. 200,000, "one of the conditions that are required." See AST, Prima Sez., "Titoli di Nobiltà," b. 2, F. Barile, Domenico, 1836 and b. 1, procuratore generale di S. M., no date, 1840. For similar examples, see the dossiers of Vittorio Asti, no date, 1825, and Major General Maurizio Bacchiglieri, b. 2, no date, 1843. For a more general discussion of the patrimonial criteria for ennoblement, see Genta, "Introduzione allo studio delle nobilitazioni sabaude della restaurazione

lineage and services of those men whom it chose to elevate to the titular nobility. As a rule, supplicants had to provide documentation of their family's "civilized" or respectable status for at least a century and of their "personal good services or those of their ancestors."[106] Whenever possible, would-be nobles relied on their purportedly close ties to old titled families to buttress their status claims.[107] Personal wealth and talent alone were rarely sufficient to overcome a lack of civilized lineage as many supplicants discovered. Indeed, royal officials thoroughly investigated the backgrounds of men seeking titles and did not hesitate to reject those who, in their judgment, lacked an acceptable pedigree.[108] Similarly, aristocratic disdain for the worlds of trade and commerce continued to influence the process of ennoblement even in the last decade of absolutism.[109]

Those postulants who successfully combined wealth, lineage, and service to enter officially into the ranks of the nobility found that a hereditary title did not translate into rapid social acceptance. From the outset, most of the families ennobled after 1815 were visibly separated from the older nobility by their lack of a feudal predicate. Social practice confirmed their separateness. Intermarriage between old and new

(1814–1847)," in *Atti della Società Italiana di Studi Araldici* (Turin, 1990), pp. 101–107.

[106] *Ibid.*, b. 5, procuratore generale, 1844.

[107] The procuratore generale supported the petition of Carlo Danese in 1826, on the grounds that one of Danese's ancestors had been the Tesoriere della Provincia di Pinerolo in 1650 and that his family had lived civilly for two centuries. For his part, the wealthy Novarese landowner, Francesco Basilico, argued in his successful bid for ennoblement in 1832 that his rank of commendatore in the knightly Ordine Militare di San Maurizio e Lazzaro as well as his "noble alliances by way of marriages contracted with the aristocratic Tarsis and Caccia families prove . . . the distinguished civility of [his] lineage." See *ibid.*, b. 7, F. Danese, Avv. Carlo, 1826 and b. 2, F. Basilico, Francesco, 1832.

[108] Despite Gioanni Cervetti's successful legal career and his impending marriage to the daughter of Count Negri di Sanfront, he was refused a title in 1829 because, the procuratore generale reported, "the Cervetti family cannot be considered genteel (*civile*) in any real sense." Similarly, the fact that the father-in-law of Matteo Merialdi had worked as a miller proved fatal to his hopes of a title in 1836. See *ibid.*, b. 5, F. Cervetti, Gioanni, 1829 and b. 14, F. Merialdi, Matteo, 1836.

[109] In 1846, for instance, Major General Mario Giacomo Barabino's petition for elevation to baronial status met with rejection after the procuratore generale learned that "his father was contractor, his mother [was] of low lineage . . . ." On the basis of this information, the procuratore concluded that Barabino was not suitable for elevation to the nobility, since he did not possess "one of the most essential prerequisites that must be present for the concession of an honorific title, namely a hundred years of gentility in the family." See *ibid.*, b. 2, F. Barabino, Maggiore Generale Mario Giacomo, 1846.

nobles remained fairly limited.[110] Likewise, the few women from recently ennobled families who managed to gain access to a box at the Teatro Regio were confined to the highest and most remote tiers, together with the prominent middle-class women.

INTERNECINE CONFLICT AND THE END OF ARISTOCRATIC PRIMACY

The virtual monopoly of political and social leadership enjoyed by Piedmontese nobles in the first half of the century rested upon fragile foundations, however. To begin with, the values and mechanisms that perpetuated aristocratic political dominance and social exclusivity aroused increasing resentment from other segments of the propertied classes who, in the words of Angelo Brofferio, "no longer wanted to be second best."[111] In the face of egalitarian pressures from below, the preservation of the nobility's hegemonic role depended upon a combination of at least three circumstances: (1) a relatively unified aristocratic political outlook; (2) the determination of successive Savoyard rulers to defend aristocratic privileges and prerogatives; (3) the willingness of the middle classes to compromise and accept a subordinate role in Piedmont's governmental order. By late 1840s, all three of these circumstances had largely disappeared.

Much like their counterparts in France and England, the nobility in Piedmont were united more by a shared pride of rank and a distinctive style of life than by any single political program or strategy. The Restoration accentuated this lack of political unity by ushering in an era of bitter ideological controversy and political discord within the subalpine nobility. Such divisiveness was less the result of internal differences in wealth and lineage than of divergent views on how to respond to the problems left in the wake of the French Revolution. While virtually all segments of the nobility abhorred social revolution and wished to avoid radical change at all costs, there was little agreement on how to achieve

---

[110] Only 2 percent of the nobles from older (pre-1722) feudal families in my probate survey ever wed individuals belonging to the Restoration nobility. While a third of the newer nobles in the same survey did establish marital ties with the pre-revolutionary nobility, most of those marriages involved daughters. Both new noblemen and their sons were considerably more likely to draw their spouses from the middle classes than from the ranks of the established nobility. See chapter 4, table 1 for marriage statistics. An additional survey of the genealogies of another fifteen families ennobled in the decades between 1815 and 1848 also reflects the rarity of marriages between new and old families. See Manno, *Il patriziato subalpino*, vols. II, V, XII, XV, XVI, XVIII, XIX, XXII, XXIV, XXV, XXVII.

[111] Brofferio, *Storia del Piemonte*, p. 84.

this goal. On the contrary, the very dominance of the nobility in Piedmontese political life meant that struggles over constitutions, representative government, and egalitarian reform were largely played out between and within aristocratic families, at least until the 1840s.

These issues tended to divide the nobility between two poles that paralleled, in many respects, the division between Bourbonists and Orleanists in France, or Tories and Whigs in England. At one extreme were the traditionalists who, in the words of Angelo Brofferio, formed a "compact, strong, and obstinate party that, clinging to the past, wanted to make no compromises with the present." Their chief opposition came from moderate proponents of innovation, who were themselves divided into "reformers," "constitutionalists," and "radicals."[112]

The most outspoken representative of the arch-conservative and ultramontane nobility was Count Clemente Solaro della Margarita. Born in 1792 into an old feudal family from Cuneo, Solaro experienced the trauma of the French Revolution first hand and it remained for him, as well as for many other aristocrats of his generation, a decisive formative experience.[113] That, and their hatred of the Enlightenment, combined with an intense devotion to both the Catholic Church and royal absolutism, were to provide the cornerstones of their political vision.

Aristocratic conservatives started from the premise that all political authority derived from God and the people thus owed unswerving obedience to their legitimate rulers. As Solaro proudly affirmed in one of his tracts, he was "an aristocrat . . . a defender of divine right, an enemy of the sovereignty of the people."[114] Solaro and his friend Count Emiliano Avogadro della Motta viewed all modern revolutions as an undiluted evil, rooted in the Protestant Reformation and Enlightenment notions of popular sovereignty, liberty, and equality. In this vision, the French Revolution represented a form of divine punishment, while the period after the fall of Napoleon became a temporary "respite granted by God . . . so that men, corrected and punished, might walk the straight and narrow."[115]

---

[112] See ibid., *Storia del Piemonte*, pp. 16–17. For analogies with the situation in England and France, see Rodolico, *Carlo Alberto . . . 1831–1843*, pp. 36–37.

[113] For the most detailed treatment of Solaro's family, education, and adolescent experiences, see Lovera and Rinieri, *Clemente Solaro della Margarita*, vol. I, pp. 2–38.

[114] Solaro della Margarita, *Gli avvedimenti politici*, p. 67. Solaro and his allies drew much of their intellectual inspiration from such early-nineteenth-century conservative thinkers as Joseph de Maistre and Louis de Bonald; de Maistre, in particular, played a direct role in the early governments of the Restoration in Piedmont. See Lebrun, *Joseph de Maistre*, pp. 26–35, 246–257.

[115] Solaro della Margarita, *L'uomo di stato*, vol. I, p. 279. For Solaro's views on revolu-

To prevent any repetition of the "great catastrophes" of the revolutionary era, Solaro and his allies advocated an integral restoration of the traditional principles associated with absolute monarchy, the Catholic Church, and the nobility. From the outset, they saw the pressing need for legitimate rulers to reassert that their authority derived from God, not the people, and to be prepared to use whatever means necessary, including force, in its defense. Above all, Solaro vehemently opposed any compromise with liberalism, a movement that he saw as paving the way for all forms of subversion by "allowing everyone to make themselves as they please according to their own whims" without regard for the "the will of the Creator." Even the smallest concessions to proponents of reform represented symptoms of royal weakness that would only embolden troublemakers and dishearten the king's faithful supporters.[116]

The political prescriptions of aristocratic conservatives rested, in turn, upon an avowedly hierarchical and corporative vision of social relations, one that maintained an exclusive role for the titled nobility in the governance of society. Indeed, Solaro insisted that differences in wealth, talents, and responsibilities which separated the various classes reflected the will of God: "He wants there to be those who obey and those who command, those who rule and those who serve, those who are rich and those who are poor."[117] While each class had a necessary part to play, the nobility had to remain in a position of superiority as the essential bulwark of the monarchy as well as the exclusive intermediary between the king and his subjects. In his view, aristocrats alone combined the social rank, wealth, and sense of honor needed to carry out the royal will and maintain the respect and deference of the lower classes.[118] While Solaro favored the ennoblement of able commoners, he saw little room for the non-nobles at the upper levels of government. As he expressed it, "I honor doctors and I hold engineers in high regard, but I am moved to pity when I see them deal with matters of state in the cabinets of princes, where neither the aphorisms of Hippocrates, nor Bramante's rules of architecture . . . have any application."[119]

At the opposite end of a rather narrow aristocratic political spectrum stood a small but influential group of nobles who questioned the

---

tion, the Reformation, and the Enlightenment, see *ibid.*, p. 276, *Gli avvedimenti politici*, p. 134 and 147, *Questioni di stato*, p. 98. For the ideas of Avogadro della Motta, see his *Saggio intorno al socialismo*, 2 volumes.

[116] Solaro della Margarita, *Gli avvedimenti politici*, p. 136; *L'uomo di stato*, vol. II, p. 12.

[117] Solaro della Margarita, *Gli avvedimenti politici*, p. 63.

[118] See *ibid.*, pp. 68–69; Solaro della Margarita, *L'uomo di stato*, vol. II, pp. 111–112.

[119] Solaro della Margarita, *L'uomo di stato*, vol. I, p. 283.

wisdom and practicality of Solaro's intransigent hostility to new ideas and movements.[120] In terms of wealth and lineage, little separated moderates from their conservative counterparts who in some cases were their own fathers and brothers. Many moderates were products of a set of distinctive generational experiences that included a relatively positive exposure to new French ideas and institutions; most came from families who had figured prominently in the Napoleonic Empire and then been excluded, at least temporarily, from political life under the Restoration. For others, like Camillo Cavour and Massimo d'Azeglio, their difficult position as cadets contributed both to their impatience with the traditional conventions of their class and to their relative openness to innovation. As a group, they also tended to be somewhat more cosmopolitan than the conservatives, with an intellectual preparation and extensive travel experiences that gave them an appreciation of political developments in France and Great Britain.[121]

Aristocratic moderates were just as concerned as their conservative adversaries with avoiding revolutionary change and preserving the power and influence of the old nobility. But in contrast to men like Solaro, they believed that the traditional order of monarchical absolutism and noble privilege had perished with the French Revolution. As Count Guglielmo Moffa di Lisio expressed it: "The world changes; the models that have come down to us from the Middle Ages . . . no longer serve us now." Echoing these sentiments, Count Ruggero Gabaleone di Salmour insisted that any viable political program in the nineteenth century had to accept that "the aristocratic structure of our old society has collapsed."[122] For the moderates, the reactionary policies favored by Solaro and his legitimist allies were actually harmful to the established social order, since they only increased the likelihood of new revolutionary upheavals.[123]

In order to forestall radical change, reestablish social harmony, and

---

[120] Included in this group were members of some of the most distinguished old families of the realm like the Alfieri di Sostegno, Taparelli d'Azeglio, Benso di Cavour, Balbo di Vinadio, Dal Pozzo della Cisterna, Asinari di San Marzano, and Provana di Collegno.

[121] On the experiences of these aristocratic reformers as a generation, see Gerbore, *Dame e cavalieri del Re*, pp. 25–28; Nada, *Roberto d'Azeglio*, vol. I; Romeo, *Cavour e il suo tempo*, vol. I; Briano, *Il Marchese Cesare Alfieri di Sostegno*; Ottolenghi, *La vita e i tempi di Giacinto Provana di Collegno*; Berti, *Cesare Alfieri*; Passerin d'Entrèves, *La giovinezza di Cesare Balbo*.

[122] See AST, Prima Sez., Archivio Alfieri di Sostegno, letter from Moffa di Lisio, as quoted in Manzone, *Il Conte Moffa di Lisio*, pp. 175–178; Gabaleone di Salmour, *Le riforme ed il patriziato*, p. 12.

[123] Any attempt to restore the old order without any changes "in the nineteenth century on the borders of France and with these ominous clouds in the sky," wrote

safeguard the position of the nobility, moderates advocated instead a strategic retreat through a program of gradual civic and political progress that avoided the extremes of reaction and revolution. This meant, in practical terms, the adoption of a some form of limited constitutional monarchy that, in the words of Moffa, "takes the initiative and gives today what might be seized . . . tomorrow" by diffusing popular discontent and slowly broadening the base of the Piedmontese political class.[124] The views of moderates on the type of constitutional order and the nature of the nobility's role in it evolved over time. Initially, Count Cesare Balbo envisioned a new parliamentary order in which the nobility continued to enjoy an official status as the political class *par excellence* in Piedmont. Drawing his inspiration from the British House of Lords and ostensibly open aristocratic class, Balbo favored a bicameral system of government that "legally constituted" the hereditary political position of the titled nobility in an upper chamber.[125]

By the 1830s, however, developments in France and the pressures of middle-class opinion at home had led many prominent moderates to abandon altogether the idea of exclusive political privileges for the nobility. In the immediate aftermath of the Revolutions of 1830, they began to envision instead a new and transformed role for old titled families, namely as Piedmont's great landlords whose political power lay in property rather than privilege. For Marchese Cesare Alfieri di Sostegno, landed property represented the vital "neutral factor" that would "confer vigor to democracy and increase the authority of the aristocracy" by tying "the citizen to the patriotic soil, made fertile by his sweat, [and] to the monarchy which protects it."[126] In his enthusiastic endorsement, Moffa pointed out how Alfieri's plan would "succeed in pleasing many people." The middle classes, as landowners, could "take part in the business [of government] with the same rights as nobles," while the entire population would be contented "since they will have

Moffa, demonstrated only "the infinite power of stupidity." See Manzone, *Il Conte Moffa di Lisio*, p. 178.

124 *Ibid.*

125 Balbo, *Pensieri ed esempi*, p. 265. For a more general discussion of Balbo's political views, see Passerin d'Entreves, *La giovinezza di Cesare Balbo*, pp. 243–250. In a similar vein, most other aristocratic reformers in the early years of the Restoration were partisans of the French constitution, which also preserved a corporative role for the nobility through a chamber of peers. See Brofferio, *Storia del Piemonte*, pp. 17–18 and Romeo, *Dal Piemonte sabaudo all'Italia liberale*, pp. 22–26.

126 Alfieri di Sostegno proposed a tri-level plan of constitutional reform based on land: small landowners would participate in municipal councils, medium ones in provincial councils, and the large landowners in a central state council. See Alfieri to Sclopis, quoted in Berti, *Cesare Alfieri*, pp. 45–46.

what every class of people wants today, namely a constitution." Above all, moderates like Moffa emphasized the benefits to the titled elite who could dominate the state, since "nobility and property are things that still sustain each other in Piedmont, the soil being, in general, owned by the nobles." In this way, the social base of the established order could be broadened without sacrificing the aristocracy's leading role. As Moffa expressed it, "if the nobility exits from power by one door, it reenters immediately through the other by means of property."[127]

These contrasting moderate and conservative visions of state organization and of the role of the titled nobility in public life largely defined the terms of intra-aristocratic political struggles in the decades after 1814, struggles that pitted father against son and brother against brother. As Angelo di Saluzzo recalled in his memoirs, ideological and private conflicts in this era became so intertwined that "the discord [was] often within the family [and] the diversity of political principles became a motive for personal animosities and even a pretext . . . for hurting a rival [or] a personal enemy."[128] Indeed, in no other state on the Italian peninsula did tensions within the old privileged orders give rise to so much bitterness and acrimony as in Piedmont, where they erupted into open rebellion, criminal prosecution, and forced exile of young men from some of the most prominent aristocratic families. Ultimately, these internal struggles produced no real winners, since they weakened the nobility as a whole precisely at a time when new forces were challenging their monopoly of political leadership.

The most dramatic and best-known instance of intra-elite conflict came only seven years after the return of the House of Savoy from Sardinia: the ill-fated Piedmontese Revolution of 1821. In the political climate that prevailed in Piedmont after the fall of Napoleon, the reactionary policies of the government as well as the mistreatment of those families associated with the French imperial regime soon angered and frustrated a group of idealistic, young aristocrats, for the most part army officers, led by Santorre Derossi di Santarosa, Carlo Asinari di San Marzano, Giacinto Provana di Collegno, and Moffa di Lisio. Motivated by a contradictory blend of Italian nationalism, Piedmontese military expansionism, constitutionalism, and loyalty to the House of Savoy, these men spearheaded a military revolt in March 1821 to force the

---

[127] Moffa to Alfieri, quoted in Manzone, *Il Conte Moffa di Lisio*, pp. 175–178. For similar views, see the comments of Gabaleone di Salmour in his *Le riforme ed il patrizi*, p. 13 as well as those of Cavour, quoted in Romeo, *Cavour e il suo tempo*, vol. I, p. 575.

[128] Zucchi (ed.), "I moti del 1821 nelle memorie inedite di Alessandro Saluzzo," p. 526.

abdication of Vittorio Emanuele I and the enthronement of the supposedly sympathetic Prince of Carignano, Carlo Alberto. While virtually
all the titled rebels favored a constitution similar to that of the French or
English which guaranteed the nobility a privileged role in government,
they wound up supporting a more democratic program modeled on
that of Spain under the pressure of events.[129]

The aristocratic rebels achieved the first objective and initially
enjoyed the sympathy of the younger generation of nobles like Roberto
d'Azeglio. Nonetheless, the new regime lasted only a week before its
lack of popular support, its failure to win over more moderate aristocrats
like Cesare Balbo, and its abandonment by Carlo Alberto, who
remained obedient to the new king, Vittorio Emanuele's brother Carlo
Felice, left it isolated and vulnerable to forces loyal to the monarchy.
The internecine character of the conflict emerged clearly in early April
when royal troops led by their noble officers under the command of
Marshal Vittorio Sallier de la Tour, supported by Austrian forces,
defeated the rebels on the battlefield of Novara.[130] The titled leaders of
the insurrection fled into exile in Geneva, while at home Count Ignazio
Thaon di Revel oversaw a sweeping purge of suspected sympathizers in
the army and bureaucracy. The events of 1821, and the repression and
disillusionment that followed them, not only strengthened the position
of the most conservative elements in the state; they also left deep divisions that continued to poison relations between and within many of
the leading families of the nobility throughout the 1820s.[131]

The following decade, divisions between aristocratic moderates and
conservatives resurfaced in less violent forms in the more open political
and economic climate of Carlo Alberto's reign.[132] Chastened by the
experiences of 1821 and alarmed by the Revolution of 1830 in France,
moderates such as Cesare Alfieri, Roberto d'Azeglio, and Camillo
Cavour began to carve out a new role for themselves by promoting a
number of educational, charitable, and cultural initiatives that prepared
the social terrain for those political reforms that, according to Alfieri,

---

[129] See Romeo, *Dal Piemonte sabaudo all'Italia liberale*, pp. 22–28.

[130] See *ibid.*, pp. 17–29.

[131] See *ibid.* pp. 29–35; Nada, *Roberto d'Azeglio*, vol. 1, pp. 101–144. Among the
nobles who went into exile were Santarosa, Lisio, Turinetti di Priero, Dal Pozzo
della Cisterna, Asinari di San Marzano, and Provana di Collegno. Massimo d'Azeglio provides some indication of the impact of his brother's marginal role in the Revolution of 1821 on family life in his memoirs. See d'Azeglio, *Things I Remember*,
p. 173.

[132] These years saw the creation of a Council of State, judicial and military reforms, and
the cautious liberalization of Piedmontese trade policies. See Romeo, *Cavour e il suo
tempo*, vol. 1, pp. 772–773.

were needed "to combat revolution." D'Azeglio, his wife Costanza, and other female relatives from the Costa della Trinità and Luserna di Rorà families took the lead in these areas, sponsoring new workhouses and poor relief shelters in the wake of the Cholera epidemic of 1834. Cavour's similar concerns led him to collaborate with Count Carlo Beraudo di Pralormo in the reorganization and reform of the Opere pie in 1838.[133] At the same time, the moderates became involved with the problems of popular education, founding in 1839, for instance, a new organization to promote the diffusion of children's shelters and schools throughout the realm.[134]

Moderates included bourgeois spokesmen in these initiatives to achieve a larger objective: the breakdown of traditional caste barriers and the forging of new political ties with influential sectors of the middle classes. Their strategy found expression in a number of new voluntary associations which they sponsored in these years. In 1839, for example, they founded a Società di ballo to encourage mixed socializing between nobles and bourgeois.[135] Two years later, Cavour and his titled friends took an additional step in this direction by launching the Società del Whist, an English-style gentlemen's club that provided a gathering place for all currents of respectable society in Turin: "old names of the ancient aristocracy, young hopefuls from the arts [and] sciences, and established figures from the banking and business worlds."[136]

In the rigidly hierarchical social world of Turin, these modest leisure, charitable, and educational activities encouraged the growth of new reference groups while sharpening divisions within both the titled aristocracy and the middle classes. Angelo Brofferio recalled a decade later how the mixed balls and socially integrated associations fueled two schisms: the one between "the blue-blooded aristocracy that did not want to *merge* . . . and the less thick-skinned aristocracy that would consent to touch the hand of bankers," and the other between "the money men who, calling themselves the *buona borghesia,* wanted

[133] See Nada, *Roberto d'Azeglio,* vol. I, pp. 230–235; d'Azeglio, *Things I Remember,* p. 306. For Alfieri's views on the need for reforms to combat revolution, see letters cited in Berti, *Cesare Alfieri,* pp. 43–47. Cognasso, "Nobiltà e borghesia," p. 240, mentions Cavour's involvement in the reform.

[134] See Rodolico, *Carlo Alberto . . . 1831–1843,* pp. 368–377.

[135] See Cavour to Paul-Émile Maurice, February 5, 1839, as cited in Romeo, *Cavour e il suo tempo,* vol. I, p. 792.

[136] In fact, the list of the Whist's founding members contained the names not only of influential patricians, but also distinguished bourgeois professional men, wealthy bankers as well as a number of prominent magistrates, army officers, philanthropists, and diplomats. See Società Camillo di Cavour, *Un secolo di vita del Whist,* pp. 19, 32–38; ACT, b. 93, Società del Whist, soci fondatori, March 1, 1841.

to be accepted, and intellectuals and professionals who did not want to be second."[137] Predictably, the moderates encountered strong opposition from both radical democratic elements and aristocratic traditionalists.[138]

The values and aspirations that underlay moderate social initiatives also informed the *Associazione Agraria Subalpina*, an organization launched by Cesare Alfieri and a small group of prominent nobles and bourgeois notables in the spring of 1842 to unite "all . . . the various elements of agricultural progress."[139] Much like comparable bodies elsewhere in northern and central Italy, the new association aimed to promote improved methods of farming and stock raising by disseminating the latest scientific information. At the same time, the association had a broader social mission of encouraging practical collaboration between nobility and the middle classes. Its founders achieved rapid success in this latter endeavor, attracting not only landowners and farmers, but also men who had little or no connection to agriculture.[140]

Despite the Agraria's egalitarian pretensions and heterogeneous membership, its titled founders displayed little inclination to share leadership with their non-noble colleagues. Indeed, aristocrats controlled most of the key offices.[141] Even so, conservatives like Solaro della Margarita denounced the Agraria and its congresses as "a pretext, a means of disguising ideas that subvert the established order."[142] These warnings did not sway Carlo Alberto who virtually guaranteed its success by sup-

---

[137] Brofferio, *Storia del Piemonte*, p. 84.

[138] For his part, Brofferio attacked the new associations as Trojan horses of the "most sublime aristocracy of Piedmont," ridiculing the very idea of class collaboration as "the brotherhood between the wolf and the lamb," see *ibid*. Titled conservatives were even more sweeping in their denunciations of the moderate initiatives. On their opposition to the new charitable agencies, see Rodolico, *Carlo Alberto . . . 1831–1843*, pp. 370–378.

[139] AST, Prima Sez., Istruzione Pubblica, Accademie ed altri Istituti Scientifici, Società Agraria, b. 8, letter of transmission of the proposed statute to Count Gallina, May 31, 1842, cited in Romeo, *Cavour e il suo tempo*, vol. II, p. 83.

[140] The moderates' initiative also received an enthusiastic reception from influential middle-class spokesmen like Lorenzo Valerio. Such sweeping support quickly translated into a massive influx of members. See Prato, *Fatti e dottrine economiche*, p. 159. For the views of Valerio, see *Letture di famiglia*, vol. I, n.44, November 5, 1842, as cited in Romeo, *Cavour e il suo tempo*, vol. II, p. 86.

[141] *Ibid.*, p. 159. Despite their avowed commitments to ideas of progress and social cooperation, men like Cavour and Alfieri remained, to some extent, the products of their class and its particular values. For Cavour's views, in particular, see his *Sui voyages agronomiques di F. Lullin de Chateauvieux*, in *Scritti di economia*, p. 66 as cited in Romeo, *Cavour e il suo tempo*, vol. I, p. 575.

[142] Solaro della Margarita, *Memorandum storico-politico*, p. 201; *L'uomo di stato*, vol. II, p. 226.

porting the first proposal and then recognizing the association as an official institution.[143]

The evolution of the Subalpine Agrarian Association quickly demonstrated, however, the enormous difficulties confronting moderates in their attempt to broaden the social base of participation in public life to the middle classes and, at the same time, preserve aristocratic leadership. In fact, the association developed less as the embodiment of harmonious social collaboration than as a forum for the expression of deep-seated class antagonisms and resentments. As Francesco Predari recalled some two decades later, "the mixture of so many varied elements with such distinct social backgrounds, wealth, education, [and] political aspirations, necessarily had to produce in short order conflicts of interest and aims."[144] The Agraria gave bourgeois spokesmen like Lorenzo Valerio an organizational base to advance their own projects and, perhaps more importantly, their own claims to equal leadership status.

These larger social tensions fueled the emergence of two rival factions within the Subalpine Agrarian Association by 1845: the one led by Valerio, the so-called "democrats," and the other appropriately named the "aristocrats" – a group led by Alfieri, Cavour, Petitti di Roreto, and Gabaleone di Salmour. The two factions soon clashed over the former's proposals to decentralize and democratize the operations of the association, as well as over the selection of a new president to replace Alfieri who resigned early in the spring of 1845.[145] Factional strife came to a head in the first months of 1846 when Cavour and his allies were voted out of the ruling council of the association, followed by governmental intervention after Cavour's father denounced the Agraria as a center of political subversion. The association was drastically restructured with royal officials nominating the president and vice-presidents and regulating all meetings and topics of discussion.[146]

The evolution of the Agrarian Association dramatically illuminated the political vulnerability of Piedmont's aristocratic ruling class on the eve of 1848. The unalloyed hostility of men like Solaro della Margarita to the idea of voluntary associations underscored how profound were the ideological differences separating titled arch-conservatives from

---

[143] Prato, *Fatti e dottrine economiche*, p. 159.

[144] Predari, *I primi vagiti della libertà*, p. 41.

[145] On the views of Cavour, see his letter to Corio, March 5, 1846, cited in Prato, *Fatti e dottrine economiche*, p. 420n and his letter to Costa de Beauregard, October, 1847 cited in Romeo, *Cavour e il suo tempo*, vol. II, p. 107n. For Petitti's rather critical judgment of the "aristocrats," see his letter to Michele Erede, March 25, 1846, cited in *ibid.*, vol. II, p. 114n.

[146] Romeo, *Cavour e il suo tempo*, vol. II, pp. 107–115.

their moderate fellow nobles. Even those aristocrats who chose to join the association did not necessarily share a common political outlook.[147] Not surprisingly, such differences precluded any coherent strategy or unified action in defense of the nobility's corporative power and privileges. At the same time, the aggressive challenge advanced by Valerio's democratic faction to aristocratic domination of the Agrarian Association showed that influential segments of the middle classes no longer accepted unquestioningly the nobility's right to lead. As a result, aristocratic reformers found themselves in the 1840s engaged in a two-front war against a rigidly traditional nobility opposed to any compromises, on the one side, and increasingly assertive and impatient middle-class proponents of more radical reform, on the other.

Above all, Piedmontese aristocrats continued to be the subordinate partners of an absolute monarch whose support was ultimately decisive to whatever power they might enjoy. While Carlo Alberto remained a profoundly ambiguous and contradictory figure with policies that oscillated between liberal reform and ultramontane reaction, he did display a certain willingness in the late 1840s to sacrifice aristocratic prerogatives in order to curry the favor of middle-class public opinion and broaden the base of support for the throne. The nobility's ability to oppose or dilute royal policies that threatened their power was hamstrung by their longstanding tradition of unwavering service to the House of Savoy. Marchese Cesare Taparelli d'Azeglio, a bitter foe of constitutional government, eloquently captured the dilemma facing traditional conservatives in an era of institutional change:

> What would happen if Piedmont became a constitutional state? Through rebellion? . . . I should certainly oppose the rebels with all I had of mind, strength, and influence . . . Should it happen with royal assent, whether obtained by persuasion or through fear of worse evil, I should conform to the royal command. Once the new constitution was established I should be its tenacious supporter. To obey the ruler is a duty with but few exceptions. Had the King agreed to any other form of monarchy, mixed or constitutional as might be, there would be no limitation to this duty.[148]

Dynastic loyalty gave defenders of aristocratic corporative power little choice but to obey their king, even when that meant their own political extinction as a separate caste.

---

[147] Marchese Massimo Cordero di Montezemolo and Count Giambattista Michelini, for instance, became leading spokesmen for the democratic faction and harsh critics of Cavour. See Romeo, *Cavour e il suo tempo*, vol. II, pp. 95–97.

[148] Quoted in d'Azeglio, *Things I Remember*, p. 273.

Significantly, conflicts within the Agrarian Association in 1846 prefigured a much more decisive political setback for the entire Piedmontese nobility in 1848. Under mounting pressure from restive democratic forces to embrace the cause of Italian unification and adopt sweeping changes at home, Carlo Alberto slid reluctantly in the direction of reform in the second half of 1847. Reform demands coincided with an intense public campaign against the nobility. Even respectable non-nobles like Pier Alessandro Paravia, a frequent presence in aristocratic salons, began to speak of the "dislike that boils up in us bourgeois against the nobility," a view echoed by foreign observers like the British ambassador who warned in November 1847 that a "class war . . . [is] not far off."[149] Anti-aristocratic sentiments took a variety of forms from wall graffiti proclaiming "death to the nobles" to anonymous pamphlets that violently attacked the hereditary nobility and demanded their immediate elimination as "dangerous enemies of constitutional liberty" and as sources of "civil discord."[150]

In the face of this aggressive reform movement, Piedmont's foremost aristocratic families displayed no more unity of outlook than they had in the past. Hardliners like Solaro della Margarita steadfastly favored a policy of royal intransigence even at the risk of a head-on collision with new forces. Other conservatives like Marchese Vittorio Amedeo Sallier de la Tour and Count Carlo Beraudo di Pralormo recognized the need for the king to introduce a constitution, but advocated one that included a chamber of hereditary peers based on wealth and "those families which have rendered significant services to the state."[151] The foremost moderate nobles – Cavour, Cesare Alfieri, Roberto d'Azeglio, and Count Pietro De Rossi di Santa Rosa – dismissed the idea of an "aristocratic high chamber" as antiquated and no longer unacceptable to middle-class opinion; they called instead for a constitution that guaranteed genuinely representative institutions as the only way to avoid violent insurrections, diffuse demands for an "ultra-democratic constitution," and insure a peaceful renewal of the country's ruling classes.[152]

This moderate position, which Alfieri, Count Giacinto Borelli, and Count Federico Sclopis di Salerano argued before the king carried the

---

[149] On the views of Paravia, see V. Cian, "Vita e coltura nel periodo albertino," p. 335; the British ambassador is cited in Rodolico, *Carlo Alberto . . . 1843–1849*, p. 7.

[150] See the anonymous tract, *Non più nobiltà ereditarie* (Turin, 1848), p. 121.

[151] See Romeo, "Una iniziativa costituzionale," vol. I, pp. 368–370.

[152] See the speech of Piero De Rossi di Santa Rosa in *Risorgimento*, February 7, 1848, as well as Cavour's letter to Giovanetti, February 1848, both cited in Romeo, *Cavour e il suo tempo*, vol. II, pp. 287, 291.

day in the wake of the February Revolution in France. In a setting of public dinners, street demonstrations and petitions at home, and mounting nationalist and democratic unrest elsewhere on the peninsula, Carlo Alberto promulgated on February 8, 1848 a new constitution, the *Statuto*.[153] Although the document left a number of questions unanswered, it clearly envisioned a government that was monarchical and representative, with legislative power shared by the king and two chambers: an elective lower chamber and an upper chamber whose members were appointed for life by the throne.

The *Statuto*, which had been co-signed by such titled luminaries as Count Ottavio Thaon di Revel, Count Ermolao Asinari di San Marzano, and Count Mario Broglia di Casalborgone, effectively demolished the position of the hereditary nobility as a legally privileged caste within the Piedmontese body politic. The new constitution recognized the existence of titles of nobility and the king's right to confer new ones, but it explicitly proclaimed the equality of all citizens before the law "regardless of their title or rank." As a result, apart from the titles attached to their names, nobles ceased to enjoy any distinctions or rights that were denied to other classes in the society. Thus, the *Statuto* attributed no official public functions of any sort to the nobility nor did it make titled status a prerequisite for any state office.[154] At least in the eyes of the law, aristocratic gentlemen now had to compete on equal terms with their former legal and social inferiors for the prizes and honors of public life.

[153] See *ibid.*, pp. 287–291 for a chronology of events leading up to the proclamation of the *Statuto*.

[154] For the articles comprising the *Statuto*, see Rodolico, *Storia del parlamento italiano*, vol. I, pp. 421–428; on their implications for the status of the nobility, see Rumi, "La politica nobiliare del Regno d'Italia," pp. 578–579.

CHAPTER 2

THE LONG GOODBYE: ARISTOCRATS IN POLITICS AND PUBLIC LIFE: 1848–1914

The Revolution of 1848 fundamentally transformed the political and legal framework within which Piedmont's titled nobility had long exercised leadership and exerted power. The triumph of constitutional government and full civil equality that year not only ended the aristocracy's virtual monopoly of high state office in the Kingdom of Sardinia; it also eliminated their last remaining institutional privileges. Indeed, the nobility ceased to exist as a separate corporative body in the new parliamentary order that emerged from the *Statuto*. Officially, only individual noble families remained and they now represented at best just one component of a much larger and heterogeneous ruling class, defined more by wealth and education than birth and privilege. Such changes unavoidably entailed a significant reduction in the direct political power wielded by the old nobility in the decades after 1848.

The loss of their formal institutional status in the state, however, did not mark the end of aristocratic involvement in politics. On the contrary, Piedmont's titled families managed to keep some of their old roles while carving out new ones for themselves that together still assured them an influential place in public life both locally and at the national level in the second half of the nineteenth century. They were able to do so in part by exploiting the more informal advantages afforded by their wealth and by the prestige they derived from generations of public service and political leadership. Especially in the system of limited suffrage that prevailed in the Kingdom of Sardinia, aristocratic landowners were well situated to exploit older loyalties in the countryside in order to become the standard-bearers of rural religious and particularist values. The ascension of their own monarch, Vittorio Emanuele II, to the throne of the new Italian Kingdom in 1861 assured Piedmontese nobles a special status in court circles and a prominent role in key institutions of the national state that emerged in the following decade. Finally, long-standing networks based on kinship and clientele relations gave old-line titled families the personal influence and patronage power to remain "unofficial" leaders at the provincial and village levels, even as their names ceased to feature prominently on electoral slates or on published rosters of government ministers, parliamentary deputies, and municipal councilors. In this fashion, nobles were able to perpetuate an older way of life while contributing to and benefiting from a distinctive political culture that rested upon local allegiances rather than stable party organizations.

THE PLACE OF THE ARISTOCRACY IN THE NEW POLITICAL ORDER

From the outset, the nobility assumed a much more modest role in the new parliamentary institutions that arose in the course of 1848. The change was immediately evident in the elections of April of that year, the first of the constitutional era. Few titled nobles chose to stand for election; those who did emerged triumphant in a mere 32 of the 204 colleges represented in the Chamber of Deputies. A sharply reduced aristocratic political presence was no less striking at the local level. The elections of November 1848 in the city of Turin, for instance, produced a new Municipal Council that included only 22 aristocrats among its 80 members, a far cry from the two-thirds majority of the *decurioni* they had enjoyed only a year earlier.[1]

Still, despite the loss of their old privileges and prerogatives, even traditional defenders of the titled nobility were inclined to accept the new constitutional arrangements, if only as the lesser of evils in the turbulent political climate of 1848. Commenting on the attitudes of the "diehards," the moderate Marchesa Costanza d'Azeglio observed how they became "all partisans of the Constitution, overcome as they are by fear and because they hope that in this manner they can save themselves through the upper chamber." This possibility found confirmation in the disappointed comments of radical democrats like Brofferio who complained that "representative government with two chambers has always been the best government for the aristocratic castes to become arbiters . . . between the people and the throne."[2] In fact, the new political order offered three potential avenues for the nobility to reassert their leadership: (1) as the closest advisors and favorites of a powerful monarchy; (2) as the dominant element in the Senate; (3) as the leaders of a

---

[1] For results of the first elections to the Chamber of Deputies, see Rodolico, *Storia del parlamento italiano*, vol. I, pp. 445–452. Data on the social makeup of Turin's municipal council is from ACT, Amministrazione, Consiglieri comunali, b. 3, vols. 7 and 8.

[2] Brofferio, *Storia del Piemonte*, parte terza, capo secondo, p. 30. For D'Azeglio's views, see *Souvenirs historiques de la marquise Constance d'Azeglio*, p. 195.

conservative party in the Chamber of Deputies closely allied to the Catholic hierarchy and with a solid base of rural support.

To begin with, the *Statuto* attributed sweeping powers to the monarch, powers that could be used to limit and, perhaps, roll back the reforms in defense of the values and institutions of the old order. The king remained "the supreme head of the state" and as such he enjoyed a monopoly of executive authority, commanded the armed forces, controlled foreign policy, and made nominations to all state offices.[3] In the exercise of their powers, it was expected that the monarchs would go on relying on the counsel of their oldest and closest tutors and advisors who came from the ranks of the nobility. The introduction of a constitution did nothing to alter the privileged access to the throne enjoyed by great titled families who continued to monopolize the key sinecures in the royal household and at court. Moreover, in the first decade after 1848, the nobility found a sympathetic patron and powerful ally on the throne. Vittorio Emanuele II was reluctant to give up his family's traditional autocratic prerogatives and resisted the restrictions that came with the introduction of constitutional government. In particular, he was hostile to any understanding with democratic elements and did not hesitate to impose his ministers of war, intervene directly in the electoral process, and engage in extra-parliamentary intrigues.[4]

The willingness of the king to use his enormous authority to ensure the nobility a prominent place in the new political order translated, in institutional terms, into *de facto* aristocratic control of the Senate. While the *Statuto* made no specific mention of the nobility among the twenty-one categories of citizens eligible for royal appointment to the Senate, the old aristocratic families confidently expected to monopolize at least four – namely those for top diplomats, high-ranking military officers, wealthy tax payers, and men whose "eminent services or achievements will have added lustre to the patria."[5] Initially, their expectations proved to be justified. The first group nominated in April 1848 read like a "Who's Who" of the titled nobility with names like Alfieri di Sostegno, Colli di Felizzano, Ferrero della Marmora, Provana di Collegno, and Taparelli d'Azeglio featuring prominently. Over the course of the year, most of the leading figures of Piedmont's old governing class were elevated to the Senate. By December 1848, the nobility accounted for a majority of the newly appointed members of the upper chamber. In accordance with the decidedly aristocratic makeup of the Senate, the

[3] *Ibid.* [4] See Mack Smith, *Italy and its Monarchy*, pp. 3–5.
[5] For a complete list of the categories of eligibility for the Senate, see Article 33 of the *Statuto*, as reprinted in Rodolico, *Storia del parlamento italiano*, vol. I, p. 424.

king picked Count Gaspare Coller as the first president of the body and nominated Marchese Cesare Alfieri di Sostegno, Marchese Antonio Brignone Sale, and Baron Giuseppe Manno to assist him as vice-presidents.[6] Despite the presence of a few prominent moderates like Alfieri and Petitti di Roreto, the more conservative landed and military nobility dominated the upper chamber from its inception. As Petitti complained in April 1848, his nomination now required him to keep "the company of a large number of reactionaries" who, he claimed, comprised "no less than five-sixths" of the Senators."[7] Since the constitution dictated that all legislation have the approval of the upper chamber, aristocratic dominance made that body a potentially important bulwark of the old ruling class and monarchical authority against the more liberal Chamber of Deputies.

In the case of the lower chamber, the nobility accounted for only a small minority of the deputies, but these deputies were well situated to play a prominent role there. At first, the various noble factions achieved an exceptional degree of political unity in response to the militancy and verbal extremism of the democratic left in 1848–1849, which drove moderates to positions virtually indistinguishable from those of the conservative old guard. More importantly, aristocratic politicians were able to dominate two of the major parliamentary groups that emerged after 1848. On the one hand, noble reformers like Cavour, Alfieri, and Massimo d'Azeglio continued to furnish both the leadership and ideas of the moderate center-right group that headed most of the governments in the ensuing decade. In fact, titled moderates accounted for all but a few of the aristocratic ministers who occupied forty-two of the seventy-one cabinet offices and provided seven of the prime ministers in the first eight governments of the constitutional era.[8]

At the same time, the majority of titled deputies and old aristocratic families identified more with the rightist coalition of royalists and clericalists led by Count Ottavio Thaon di Revel, which included in its ranks Cavour's older brother, Marchese Gustavo Benso di Cavour.[9] With its

[6] See ibid., pp. 408–409; Segretariato Generale del Senato, Elenchi storici e statistici dei senatori, provides data on nobles in the Senate. Nobles accounted for forty-six of the eighty-seven new senators.

[7] Petitti's comments are from a letter to Michele Erede which is quoted in Romeo, Cavour e il suo tempo, vol. II, p. 375.

[8] For the composition of the governments during the legislative sessions of the Subalpine parliament, see Rodolico, Storia del parlamento italiano, vol. III, pp. xxix–xxxii. During this period, all but one of the eight prime ministers were aristocrats.

[9] For Gustavo di Cavour's place in Piedmontese political life, see Monale, "Lineamenti generali per la storia dell'Armonia," 475–482.

close ties to the Catholic Church and the court, and its solid base of support in the countryside, Thaon di Revel's group seemed to offer the best prospects for becoming a genuine conservative party that institutionalized aristocratic influence in the Chamber of Deputies in a way similar to that of the Tories in England or the agrarian conservatives in Prussia. Members of this group were, for instance, among the strongest advocates of expanded suffrage, convinced that, in the words of Count Luigi Torelli, it would lead to "the parties [which] have until now had to deal with eighty or one hundred electors for each deputy, losing the game with the entire population, over which will prevail the influence of the landowners."[10]

The possibilities of a conservative party guided by aristocrats and supported by the church found their clearest expression in the elections of November 1857. After a campaign in which priests and prelates aggressively mobilized the faithful, voters elected a substantial bloc of conservative deputies that included more than fifty nobles. Cavour, for one, recognized the potential benefits of these results: "Although the larger part of these counts and marquises are personally hostile to me, I rejoice to see them in the bosom of Parliament. Practical acquaintance with affairs will enlighten them, will moderate them, and in a given time will transform them into Tories from the Clericalists they are now."[11]

The elections of 1857, however, proved to be the exception rather than the rule. The Piedmontese nobility achieved considerably less success than their Prussian counterparts in carving out an institutional role for themselves in the new constitutional order. Indeed, events in the first decade after 1848 revealed the inability of the throne, the upper chamber, or the parliamentary right to provide a stable and enduring base for reasserting the political authority of the nobility. Early on, various factors tended to limit the value of the Senate as a vehicle of aristocratic power. While the upper house was theoretically equal in status to the Chamber of Deputies, in practice it quickly assumed a subordinate and secondary role in the legislative and governing process. To begin with, the advanced age and conservatism of its members prevented the Senate from developing into an arena of significant conflict

---

[10] See Torelli to Pinelli, April 26, 1849, as cited in Romeo, *Cavour e il suo tempo*, II, p. 384n. Even notorious die-hards like Solaro accepted the legitimacy of the *Statuto* as a royal decree; what they sought was a narrow interpretation of its articles that guaranteed "the protection of religion, the independence of the Monarchy, the peace and the prosperity of the country." See Solaro della Margarita, *Agli elettori del collegio di Borgomanero*, p. 46; *Discorso secondo alla nazione*, p. 5, both titles cited in Monaco, *Clemente Solaro della Margarita, pp. 333–336*.

[11] Luigi Chiala, ed., *Lettere edite ed inedite di Camillo Cavour* (Turin, 1882–1887), vol. II, pp. 506–507, quoted in Thayer, *The Life and Times of Cavour*, I, p. 466.

and debate. More importantly, the upper chamber failed to win the power to compel the resignation of a government or the right of financial initiative enjoyed by the Chamber of Deputies. As a result, by 1861 the Senate possessed little more than the power to delay legislation, a power that did not give its aristocratic members a particularly constructive role in the political process.

More importantly, the political influence of the nobility suffered as a consequence of the mounting conflicts between church and state in the 1850s. These conflicts not only divided the nobility, but they also effectively disrupted the traditional alliance of throne, sword, and altar in Piedmont, limited the influence of clerical aristocrats at court, and forced an otherwise autocratic Vittorio Emanuele II to accept the mechanisms and methods of parliamentary government. The king's anti-Austrian policies and his territorial ambitions in Italy as well as the efforts of successive governments to abolish the unconstitutional privileges still enjoyed by the church in Piedmont put him on a collision course with the Vatican and its conservative Catholic supporters from 1850 onwards. Steadfast clerical intransigence, on the one hand, and a growing anti-clericalism in parliament, on the other, sabotaged efforts to settle this conflict in 1854 and relations between the House of Savoy and the Vatican deteriorated dramatically in the second half of the decade. The resulting crusade of the Vatican against the Risorgimento proved, in the long run, to be especially damaging to the political fortunes of the traditionalist right not just in Piedmont, but throughout Italy. In the absence of the church's support, conservatives were unable to link the powerful ideological appeals of nationalism and religion to mobilize a vast Catholic electorate against progressive legislation and in favor of authoritarian rule.[12]

In the short run, the crisis in church–state relations put Piedmontese aristocratic conservatives in an untenable position. What should have been their primary source of strength – the enormous influence of the church – became increasingly directed against royal authority and thus evolved into a political liability. Weakened by royal resentment of the clericalists and torn by contending dynastic and religious loyalties, Thaon di Revel's parliamentary right never achieved any enduring political cohesion largely as a result of divisions that found personal expression in clashes between Thaon di Revel and hardliners such as Solaro della Margarita and Avogadro della Motta.[13] In fact, the split between

---

[12] See Woolf, *A History of Italy, 1700–1860*, pp. 438–439; Thayer, *Italy and the Great War*, pp. 107–124.
[13] See Monaco, *Clemente Solaro della Margarita*, pp. 128–131.

church and state accentuated divisions within the nobility as a whole; some men such as Count Roberto Beraudo di Pralormo, the son of one of Carlo Alberto's most trusted ministers, resigned from their posts and withdrew into internal exile, while others merged into a larger and more heterogeneous liberal ruling class.[14]

Ironically, the policies and tactical brilliance that made Count Camillo Benso di Cavour the foremost aristocratic political figure of the era also contributed significantly to limiting aristocratic leadership in the new parliamentary order. While Cavour shared many of the prejudices of his class, he was committed to the renewal of Piedmont's political elite through a judicious merger of the liberal-minded nobility with moderate elements of the middle classes. Accordingly, he viewed aristocratic leaders of the right as among his chief adversaries and sought to reduce their power and influence. Cavour was the key figure in the various parliamentary maneuvers in the mid-1850s that sabotaged plans for a conservative government headed by Thaon di Revel and led to the rupture of relations between Vittorio Emanuele II and the largely aristocratic forces of clerical conservatism in Piedmont. His commitment to political renewal, however, found its most important expression already earlier in the decade in what Thaon di Revel denounced as the *Connubio*: Cavour's coalition with the left center.[15] To enhance his own personal power and to forge a more solid parliamentary base for both a constitutional monarchy and liberal reform, Cavour engineered in 1852 an unprecedented parliamentary alliance of the right center and left center in support of a program of "civil and political progress." As a result of this alliance, he succeeded in dividing the left and freeing the government from its dependence on the votes of the traditional conservatives. But, in the process, he also condemned those nobles who did not share his views to political isolation and impotence and created another obstacle to the development of an organized stronghold of aristocratic political influence.[16]

Students of Italian history have long considered the *Connubio* as the pivotal event that inaugurated a "transformist" system of parliamentary government based on constantly shifting majorities composed of small groups rather than on two major parties, one progressive and the other conservative, which alternate in power as in Great Britain and the

---

[14] Count Roberto Beraudo di Pralormo was a member of the diplomatic corps who was elevated to the ambassadorship in Rome in 1853. Two years later, his "Catholic cavalier's faith" led him to resign his position. See Archivio privato Beraudo di Pralormo, funeral oration of Professor B. Bona, 1857.

[15] See Thayer, *The Life and Times of Cavour*, vol. I, p. 142.

[16] See Perticone, "Il regime costituzionale," 719–737.

United States.[17] Whatever were its consequences for the cause of liberalism and national unification, Cavour's broad centrist coalition struck an immediate blow to aristocratic political pretensions by making it considerably more difficult for the nobility to build and lead a genuine conservative party. Aristocrats were certainly not excluded from politics, but their participation became that of local notables engaged in the pursuit of immediate political advantages rather than that of leaders of an organized party committed to the defense of the traditional interests and values associated with the nobility.

These developments in the decade after 1848 shaped the active, but decidedly ambivalent role played by the Piedmontese aristocracy in the events leading to the creation of a unified Italian state between 1859 and 1861. On the one hand, as any textbook notes, Vittorio Emanuele II and a small core of largely patrician moderates were the chief architects of unification. Moreover, the nobility as a group participated in disproportionately large numbers in the struggles for national independence. Thus, 148 men or roughly half the membership of the aristocratic Società del Whist, served as officers in the military campaigns of 1859, while another 80 took part in the expeditions into Central Italy in 1860–61.[18] The old titled nobility, in general, accounted for most of the high-ranking army officers and diplomats who implemented Cavour's initiatives in these years. Indeed, they contributed two-thirds of the lieutenant-generals and nearly all the top commanders who led the Piedmontese army in the campaigns of 1859–60 as well as 36 of the 43 ranking members of the diplomatic corps who handled the delicate negotiations with the Great Powers that accompanied the military operations.[19]

On the other hand, aristocratic enthusiasm for the House of Savoy's leading role in the campaign to unify the Italian peninsula was far from unalloyed or unanimous, especially after the transfer of Nice and Savoy, the cradle of the dynasty, to France in 1860. While some titled members of Thaon di Revel's party made a show of reassuring foreign visitors that all segments of the nobility were "tous maintenant un cœur et une âme" in support of Cavour, other nobles voiced considerably more negative and pessimistic views of the new situation in their private correspondence. Count Edoardo Crotti di Costigliole, for instance, warned in a letter to Count Emiliano Avogadro della Motta in April 1860 that

[17] For a discussion of the issues of the *Connubio* and transformist tradition in Italian political life, see Romeo, *Cavour e il suo tempo*, vol. II, pp. 572–577.
[18] See Società Camillo Cavour, *Un secolo di vita del Whist*, p. 84.
[19] See *Calendario Generale del Regno di 1859* and Boldrini and Alberti, "Il patriziato italiano," p. 219.

"the political horizon is becoming ever darker."[20] In a similar vein, Countess Sofia Valperga di Masino complained to her brother Marchese Alessandro Compans di Brichanteau the following year how "it would be impossible to carry out a program blacker . . . than that [of Cavour]."[21] Even after the premature death of Cavour in 1861, Solaro della Margarita referred to him as the "man who destroyed the old monarchy and left the one which presumed to replace it more uncertain, more imperiled."[22]

Such private judgments confirm the portrait of an obedient, but frightened and resentful aristocracy that emerges from the memoirs of the neo-noble and liberal sympathizer, Baroness Olimpia Savio di Bernstiel. In her account, old feudal traditions of duty and loyalty to the throne led noble officers to "struggle through months under fire, shedding their own blood and sacrificing their lives for a political goal they detested." In fact, more traditional elements of aristocratic society in Turin in 1860, according to the Countess, saw their intimate little world of "family, legation, regiment, and court" threatened by the moderates' campaign to unify the peninsula; they considered the tremendous influx of *émigrés* from other regions as little more than "an intrusion from Italy . . . into our house." For them, Piedmont's little ship of state was being pushed by "new men into unknown waters in the midst of a great storm" and consequently they were "openly hostile to an enterprise [they] considered as demagogic madness, convinced that the ship, crew, and captain would sink." Baroness Savio found evidence of their displeasure not so much in any public pronouncements as in their ostracism of *émigrés*, ostentatious refusal to speak Italian, and constant mockery of those nobles like Cavour and d'Azeglio who had embraced the cause of liberalism.[23]

Developments that followed Piedmont's fusion into a unified Italian state in 1861 seemed to confirm some of the worst fears of the more traditional aristocratic families and justify the Countess Balbo Bertone di Sambuy's nostalgic lament that "we in our little Piedmont used to be

---

[20] AST, Sez. Riunite, Archivio Avogadro della Motta, B.156, letter from Crotti di Costigliole, April 7, 1860. The positive appraisal of the political situation was attributed to a parliamentary deputy of the right who was an in-law of Count Thaon di Revel by François Marcet in letter to Edward Rommily, date June 4, 1859. See Carew Hunt, "Cavour e Francois Marcet," p. 339.

[21] AST, Sez. Riunite, Archivio Compans di Brichanteau, c. 5, b. 14, f. 2, letter from Sofia Valperga di Masino, no date 1861.

[22] AST, Sez. Riunite, Archivio Avogadro della Motta, b. 156, letter from Solaro della Margarita, July 10, 1861.

[23] See Ricci (ed.), *Memorie*, vol. 1, pp. 293–297.

quite happy without these brothers from another bed."[24] From the
outset, the limited material and human resources of the House of Savoy
and the Piedmontese governing classes, whose old territories had represented no more than one-eleventh of the peninsula, made it virtually
impossible for them to exercise a dominance in Italy comparable to that
enjoyed by the Prussian monarchy and Junker aristocracy in Germany.[25]
As a result, the process of state-building in the new Kingdom of Italy
entailed a far greater number of concessions to the political elites of the
old regional states, concessions that only further eroded the subalpine
nobility's already fragile claims to preferential treatment and governmental leadership. Thus, Vittorio Emanuele's practice of not appointing
too many high public officials from his old Sardinian kingdom to positions in the new state helped to blunt any accusations of regional favor-
itism, but came largely at the expense of the nobility .[26]

Piedmont's titled nobility suffered a far more direct and permanent
blow to its collective prestige and claims to leadership with the transfer
of the capital from Turin to Florence in the mid-1860s. Old-line
families with a long history of state service were uprooted from their
ancestral homes and cherished way of life, while those who remained
saw their territorial base of power suddenly reduced to a provincial
backwater as the international diplomatic corps and the court, the
familiar centerpiece of aristocratic society, abandoned the city. Not surprisingly, the scions of such ancient titled families as the Luserna di
Rorà, Asinari di San Marzano, and Cavalchini Garofoli became the
most outspoken proponents of "Piemontesismo" and led many of the
protests and demonstrations that greeted the decision in the soon to be
abandoned capital.[27] After the transfer, the feudal families who had traditionally served the Savoyard dynasty, now found themselves an even
smaller minority within the new and considerably larger national political class that slowly emerged in the ensuing decades.

THE SLOW RETREAT FROM POLITICAL OFFICE

The introduction of a constitutional parliamentary system of government into the new Kingdom of Italy fundamentally altered and reduced

---

[24] The Countess di Sambuy is quoted in Castronovo and d'Orsi, *Torino*, p. 14.
[25] For a more general discussion of the role of the nobility in Italian life after 1861, see
Meriggi, "La borghesia italiana," pp. 167–170, 180–182.
[26] On the changing role and political significance of the Piedmontese nobility, see
Villari, *Italian Life*, pp. 18–19.
[27] On the role of the nobility in the local reaction to the transfer of the capital to
Florence, see Ricci (ed.), *Memorie*, pp. 122–131; and more generally, Castronovo
and d'Orsi, *Torino*, pp. 5–17, 34–35.

the role played by many of the old elites in political life after 1861. Between unification and World War I, direct aristocratic involvement in parliament and government declined inexorably as the size of the electorate grew and the clerical or "black" nobility retreated into internal exile. This decline at the political level, however, was neither rapid nor cataclysmic.

Initially, there was a sizeable contingent of Italian aristocrats in national government. In 1861, for instance, 171 or 38 percent of all the men elected to the Chamber of Deputies were nobles.[28] The presence of the blue bloods within Italy's governing classes remained pronounced in the era of the *Destra Storica* (1861–1876) when titled army officers and landowners accounted for 43 percent of the top office holders.[29] At the cabinet level, nobles occupied the post of prime minister in six of Italy's first eleven governments and filled nearly a third of all the ministerial posts in the opening fifteen years of national life.[30] Vittorio Emanuele and his successors also assured a sizeable aristocratic presence in the upper house of parliament. In the last four decades of the nineteenth century, the House of Savoy elevated 440 nobles, or nearly 40 percent of the total, to lifetime seats in the Senate.[31]

From the outset, the families of the Piedmontese nobility contributed a disproportionately large share of the titled deputies and officials who served in Italian political life after unification. While they no longer enjoyed their monopoly of high office, they were better placed than any of the other old regional elites to assume an active role in national government. In sharp contrast to most of the other old patrician or feudal classes on the peninsula, who either had long been excluded from government by foreign rulers or else had linked their political fortunes to defeated dynastic houses and actively opposed unification, the Piedmontese aristocratic families enjoyed close ties to the new national monarchy as well as longstanding traditions of governmental leadership and service that favored them after 1861.[32] Not surprisingly then, they furnished a third of the nobles who occupied ministerial posts in the governments of the *Destra* and over a fifth of the aristocratic senators appointed between 1860 and 1900. The subalpine nobility also achieved

---

[28] See Boldrini and Alberti, "Il patriziato italiano," p. 215; Baldi Papini, *La nobiltà e il diritto nobiliare*, pp. 70–71.

[29] Farneti, "La classe politica," pp. 285–289.

[30] See Missori, *Governi*, vol. III, pp. 15–39. I have included undersecretaries as well as ministers in my totals.

[31] Statistics on nobles in the Italian Senate were compiled on the basis of data drawn from Segretariato Generale del Senato, *Elenchi storici e statistici dei senatori*.

[32] For a discussion of the limited political role played by the old regional nobilities after 1861, see Meriggi, "La borghesia italiana," pp. 167–168.

some success at the ballot box and thereby continued to be over-represented in the Chamber of Deputies. An average of sixteen nobles, or roughly a third of the entire Piedmontese contingent, served in the lower house of parliament during the first five legislatures.[33]

Of course, the large number of Piedmontese aristocrats among the elected officials in Rome did not signify the presence of any aristocratic party. Likewise, those nobles who held elective offices at the national level in the late nineteenth century did not advance an "aristocratic" political strategy or even display a pattern of voting that distinguished them from their untitled governmental colleagues. While they tended initially to concentrate in the ranks of the *Destra*, the most successful of Piedmont's noble deputies were no different from other segments of the lower chamber in having to engage in the politics of compromise and concession. Indeed, survival in Italy's turbulent parliamentary arena made it imperative that they, like any other notables, build up personal bases of power and pursue policies that yielded immediate political advantages. As a consequence, their social position appears to have had little impact on the specific stances they assumed in the Chamber of Deputies.

The absence of any aristocratic political consensus in Piedmont emerges clearly from a comparison of the voting records of five titled deputies in the 1870s: Marchese Carlo Compans di Brichanteau, Count Cesare Valperga di Masino, Count Ernesto Balbo Bertone di Sambuy, Baron Annibale Marazio, and Count Cesare Saluzzo di Monterosso. The proposal to abolish the highly controversial *macinato* tax, for example, enjoyed the support of Compans and Saluzzo, but was opposed by Valperga and Marazio, while di Sambuy abstained. Compans and Saluzzo found themselves on opposite sides when the chamber voted on Zanardelli's internal policies. Compans backed the government, while Saluzzo joined the other four in opposition. Similarly, on the proposal to modify income tax rates, Compans and Saluzzo parted company. Compans joined Valperga and di Sambuy in abstaining; Marazio and Saluzzo voted in favor of the change. Only the plan to alter the tax on sugar generated any sort of agreement. Saluzzo abstained and the other four voted against the proposal.[34] Despite mounting social unrest and the emergence of a socialist party, little had

---

[33] Data on aristocratic deputies from Piedmont is drawn from Malatesta (ed.), *Enciclopedia biografica e bibliografica italiana*, 3 vols. For the Piedmontese nobles who served in the governments of the *Destra*, see Missori, *Governi*, vol. III, pp. 15–39; for the titled senators from Piedmont, see Segretariato Generale del Senato, *Elenchi storici e statistici dei senatori*.

[34] For the voting records of these deputies see, *La Gazzetta Piemontese*, May 17, 1880.

changed two decades later when Piedmont's leading aristocratic deputies, Compans di Brichanteau and Marchese Cesare Ferrero di Cambiano, stood at opposite ends of the Liberal party, voting differently on fourteen of twenty-two parliamentary resolutions between 1896 and 1903.[35]

Aristocratic status, however, was certainly not irrelevant to the political identities of Piedmont's titled deputies. On the contrary, the emphasis given by both friends and foes to the exalted social position and distinctive traditions of noble candidates and their families strongly suggests that such status continued to exercise a powerful, but double-edged hold on the public imagination in late-nineteenth-century Piedmontese society. On the one hand, supporters of an aristocratic candidate made a point of highlighting the past leadership and accomplishments of their man's family as well as his sense of style and those character traits of his which ostensibly expressed the traditional ethos of the nobility. Patrician political figures were praised not only for their elegance, refinement, and sense of dignity, but also for their integrity, devotion to duty, military prowess, and special deep attachment to the country. According to his admirers, Count Ernesto Balbo Bertone di Sambuy was one of Turin's "most elegant and decorative mayors," a "cultivated and refined" gentleman with "noble, chivalrous ideals."[36] One of the supposed virtues of Arturo Perrone di San Martino, a deputy of the *Destra* who served in parliament between 1870 and 1895, derived, in the words of his backers, from his belonging "to that old and glorious Piedmontese patriciate that has given so much . . . to the rebirth of Italy"; his family was "one of Piedmont's most renowned."[37] The electoral propaganda of Marchese Cesare Ferrero di Cambiano, another deputy of the *Destra* and an undersecretary in two different governments, used remarkably similar language, noting that he belonged to the "old Piedmontese aristocracy which has already given our fatherland so many men of great talent and strict scruples."[38] In like fashion, the clerical backers of Baron Alessandro Cavalchini Garofoli in the parliamentary elections of 1896 portrayed him as a "perfect gentleman who worthily carries on the Catholic traditions of the old nobility."[39] On other occasions, the manipulation of the prestige associated with aristocratic status was more subtle, but no less evident. Thus, Marchese Carlo

---

[35] See "Prospetto dei principali voti per appello nominale dati dagli ex onorevoli di Torino e provincia," *Il Grido del Popolo*, October 30, 1904.

[36] See *La Stampa*, February 25, 1909.

[37] *La Gazzetta Piemontese*, November 22–23, 1890.

[38] See ACT, Collezione Simeom, C, n. 5412, *La Bandiera Liberale*, November 5, 1904.

[39] See *ibid.*, C, n. 5415, Associazione degli Elettori Torinesi, 1896.

Compans di Brichanteau belonged to a family that had "performed beneficial deeds in the college of Caluso for more than 300 years," Count
Carlo Felice Nicolis di Robilant was an "excellent soldier [and] a
perfect gentleman," Count Emilio Gromis di Trana represented "the
perfect specimen of a Catholic gentleman," Genova Thaon di Revel
stood for "morality, a sense of duty, devotion to the patria, and loyalty
to the king," while Marchese Vittorio Scati Grimaldi di Casaleggio displayed a "chivalrous loyalty" and descended from an "eminent family
in which a tradition of duty has been consecrated in service to the king
and the country."[40]

On the other hand, proud aristocrats who chose to compete for elective office in the late nineteenth and early twentieth centuries had to
pay a high personal price in the form of public abuse and vilification
from political adversaries who also made an issue of their social status.
As the *Gazzetta Piemontese* lamented in 1880, rival candidates sought to
revive memories of the earlier divisions between aristocrats and democrats, exploiting "the old antagonism with all its caste prejudices."[41]
Not surprisingly, certain negative stereotypes of the nobility were
evoked in order to depict blue bloods in politics as arrogant, caste
conscious, autocratic reactionaries. The enemies of Count Balbo
Bertone di Sambuy, for instance, portrayed him as a "disdainful, dog-
matic . . . feudal authoritarian, locked into a dream of anachronistic oli-
garchy." According to his campaign rivals, Marchese Compans di
Brichanteau had transformed the college he represented in parliament
into a "refuge where [he] imposes the feudal yoke of olden times."
Likewise, the adversaries of Marchese Ferrero di Cambiano denounced
his "arrogance" which they attributed to his "high lineage" and accused
him, a large landowner in his college, of maintaining a "fief – over
which he exercises his high sovereignty."[42]

This anti-aristocratic rhetoric does not appear to have been especially
efficacious in the cases of Compans, Balbo Bertone, and Ferrero, who
all enjoyed long and rather successful careers in politics. Nevertheless, it

---

[40] For the descriptions of Gromis and Scati, see *L'Italia Reale–Corriere Nazionale*, June
9–10, 1895; for Thaon di Revel and Compans di Brichanteau see respectively, AST,
Sez. Riunite, Archivio Thaon di Revel, electoral leaflet, Chivasso, 1867 and
Archivio Politico Compans, b. 1, campaign poster 1904; for Nicolis, *La Gazzetta Piemontese*, November 10, 1870.

[41] See *Gazzetta Piemontese*, May 15, 1880.

[42] For criticisms of Balbo Bertone di Sambuy, see *La Stampa*, February 2, 1909. The
attack on Compans di Brichanteau appeared in a leaflet distributed by his foe, Cesare
Facelli, during the parliamentary electoral campaign of 1904; see AST, Sez. Riunite,
Archivio Politico Compans, b. 1. The attack on Ferrero di Cambiano appeared in *Il
Grido del Popolo*, October 30, 1904.

does indicate part of the costs paid by men from old-line families who chose to participate directly in a parliamentary system characterized by petty, vulgar, and often personally demeaning political contests. Piedmontese nobles were especially ill suited and ill disposed by tradition and training to the rough and tumble of electoral campaigns or the crude interest bargaining in Rome. Much like their Junker counterparts, their arrogance, caste-consciousness, and disdain for machine politics tended to make them less effective as parliamentary politicians.[43] Marchese Roberto d'Azeglio anticipated the difficulties confronting aristocrats in the new political order as early as 1849 when he complained of feeling "continually jostled by this crude, vulgar, boring, bruising element that is steadily infiltrating the social body and that will end by canceling the refined style and distinguished manners which reveal education [and] *le rang*."[44] Especially after the electoral reform of 1882 which quadrupled the size of the electorate and required candidates to actively court the voters, the pursuit of elective office became a decidedly less attractive and socially acceptable avocation for men from the subalpine nobility.

In fact, the decades after 1876 saw a general retreat of nobles from Piedmont and other regions of the country from direct participation in national political life. The fall of the *Destra* and suffrage reform led to a noticeable decline in the number of Italian aristocrats in high elective office, although there were some significant fluctuations at the end of the century. Nobles from all regions made up a mere 16 percent of the governing class in the three decades after 1876. Only fifteen of them served in the governments of Depretis and Crispi between 1876 and 1896. The number of nobles at the cabinet level rose sharply again in the turbulent years between 1896 and 1900 when more of them occupied ministerial posts than during the entire reign of the *Destra*. Still the number of nobles in high office was rather modest, especially when compared with the government of Germany and Great Britain in the same era, when virtually all chancellors or prime ministers were aristocrats. Aristocratic involvement in the Chamber of Deputies proved to be somewhat more stable. Throughout the second half of the nineteenth century, the number of noble deputies serving in the lower house of parliament fluctuated between 117 and 155; they accounted for between 23 and 31 percent of the total. Not until the elections of

---

[43] For the case of the Junkers in politics, see Retallack, *Notables of the Right*.

[44] See *Souvenirs historiques de la marquise Constance d'Azeglio née Alfieri*, p. 448, as cited in Falletti, *Saggi*, pp. 155–157.

1904 did their numbers fall below 100 and only thereafter did the aristocratic presence in the Chamber of Deputies drop off steadily.[45]

On the whole, the Piedmontese nobility conformed to this general
pattern of retreat from the national political arena after 1876. Only thirteen men from local titled families served in any of the Italian governments from the fall of the *Destra* to the outbreak of World War I, and
four of them were new nobles who had acquired their titles in the
second half of the nineteenth century. Similarly, the advent of the
Sinistra witnessed a precipitous drop in the number of nobles elected to
parliament. In the five legislative sessions between 1876 and 1892, an
average of eight titled deputies out of approximately forty-eight, or half
as many as in the previous fifteen-year period, represented the provinces
of Piedmont. Still, Piedmontese nobles proved to be somewhat more
reluctant to abandon national political office than their titled counterparts elsewhere on the peninsula. Their numbers actually rose again
after 1892, averaging around twelve per session in the next two decades;
in the last pre-war elections, held in 1913, they accounted for over a
fifth of all aristocrats elected to parliament.[46]

The same decades also saw the Piedmontese nobility slowly dis-
engage from positions of direct political leadership at the local level.
Prominent old-line aristocrats like the Marchese Emanuele Luserna di
Rorà, Count Cesare Valperga di Masino, and Count Ernesto Balbo
Bertone di Sambuy were among the group of nobles who virtually
monopolized the mayor's office in Turin until World War I, but increasingly these men were drawn from the ranks of the newly ennobled;
four of the last seven mayors of Turin before 1914 had received their
titles after 1861.[47] As a rule, nobles occupied a quarter of all the seats in
the municipal council until the early 1880s and typically dominated the
committees concerned with finance, education, charitable activities,
and local cultural institutions. Thereafter, their numbers began to
shrink. The nobility accounted for only about a fifth of the council in
the 1880s and 1890s, although they continued to preside over the committees that regulated local taxes and managed the Civil Museum,
Teatro Regio, the charitable Opera Pia San Paolo, and the Royal Work

---

[45] See Boldrini and Alberti, "Il patriziato italiano," p. 215; Baldi Papini, *La nobiltà e il
diritto nobiliare*, pp. 70–71; Missori, *Governi*, pp. 40–101; Farneti, "La classe politica,"
pp. 290–292.

[46] See *Rivista Araldica*, November, 1913, for names of the ten Piedmontese nobles
elected to the Chamber of Deputies. They were part of a national contingent of
seventy-eight nobles; see Baldi Papini, *La nobiltà*, p. 71.

[47] For a complete list of the mayors in Turin from 1848 until 1913, see *Annuario del Municipio di Torino, 1912–1913* (Turin, 1913), p. 111.

House.[48] By the last decade before the war, old titled families had largely disappeared from local political office in Turin. In the municipal elections of 1914, for instance, only six nobles won seats on the city council and four of them were newly ennobled men with few ties to traditionally prominent aristocratic families.[49] The situation varied somewhat in smaller provincial centers like Cuneo where the ranks of nobles serving on the municipal council swelled during the Giolittian era, but even here their numbers remained relatively modest.[50] Judging by these patterns of office-holding, it would appear that the Piedmontese nobility had lapsed into irreversible decline and ceased to be a significant component of the governing classes, either in Rome or at the local level by the beginning of World War I.

THE SURVIVAL OF ARISTOCRATIC INFLUENCE IN PUBLIC LIFE

Direct participation in the formal electoral process, however, provides only one measure of the political role played by Piedmontese nobles in the half century after Italian unification. Even as men from old aristocratic families ceased to serve as deputies and municipal councilors, they continued to enjoy less contentious and more dignified forms of influence through their entrenched positions in the court, army, and diplomatic corps, their patronage of the arts and charities, their leadership of a host of new voluntary societies, and their activities as power-brokering notables in political clubs and organizations at the local level. At the same time, titled families also benefited from participation in an exclusive network of kinship and friendship relations, reinforced by shared school, club, and professional affiliations that offered them informal, but perhaps equally important channels of private influence.

The Italian state continued to offer the nobility various institutional bases of power that were less vulnerable than parliament or municipal government to the vagaries of the ballot box. First and foremost was the monarchy itself which played an obscure but powerful role in the formulation of both foreign and military policies, and enjoyed a strong influence over the choice of government ministers. In the exercise of their prerogatives, both Vittorio Emanuele II and his successor Umberto I relied on a small group of close and trusted advisors drawn

---

[48] See Archivio Comunale di Torino, b. 3, vols. 7–8, "Elenco Componenti Consiglio Comunale" for the years, 1861, 1865, 1870, 1875, 1881, 1885, 1890, 1895, 1900.

[49] See *Annuario del Municipio di Torino, 1913–14* (Turin, 1914), pp. vi–xx.

[50] See Mola, *Storia dell'amministrazione provinciale di Cuneo*, p. 535. In 1894 there were six nobles on the municipal council; in 1913, eleven were elected.

almost exclusively from their old nobility. On the whole, the House of Savoy viewed with suspicion "that assorted *antipasto* of nobles of all shapes and descriptions" which they had acquired with unification, preferring to rely on those families who had served them for centuries.[51] As a result, aristocratic courtiers from Piedmont were in a privileged position to affect royal policy throughout the second half of the nineteenth century. While the paucity of documentation on the monarchy precludes any precise measure of their clandestine activities, they certainly alarmed foreign and domestic critics alike, who frequently warned of the "secret and unconstitutional influences" of a "court party" that, in their view, disdained parliamentary procedures and bore special responsibility for royal support for reaction at home and imperialism abroad.[52]

Much like the new monarchy, the Italian state that emerged in the 1860s was also largely an extension of the institutions of the Kingdom of Sardinia to the rest of the peninsula. Accordingly, the same titled Piedmontese generals and diplomats, who spearheaded the program of unification, proceeded to occupy comparably high stations in the Italian military and diplomatic services which served as bastions of aristocratic values and traditions after 1861. In the case of the Italian army, a relatively small group of aristocratic officers assumed a disproportionately large share of the command responsibilities. Nearly a decade and a half after unification, Piedmontese nobles accounted for less than 5 percent of the army officer corps, but still featured prominently among the senior commanders. Indeed, two of the three *generali d'armata*, a third of the lieutenant generals, more than a quarter of the major generals, and roughly a third of the military staff attached to the royal family came from their ranks. The dominant position of titled officers from the old Sardinian kingdom was especially striking in the cavalry where they commanded five of the six brigades and half the regiments.[53] The same small group of aristocratic military men was also actively involved in the political life of the country. Titled army families from the region contributed fifty-three men to the Chamber of Deputies and sixty-three to

[51] The expression is Luigi Barzini's in his *From Caesar to the Mafia*, p. 103.

[52] See Mack Smith, *Italy and its Monarchy*, pp. 34, 86, 123, 141 for references to this court party. Mack Smith explores the paucity of documentary evidence concerning the activities of the House of Savoy, pp. ix–x. On court life and organization, see Antonelli, *Il Ministero della Real Casa*.

[53] For the army command structure, see *Il Palmaverde. Almanaco universale per l'anno 1874* (Turin, 1874), pp. 143–153. Lucio Ceva estimates that nobles from all regions of the peninsula supplied only 6.5 to 7 percent of the army officers in 1863 and 3 to 4 percent in 1887; see his "Forze armate e società civile," p. 285.

the Senate, while another thirteen occupied high cabinet posts in various governments between 1861 and 1914.[54]

Of course, the Piedmontese could not maintain such a dominant presence in the armed forces in the face of organizational expansion, technological innovation, and political change in the decades before World War I. Nonetheless they remained influential at the commanding heights of the military establishment and in the cavalry into the early twentieth century. In 1905, for example, ten of the forty-eight lieutenant generals came from a restricted circle of old-line military families. The same families also furnished the commanders of the cavalry school and three of the eight cavalry brigades on the eve of the Great War.[55]

In a similar fashion, men from the Piedmontese nobility continued to play an important role at the upper levels of the Italian diplomatic establishment after the fall of the *Destra* and the aristocratic exodus from direct participation in the electoral process. Between 1870 and 1900, for instance, they filled nearly a third (30 percent) of the ambassadorial posts, including those in London, Paris, Vienna, Berlin, and Moscow. More importantly, they largely defined the values, standards of comportment, and language for the diplomatic corps as a whole.[56]

At the same time, the scions of many aristocratic families, who no longer ran for political office, continued to exercise cultural and social leadership in other areas of public life at the local level, where such assets as leisure, connections, and prestige stood them in good stead. Here they were able to reassert their status within the community by cultivating an image of themselves as dignified and disinterested symbols of order and continuity who stood above the sordid battles of the political arena. In this guise, they directed much of Turin's religious and secular philanthropy and presided over or served on the boards of most of the city's leading cultural and public health institutions as well as a host of new voluntary sporting and leisure-time associations that emerged in the second half of the nineteenth century.

Count Ernesto Balbo Bertone di Sambuy, perhaps the leading patron of the arts in Turin at the turn of the century, represents a classic case in point. After retiring from the Chamber of Deputies and the mayor's office, Count Ernesto went on to contribute his time, prestige, and

---

[54] Segretariato Generale del Senato, *Elenchi storici e statistici dei senatori*, and Malatesta (ed.), *Ministri, deputati e senatori dal 1848 al 1922.*

[55] See *Annuario Militare del Regno d'Italia 1905*, vol. I, pp. 3–7; ibid., *1914*, vol. I, pp. 4–8.

[56] Data on the social composition of Italian ambassadors is drawn from the *Calendario Generale del Regno d'Italia* for the years 1870, 1880, 1890, and 1900. See Romano, "Le nobiltà, lo stato," pp. 529–540, for a discussion of the influence of the nobility within the diplomatic establishment.

glamour to a wide range of civic activities. In the last decade of his life, he still sat on five municipal commissions, chaired the boards of the Circle of Artists, the Royal Albertine Academy of Fine Arts, the Society for the Promotion of the Fine Arts, and the Friendship Choral Circle, served as a founding member of the Society for Archeology and Fine Arts, and was honorary president of the Subalpine Photography Society. Nor did di Sambuy neglect his philanthropic and recreational responsibilities. During the same period he also presided over the board of the Hospital for Infectious Diseases (Ospedale delle Malattie Infettive) and the local hunting society, Società dei Paper-Hunts, and served as vice-president of the Turinese Horse-Racing Association and honorary president of the Royal Botanical-Agricultural Society of Piedmont. As Turin's leading daily newspaper, La Stampa, observed in its obituary notice in 1909, "Count di Sambuy was justly considered by the Turinese as one of the most eminent personalities of the city."[57]

Although few aristocratic gentlemen could boast of such an impressive range of activities, many followed a similar itinerary. At the beginning of the twentieth century, there was still scarcely a hospital, orphanage, asylum, or shelter that did not have aristocrats chairing and sitting on its board. The same men or their wives and daughters featured prominently as the chairmen, directors, and chief patrons and patronesses of most other charitable agencies in the city, including the Red Cross, the Congregation of Charity, and the royal institutes for the deaf, dumb, and blind. In 1900, for example, Baron Orazio Galleani di S. Ambrosie and Marchese Filippo Morozzo della Rocca di Bianze served respectively as the president and vice-president of the local branch of the Italian Red Cross and members of the Della Chiesa della Torre, Luserna di Rorà, Valperga di Masino, Ferrero di Cambiano, and Radicati di Brozolo families served on its board, while a dozen titled ladies directed its Women's Auxiliary.[58]

As the interlocking directorships of Balbo Bertone di Sambuy suggest, aristocrats also played a prominent role as patrons of the arts in Turin. The city's major cultural institutions recruited heavily from the ranks of the nobility for their trustees, presidents, and directors. In 1900, for instance, titled gentlemen concentrated in their hands all but three of the more important cultural directorships in the city. In addition to Count Ernesto, Count Luigi Avogadro di Quaregna and Count Ales-

---

[57] For information on Count Ernesto's many activities, see La Guida di Torino, for the years 1895 and 1900. A lengthy obituary appeared in La Stampa, February 25, 1909.

[58] In 1900, aristocrats presided over half of these societies and were well represented on the boards of all but one of the fifty-two listed in the Guida di Torino, 1900, pp. 489–545.

sandro Baudi di Vesme served respectively as the directors of the Royal Armory and Royal Picture-Gallery, while Baron Domenico Carutti di Cantogno and Count Edoardo Scarampi di Villanova chaired the boards of the Royal Deputation for the Study of the History of the Fatherland and the Concert Society.[59]

The old families played an equally visible role at the turn of the century in the new world of sports and recreation clubs whose boards were littered with aristocratic luminaries. Count Roberto Biscaretti di Ruffia, alone, was president of the local chapter of the Italian Rowing Club and of the Cyclists Club, and sat on the boards of the Gymnastics Society and Club d'Armi. Other patrician dignitaries like Marchese Carlo Compans di Brichanteau, Count Emanuele Cacherano di Bricherasio, Count Paolo D'Oncieu de la Batie, Casimiro Faà di Bruno, and Giuseppe Lovera di Maria presided over the hunting, horse-racing, tennis, and veterans' social associations such as the Circolo Militare and the Circolo Ufficiale a Riposo ed in Congedo. Likewise, the nobility were well represented on the boards of the clubs devoted to mountaineering, gymnastics, skating, soccer, skeet-shooting, chess, and bird-watching.[60]

It is difficult to assess what sort of power aristocrats actually enjoyed as a result of the leadership they exercised in these various civic activities. On the one hand, such leadership offered the possibility of a new and potentially influential role for the traditional upper classes in an increasingly egalitarian society. On the other hand, their involvement in this area can also be dismissed as frivolous and purely decorative in character, and thus as further proof of the nobility's growing marginalization and trivialization.[61]

In the case of Piedmont, civic leadership does seem to have enhanced the stature of aristocrats as "natural leaders" in the community and thereby made it easier for them to continue acting as influential behind-the-scenes "king-makers" at the local level. They were clearly favored in this role by a parliamentary system that lacked large, organized, and disciplined parties. The so-called Liberal party, which dominated Italian parliamentary life, was itself little more than a loose-knit federation of local political clubs. The predominance of such small informal groups held together by the prestige of notables and municipal or village loyalties rather than by clear principles, worked decidedly to the advantage of respected members of old titled families who exploited their image of

---

[59] Ibid., pp. 559–671.   [60] Ibid., pp. 672–678.
[61] For a brief discussion of the meaning of these activities in the British context, see Lieven, *The Aristocracy in Europe*, p. 152.

non-partisan public service to orchestrate electoral campaigns long after they distanced themselves from personal involvement as candidates.

In the last three decades of the nineteenth century, aristocratic notables commonly chaired the assemblies of liberal-monarchist electors who selected candidates. They also featured prominently on the *ad hoc* electoral committees that set the agendas and coordinated the campaigns. Weeks before the parliamentary elections of November 1870, for example, Count Cesare Ponza di San Martino was picked to preside over a gathering of monarchist electors in the province of Turin who, according to press accounts, voted unanimously to give him the mandate to form a "committee to coordinate the electoral movement."[62] Similarly, the two top officials of the Constitutional Association of Turin in 1880 were Count Ferdinando Avogadro di Collobiano and Count Carlo Boncompagni di Mombello; the same year Marchese Carlo Compans di Brichanteau and Count Guido Valperga di San Martino sat on the ruling council of the Turinese Progressives Association. Nor was the organizational presence of the nobility in electoral politics limited to the Piedmontese capital. In the 1890s, Marchese Tommaso Ferrero della Marmora was a key political mediator in the province of Vercelli, while in Cuneo men like Count Lanfranco Lunel di Cortemiglia, Count Ferdinando Galli della Mantica, and Baldassero Incisa di Camerana played a leading role on the local electoral committees.[63]

The ascendance of a fellow Piedmontese, Giovanni Giolitti, to national leadership appears, if anything, to have enhanced the influence of nobles behind the scenes in the first decade and a half of the new century. In 1900, Count Ernesto Balbo Bertone di Sambuy and other titled notables took the lead in promoting the Unione Liberale-Monarchica in Turin to overcome, in the words of Count Ernesto, "divisions within the grand old constitutional party" and to combat the socialist "anti-constitutional party."[64] During the campaign prior to the parliamentary elections of 1904, Marchese Rinaldo Tornielli di Borgolavezzaro, ex-deputy and "one of the most eminent personages of that college," chaired the campaign committee of the constitutional forces in Novara, while his cousin, Count Giuseppe Tornielli Brusati di

---

[62] *Gazzetta Piemontese*, November 8, 1870.
[63] For accounts of the activities of these aristocratic power brokers, see *Gazzetta Piemontese*, April 19, May 10 and 11, 1880 and November 3–4, 1890.
[64] *La Stampa*, May 25, 1900. It was Count di Sambuy who called a meeting of some 200 liberal-monarchist electors that month, at which he launched the idea of such a political association. Another gathering two months later officially proclaimed its founding. See ACT, Collezione Simeom, n. 4566, for printed documents pertaining to the origins of the Unione Liberale.

Vergano served as president of the Unione Liberale Monarchica in the third electoral college of Turin. In its coverage of the parliamentary campaigns of 1909, the local press listed the names of a half dozen nobles as being among the most influential electors in the province of Cuneo. The same year and again during the elections of 1913, titled notables like Marchese Vincenzo Ricci, Count Carlo Arborio di Gattinara, Count Max Leonardi, Marchese Ernesto Del Carretto di Moncrivello, and Alessandro Arborio Mella provided much of the organizational leadership for the anti-socialist political forces in both the provinces of Vercelli and Novara.[65]

As these many examples indicate, emphasis on the shrinking number of aristocratic office holders in the late nineteenth century partially obscures the extent to which prominence in public affairs at least on the local level continued to be associated with inherited titles and the lineal qualifications of the nobility to community leadership. At least up to 1914, some of the old aristocratic families were able to adapt fairly effectively to new circumstances in ways that delayed and cushioned the political decline of their social class. They were able to do so, in large part, by exploiting the prestige, glamor, and respect attached to their names to retain influence within a still fragmented and loosely organized liberal political order.

ARISTOCRATS AND CATHOLIC LAY POLITICS IN PIEDMONT

The involvement of prominent aristocrats in Liberal–Monarchist politics paled in comparison to the central role they played in the slow and difficult construction of a Catholic movement in the region during the second half of the nineteenth century and the first decades of the twentieth. A new alliance between the sword and altar had already begun to take shape in the decades before unification. Although the names of old titled families appeared more rarely within the ranks of the high clergy after 1815, nobles were in the vanguard of the organizations of laity that arose during the Restoration in support of the church. Marchese Cesare Taparelli d'Azeglio, for instance, was the moving spirit behind Catholic Friendship (Amicizia cattolica), an influential society set up in the 1820s to provide a militant defense of religious orthodoxy and monarchical legitimacy, whose founding members also included several illustrious local nobles. After the closing of Catholic Friendship, its work was continued by the Laity of the Virgin Mary (Oblati di Maria

---

[65] See *La Stampa*, October 19 and November 1, 1904; March 3, 4, and 5, 1909; and October 5 and 9, 1913.

Vergine) in which Count Solaro della Margarita, Count Rodolfo de Maistre, Marchesa Giulia Falletti di Barolo, Baron Charles Hubert De La Tour, and the father and brother of Cavour featured prominently.[66]

These early initiatives set the stage for the titled nobility to act as the principal defenders of the Catholic Church in the decade after 1848. In 1850, for instance, such renowned moderate conservatives as Count Ottavio Thaon di Revel and Count Cesare Balbo di Vinadio withdrew their support from the government and joined the largely aristocratic clerical opposition to the Siccardi Laws, which aimed to abolish ecclesiastical courts and the right of asylum, to limit the number of religious holidays, and to restrict the property rights of church bodies.[67] Two years later, an impressive array of titled dignitaries that included the brothers of two government ministers, Alberto Ferrero della Marmora and Marchese Roberto Taparelli d'Azeglio, as well as Thaon di Revel, Balbo, and the intransigents, Solaro della Margarita and Marshal Vittorio Sallier de la Tour, spearheaded the victorious resistance in the Senate to Cavour's civil marriage bill. During the same period, aristocratic courtiers used their influence to urge the king to make peace with the Vatican. Again, when the government moved to reform the religious corporations in the Kingdom of Sardinia in the winter of 1854/5, the prime minister's brother, Marchese Gustavo Benso di Cavour, Count Giorgio De Viry, Marchese Lodovico Pallavicino-Mossi, and Count Solaro della Margarita led the parliamentary opposition.[68] Aristocratic political engagement on behalf of the church continued in the first decade after unification when another old Piedmontese noble, Count Edoardo Crotti di Costigliole, served as one of the last two Catholic deputies to sit in parliament before his expulsion in 1867.[69]

The Vatican's loss of temporal power in 1870 and the ensuing church boycott of domestic Italian politics, embodied in Pius IX's *non expedit* of 1874, did not fundamentally alter the Catholic loyalties of the bulk of Piedmont's old titled families. In a survey carried out in the mid-1870s, for instance, Leandro Carpi found that a large part of the Piedmontese nobility "and especially the younger generation" were "enrolling in the black international [and] associating with that party which hopes to res-

---

[66] See De Rosa, *Storia del movimento cattolico*, pp. 25–35. On the limited presence of the nobility within the local church hierarchy, see Chevallard and Frova, *Cronaca di Torino*, p. 7. After 1814, only one archbishop of Turin, Alessandro Riccardo di Netro (1867–1870) came from a titled family, while Stanislao Gazelli di Rossana served as vicar of the Cathedral between 1883 and 1897. For the life of the latter, see di Robillant, *Un prete di ieri*.

[67] Thayer, *The Life and Times of Cavour*, vol. I, pp. 120–122.

[68] *Ibid.*, pp. 214–216, 311, 335, 341.

[69] See De Rosa, *Storia del movimento cattolico*, p. 129.

urrect theocratic absolutism on the ruins of constitutionalism and national independence."[70] The prefect of Alessandria voiced similar concerns the following decade when he warned of the strength of the "clerical party" in his province which he attributed in part to the "not negligible influence exercised by the clergy over . . . the Piedmontese aristocracy."[71]

While Carpi and state officials accurately captured the political sympathies of probably most subalpine nobles, they exaggerated the intransigence of their views on church–state relations, which in fact diverged from those of the Vatican and clerical hardliners in other regions. In the decades after 1870, the Catholic movement in Piedmont continued to be dominated by the old landed aristocratic families who were linked to larger strata of artisans and peasants through the mediation of the clergy.[72] Under the leadership of men like Count Cesare Valperga di Masino, Count Alessandro Provana di Collegno, and Count Cesare Trabucco di Castagnetto, the Piedmontese Catholic forces took a conservative but distinctively conciliatory approach to relations with the monarchical state, one that reflected the nobility's traditional allegiance to the House of Savoy. Count Ernest Balbo di Sambuy captured the essence of this approach in a testamental epistle to his oldest son:

> Unfortunately we live in difficult times when human passions are seeking to dig a deep abyss between *Religion and Patria*. You must be at the same time a good Christian and an exemplary patriot. For only this way, will you belie such a fatal prejudice and contribute to that necessary and beneficial peace which will make our country great and respected without disturbing your conscience.[73]

The relatively accommodating approach of Piedmontese nobles led them to take an active part in various political initiatives as well as in the creation and development of a wide range of Catholic lay organizations in the region after 1870. In 1878, for instance, Count Valperga di Masino launched the idea of mobilizing Catholic voters within a national Conservative party, the goal to "correct and improve [liberal institutions], but not destroy them."[74] While his proposal initially won

---

[70] Carpi, *L'Italia vivente*, vol. I, p. 152.

[71] Archivio Centrale dello Stato, Gabinetto di Prefettura, "Spirito pubblico," Alessandria, July 15, 1884, b. 2, f. 1.

[72] See Traniello, "Le origini del movimento cattolico," pp. 37–38.

[73] *Ufficio di Successioni* b. 788, f. 17, testament of Count Ernesto di Sambuy, dated November 2, 1889.

[74] See Valperga di Masino's letter in the Turinese paper, *Risorgimento*, November 30, 1878 as quoted in De Rosa, *Storia del movimento cattolico*, p. 227.

support from various Catholic luminaries, intransigent elements managed to prevent its realization.

Piedmontese "black" aristocrats met with greater success closer to home where four of them – Baron Antonio Manno, Marchese Vittorio Scati Grimaldi di Casaleggio, Count Francesco Arnaldi di Balme, and Count Vittorio Roberti di Castelvero – set up the Unione Conservatrice in Turin a few years later. The Union in turn promoted the creation of the Lega di Difesa Agraria, the lobbying organization largely responsible for the introduction of agricultural tariffs in the late 1880s. In the following decades, the Unione Conservatrice became the institutional bastion of clerical conservatives, whose simultaneous control of the Catholic banks in Piedmont gave them a powerful economic and political hold over a much larger bloc of small peasant farmers.[75]

These larger organizational initiatives rested in turn upon the grassroots activities of aristocratic families who became the chief patrons and financial backers of Catholic associations of laborers and mutual aid societies at the local level, especially in those areas where their landed estates were situated. Count Carlo Broglia di Casalborgone, for instance, established and, until his death in 1891, served as honorary president of the Workers and Farmers Society (Società Operai ed Agricoltori) of Casalborgone, an organization intended to "promote the instruction, morality, and well-being" of its members. Likewise, Count Giulio Cesare Balbiano di Aramengo was a founding member and promotor of the Catholic Workers Union of Chieri, while Count Ferdinando Avogadro di Collobiano acted in a similar capacity on behalf of the Workers' Society of Carisio.[76]

Such involvement forged a network of loyalties and alliances that helped assure aristocratic dominance of the Piedmontese clerical-moderate movement which emerged in the considerably more favorable political climate of the Giolittian era. In fact, a group of prominent Catholic nobles, united in the so-called Circolo del Tüpinet, were the chief financiers and leaders of a much wider range of organizational initiatives in the years after 1895. That year, Baron Carlo Ricci des Ferres oversaw the creation of the "Secretariat for the People" with the

---

[75] For an account of the history of the Unione Conservatrice, see ACT, Collez. Simeom, C, n. 4568, *Il Momento*, April 22, 1907.

[76] See AST, Archivio Broglia di Casalborgone, b. 3, letter of condolence, Soc. Operai ed Agricoltori di Casalborgone, September 25, 1891; for the activities of Balbiano and Avogadro di Collobiano, see respectively Archivio privato Balbiano di Aramengo, b. 19, letter dated January 20, 1878 and *Gazzetta del Popolo*, October 10, 1904.

aim of providing free legal consultation. The following year another member of the Tüpinet Circle, Count Luigi Caissotti di Chiusano, who was scion of a wealthy landed family from Cuneo, founded and served as the president of the Turinese Agricultural Federation (FAT), which soon guided the activities of 139 rural unions and cooperatives of small peasant proprietors and sharecroppers.[77] By 1914, the FAT was part of a much larger regional network of approximately 1,000 Catholic banks, credit unions, and cooperatives that specialized in providing assistance to urban artisans and small merchants as well as to peasant farmers in the countryside. Significantly, Caissotti and some twenty men from titled families were founding members, stockholders, and top officers.[78]

Other prominent nobles from the Tüpinet occupied commanding positions within the local clerical-moderate propaganda apparatus. Thus, in 1903, Baron Romano Gianotti, Baron Carlo Gamba, Count Giulio d'Harcourt, and Baron Carlo Ricci des Ferres provided the initial financing for a new newspaper, *Il Momento*, which became the principal organ of the Turinese Catholic movement before World War I. Under the overall direction of Baron Ricci des Ferres and Cardinal Agostino Richelmy, *Il Momento* assumed an editorial stance in favor of active Catholic participation in political life, collaboration with other "constitutional" forces, energetic resistance to the Socialist party, and nationalist positions in foreign policy.[79]

The leadership exercised by aristocratic notables in these economic and social initiatives virtually guaranteed them a prominent role in the resurgence of Catholic political activity that began after the relaxation of the *non expedit* in 1904. Indeed, many of the same men chaired and sat on the boards of the organizations that formulated electoral policies and strategies in the decade before World War I, namely, the Conservative Union, the Catholic Electoral Union, and the Diocesan Directorate for Catholic Social Works (Direzione Diocesana delle opere sociali cattoliche).[80] These organizations became especially important after the suf-

---

[77] See Zussini, *Luigi Caissotti di Chiusano*, pp. 53–66. On the social makeup and activities of the Circolo del Tüpinet as well as the founding of the Segretariat, see Salvadori, *Il movimento cattolico a Torino*, pp. 141, 159–160.

[78] Falco, "L'organizzazione bancaria cattolica," pp. 643–709. For statistics on Catholic social institutions in Piedmont, see Salvadori, *Il movimento cattolico a Torino*, pp. 74–75.

[79] Salvadori, *Il movimento cattolico a Torino*, pp. 90–91; Frassati, *Torino come era*, p. 242.

[80] Count Cesare Balbo di Vinadio and Baron Ricci des Ferres were the principal representatives of the nobility on the board of the Conservative Union; while Marchese Crispolti, Count Caissotti di Chiusano, and Marchese Rovasenda di Rovasenda sat on the board of the Catholic Electoral Union. Rovasenda along with Count Avogadro della Motta and Marchese Corsi also were directors of the Diocesan Directo-

frage reform of 1911 which resulted in an enormous expansion of the electorate. First in the parliamentary elections of November 1913 and then again in the municipal elections in the summer of 1914, the Catholic political associations proved to be far more effective than their Liberal allies at mobilizing mass constituencies and challenging the Socialists.[81] Accordingly, at least some old-line nobles were once again enjoying substantial political influence as patrons and paymasters of an increasingly important segment of the "constitutional" forces in Piedmont on the eve of World War I.

INFORMAL NETWORKS OF ARISTOCRATIC INFLUENCE

In addition to their role as behind-the-scenes power brokers within the Liberal-monarchist and clerical-moderate political camps, Piedmontese nobles also continued to have access to informal means of influence that co-existed with and often worked through the official institutional channels of power. Indeed, such largely invisible forms of influence gave a much wider network of old established families, who had largely abdicated the responsibilities of government for sports or other leisurely pastimes, the possibility of affecting the political and bureaucratic decision-making processes and thereby of exercising patronage within their communities. These families were still able to do so because they remained part of a cohesive and self-conscious social elite united by ties of kinship as well as by shared backgrounds, education, ideals, and prejudices that put them on close, if not familiar terms, with a smaller number of individuals who did continue to hold official positions of power in the Italian state. Accordingly, intra-family ties, school friendships, and exclusive professional and club affiliations all combined to give well-connected aristocratic families privileged access to a wide range of powerful figures in the military hierarchy, the political class, and at court.[82]

Of course, such patronage and clientele relations were not the unique and exclusive preserve of the titled nobility. The dominant political force in Italy in the pre-war era, the Liberal party rested upon

---

rate. See Soave, "Las nascita della Democrazia Cristiana," p. 61; Salvadori, *Il movimento cattolico a Torino*, pp. 150–160; Falco, "L'organizzazione bancaria cattolica", pp. 643–709.

[81] Salvadori, *Il movimento cattolico a Torino*, pp. 229–249 provides a detailed description of the electoral campaigns and outcomes.

[82] For a more theoretical discussion of the importance of these informal networks, see Cohen, *Two-Dimensional Man*, pp. 110–114; Hansen and Parrish, "Elites versus the State," pp. 257–277.

organizations of local notables who, regardless of their own social status, personally dispensed favors and exercised influence on behalf of their dependents and constituents. Such arrangements, however, benefited some groups more than others. Old-line aristocratic families, in particular, were well suited to take advantage of these unofficial and in-direct mechanisms as a result of their social cohesion as well as their rare concentration of wealth, prestige, and important political connections.

Marchese Carlo Compans di Brichanteau stood at the center of one of the more stable of these largely invisible networks of aristocratic power and influence. Compans was perhaps the most prominent noble politician of his generation in Piedmont. After a brief stint as a cavalry officer in the 1870s, he embarked upon a parliamentary career that extended over five decades and included appointments as a ministerial under-secretary in four governments; in the Chamber of Deputies he presided over the Agrarian Parliamentary Group and participated in a number of other important governmental commissions. As the scion of an old subalpine feudal family, he also enjoyed excellent connections at court, where he was a frequent presence, both at public functions and in private audiences with the king and queen. At the same time, Compans was one of the most influential power brokers on the provincial level whose support was eagerly sought out by other political hopefuls. He had several terms on both the municipal and provincial councils of Turin and either chaired or sat on the boards of a long list of institutions that included the leading civic association, the association of urban property-owners, a large insurance company, four agricultural societies, and three philanthropic agencies as well as the fencing, hunting and mountain-climbing, and horse-racing clubs.[83]

The power exercised by Compans di Brichanteau both in Rome and at the local level directly benefited a circle of over sixty aristocratic families between 1889 and World War I. Significantly, family ties and exclusive social contacts took precedence over political or ideological allegiances within this circle. While Compans was associated with the left faction of the Liberal party throughout his career, his titled clients included more traditional conservatives like General Carlo Nicolis di Robilant and Catholic aristocrats such as Baron Carlo Ricci des Ferres.

The most immediate beneficiaries were a more close-knit group of eighteen families, a large "cousinhood" linked to the titled notable by extended maternal and paternal kinship ties. In the quarter century

[83] For information on Compans' many offices and activities, see AST, Sez. Riunite, Archivio di famiglia Compans, b. 4, f. 8 and Archivio Politico Compans, b. 1, 6, 29, 142; *Guida di Torino, 1900*; and *Consiglio Provinciale di Torino. Estratto di verbale dell'Adunanza, 22 dicembre 1925* (Turin, 1926), pp. 2–6.

before the war, Compans was constantly intervening on behalf of an army of cousins who, in the words of Rolando Pallavicino "have taken advantage of the affinity that runs between your family and mine" to request and receive his protection and assistance.[84] Some cousins like Stanislao Nicolis di Robilant, relied on Compans' influence within the local Liberal-monarchist associations to advance their own political careers at the municipal level. More commonly, Compans used his connections to help relatives gain entry into the officers' or diplomatic corps or other state offices, and then later to win choice assignments, promotions, and timely transfers. In 1912, for instance, his support of his cousin Ferdinando Pallavicino's candidacy for admission to the Military School of Modena proved crucial, leading his sister-in-law to express her "gratitude for [his] affectionate and very efficacious protection in such a difficult competition." Pallavicino's case was far from exceptional; Compans had already performed similar services for dozens of other relatives during the previous two decades. And judging by their effusive letters of gratitude, his intervention was usually quite effective.[85]

Favors and assistance did not flow exclusively in one direction within this cousinhood. In 1887, for instance, Compans advanced the career of one of his clients by seeking the help of his cousin and a former foreign minister, Count Carlo Felice Nicolis di Robilant, who for his part promised "to do everything possible on his behalf."[86]

Compans di Brichanteau's correspondence also reveals the presence of a much wider group of aristocratic families who entered into his network of influence through friendships and connections developed in select private schools, the army officers corps, and the gentlemanly Società del Whist. Thus, when Compans helped launch the diplomatic career of his oldest son, Alessandro, in 1902, he relied on contacts and friendships that originated in the Reale Collegio Carlo Alberto, the preferred educational institution of the Piedmontese nobility in the second half of the nineteenth century. In other instances, such as the one brought to the titled notable's attention by Count Remigio Panissera di Veglio in 1890, it was a matter of coming to the aid of an "old comrade

---

[84] For Pallavicino comments, see his letter to Compans, September 2, 1896 in AST, Archivio di famiglia Compans, cat. 5, b. 14, f. 1. The concept of cousinhood is explored in greater detail in Cohen, *Two-Dimensional Man*, pp. 110–118.

[85] AST, Archivio di famiglia Compans, b. 4, f. 5, letter from S. di Robilant, June 2, 1905; letter from Nellina (Leontina) Pallavicino (nee Pallavicino-Mossi), September 5, 1912. Cat. 5, b. 14, f. 1 in the same archive contains a large number of letters from various cousins regarding diplomatic careers and military advancement.

[86] See *ibid.*, Archivio Politico Compans, b. 56, letter Nicolis to Compans, April 30, 1887.

in arms" in the cavalry.[87] Informal interaction among schoolmates and fellow officers continued within the dining and sitting rooms of the Whist, which provided a screen of privacy far from the public view and the formal structures of power. As their letters indicate, both Count Carlo Cordero di Vonzo and Count Paolo Rati Opizzoni, for example, made use of the club's exclusive confines to meet with Compans to discuss matters of common concern and to arrange favors.[88] For yet others like Countess Maria di Viry and Count Guido San Martino Valperga, more casual encounters in urban palaces and country houses provide the settings to discuss problems and seek assistance from the powerful parliamentary notable. In November 1892, Countess di Viry, for instance, wrote to remind Compans of "the subject of our conversation at the Pallavicini ball and [your] kind promises that have encouraged me to rely on your influence at the highest levels . . . knowing that for you *volere è potere.*"[89]

More importantly, access to the influence and connections of Compans di Brichanteau also permitted aristocratic families to preserve some of the halo of social custom in those communities that had once been their fiefs well after they had ceased to exercise any police or judicial powers. Above all, with his aid they were able go on playing their traditional role as benevolent patrons who protected the residents of their old rural enclaves and mediated their relations with the legal system and state administration. In fact, most of Compans' correspondence with other nobles involved favors for third parties of more modest social origins. Not surprisingly, most of the beneficiaries of aristocratic contacts resided in areas where the titled petitioner's family had its estates and where it had long exercised predominant influence.

Assistance assumed a variety of forms. On occasion, it simply involved soliciting the aristocratic leader's support for the bestowal of an honorary title on some village notable. After he was approached by Count Giulio d'Harcourt d'Azeglio in 1891, for example, Compans intervened on behalf of a certain Ippolito Negro from the village of

---

[87] AST, Archivio Politico Compans, b. 57, letter from Count R. Panissera di Veglio, no date, but 1890. For Compans' efforts on behalf of his own son, see letter dated November 9, 1902 in *ibid.*, Archivio di famiglia Compans, cat. 4, b. 11, f. 1.

[88] In December 1889, for instance, Cordero wrote Compans that he had planned to meet him at the club "in order to refer to you what I have learned about the "known business." The same month Compans wrote back, asking Cordero to remember him to "d'Aglie, Dalla Valle, and are many friends who help you kill time in your elegant . . . Whist-Club." See AST, Archivio Politico Compans, b. 60. For Count Rati Opizzoni, see his letters to Compans in February and March 1890 in *ibid.*, B.56.

[89] *Ibid.*, Archivio di famiglia Compans, b. 4, f. 5, letter November 20, 1892.

Azeglio who wished to be decorated with the Cross of the Knights of the Crown of Italy. In his letter to d'Harcourt announcing a favorable outcome, Compans wrote that he was moved to act chiefly by "the affectionate esteem which you have always professed for . . . Negro." For his part, d'Harcourt responded that the decoration "has given me a great pleasure as it has for the entire village of Azeglio and the surrounding villages." It was only fitting then that d'Harcourt, as the key go-between and the principal local landowner, presided over the public luncheon which took place later in the village to celebrate the event.[90]

On other occasions, blue-blooded patrons intervened on behalf of their local clients who had legal difficulties or who needed help in matters of hiring, transfers, and promotions within the state administration. When a petty merchant in the village of Monforte forgot to renew a state license in 1889 and, as a result, faced a heavy fine, Marchese Alberto Scarampi del Cairo, whose family had long been prominent landlords in the territory, intervened with his "affectionate cousin." Compans, in turn, immediately contacted the appropriate authorities; they assured him that they had suspended the fine on the basis of his recommendation.[91] Countess Irene San Martino di Strambino invoked "the already ancient friendship that links our families" in order to get Compans' help in winning a transfer of the local station master to another locale whose climate was healthier for his sick wife.[92] Conversely, Count Vittorio San Martino d'Aglie sought the "protection" of Compans for his client who wished to avoid a job transfer. Countess Costanza Ricardi Lomellini requested similar protection for a local mailman who had been fired for criticizing the postal system.[93] Citing his "influence with Prime Minister Crispi," Marchesa Maria Radicati di Brozolo solicited Compans' backing for the request of "my little village of Camerano-Casaco which desires to see Marco Bersano nominated as mayor."[94] A host of other aristocratic relatives, friends and acquaintances like Duke Alfonso Arborio Gattinara di Sartirana, Countess

---

[90] See AST, Archivio Politico Compans, letters Compans to d'Harcourt, January 31, 1891 and d'Harcourt to Compans, February 4, 1891. At the request of his cousin, Adele di Villanova, Compans performed a similar service for the mayor of Valperga, where her family went in the summer to their castle. See *ibid.*, Archivio di famiglia Compans, c. 5, b. 14, f. 1, letter A. di Villanova to Compans, August 6, 1905.

[91] Both Scarampi's letter to Compans and the letter Compans received in response to his intervention are in *ibid.*, Archivio Politico Compans, b. 55.

[92] *Ibid.*, b. 55, letter, I. di Strambino, October 17, 1889.

[93] AST, Archivio Politico Compans, b. 56, letter Ricardi Lomellini, no date, but late 1889; *ibid.*, b. 60, letter S. Martino d'Aglie, November 26, 1890.

[94] *Ibid.*, b. 56, letter Radicati to Compans, December 1889.

Edmena Nicolis di Robilant, Marchesa Aurelia Di Saluzzo di Paesana (née Cacherano di Bricherasio) took the same approach, writing to Compans to push their candidates for vacant state posts in their respective rural bailiwicks.[95]

In this fashion, well-connected nobles were able to use the institutional framework of the state not only to preserve some of their traditional influence and prestige, but also to perpetuate older cultural patterns of paternalism and deference – at least outside of the big cities – into the first decade of the twentieth century. In the rural hinterlands of Piedmont, the leadership of old-line families proved to be particularly resistant to erosion, especially in those localities where their country houses and estates were located. As late as 1910, nobles still served as the mayors of more than forty rural communes, which in many cases had once been their family fiefs. That year in the province of Alessandria, for instance, the mayors of Rocchetta Tanaro, Pomaro Monferrato, and Francavilla Bisio were respectively Marchese Enrico Incisa della Rocchetta, Marchese Luigi Dalla Valle di Pomaro, and Marchese Alessandro Guasco di Bisio, while in the province of Cuneo a similar pattern of family continuity prevailed in more than half a dozen communes.[96] In fact, a few old families in the Cunese, like the Falletti di Villafalletto and Beccaria Incisa di Santo Stefano, forged local dynasties in their former fiefs that extended from the late 1850s to the mid-1920s.[97]

As these cases attest, the political influence and power enjoyed by aristocratic families in Piedmont in the last decades before World War I combined elements of the old and the new, the traditional and the modern. While nobles lost their corporative privileges and domination of high office with the introduction of civil equality and parliamentary government after 1848, they were still able to take advantage of deeply embedded social patterns and cultural values to redefine older political roles and to carve out new ones for themselves in the second half of the century. Thus, they were able to convert their longstanding ties with the House of Savoy, the Catholic Church, and their rural dependents into vital support for the conquest of important positions within the new national army and diplomatic corps, leadership in the rapidly expanding world of voluntary associations, and new forms of local power brokering and patronage in an increasingly democratic political

---

[95] *Ibid.*, b. 56 and 60.
[96] See *Calendario Generale del Regno d'Italia* (Rome, 1910) for a complete list of all mayors in Piedmont.
[97] See Mola, *Storia dell'amministrazione provinciale di Cuneo*, pp. 577–587.

arena. Significantly, these roles did not require nobles to abandon those customs and practices that had traditionally defined the collective identity of the Piedmontese nobility. On the contrary, they often allowed old-line aristocrats to represent themselves in public in ways that enhanced and reinforced the prestige and dignity associated with hereditary titled status.

CHAPTER 3

OLD MONEY: THE SCALE AND STRUCTURE OF ARISTOCRATIC WEALTH

The success of the nobility in perpetuating their leadership and influence in public life in the second half of the nineteenth century depended to no small extent on their ability to also remain a part of the wealthy upper class within Piedmontese society. Much as elsewhere in Europe, inclusion in the hereditary nobility of Piedmont had traditionally implied wealth, if only because an aristocratic way of life presupposed a certain level of affluence. As a high court official expressed it in the 1840s, a respectable aristocrat needed "a patrimony sufficient to sustain with splendor the decorum of the noble title."[1]

Such wealth, however, became even more essential in an era when nobles no longer enjoyed corporative privileges. To begin with, a sizeable unearned income made possible the extensive leisure time that titled ladies and gentlemen required in order to occupy honorary offices and take part in the activities of voluntary political, religious, philanthropic, cultural, and recreational associations and clubs. More concretely, wealth was a prerequisite for old aristocratic families who wished to play the roles that gave them the greatest prestige and influence in the decades after 1848, namely those as organizational founders, patrons, and financiers.

This chapter will examine the issue of aristocratic wealth by addressing the following questions: How rich were Piedmontese nobles? What was the range of wealth-holding within the nobility? What forms did aristocratic wealth take? How successful were titled families at preserving and/or enlarging their material assets? The answers to these questions rest principally on data drawn from a survey of all surviving probate returns in the city of Turin for the estates left by both men and

---

[1] AST, Prima Sez., Titoli di Nobiltà, b. 5, procuratore generale del re, criteria for ennoblement, 1844.

women from titled aristocratic families as well as by a more select group
of bourgeois, wealthy but untitled individuals, for the periods 1862 to
1885 and 1901 to 1912. Probate returns have been supplemented in turn
with information from family papers, luxury tax records in Turin,
Piedmontese land registries, biographical sources, and both published
and unpublished genealogies.[2]

What place did old line titled families occupy within the wealthy
elite of Piedmont? Great wealth had been synonymous with aristocratic
status at the beginning of the nineteenth century, when the wealthiest
individuals in the realm were virtually all nobles.[3] Probate returns
reveal, however, that this situation began to change in the second half
of the century. Indeed, the years from 1862 to 1912 saw the titled
nobility lose their position of absolute preeminence within the local
elite of wealth as the comparative statistics in table 3.1 attest.

Aristocratic families still dominated the upper reaches of the wealthy
class in the first decade after unification. Titled nobles enjoyed a preponderance of the largest fortunes, accounting for over half their
number and two-thirds of their total value in the period from 1862 to
1873. Thus, wealthy blue bloods, and not businessmen, merchants, and
bankers, remained the richest individuals in Piedmontese society.
During the following decade, the mean value of fortunes of nobles continued to exceed that of wealthy non-nobles, but it had declined
slightly. Moreover, aristocrats now represented a minority of the richest
Turinese in probate. The agricultural depression of the 1880s and early
1890s accelerated these trends by temporarily slashing farm incomes and
property values. As a result, the dominance of the bourgeois wealthy
had become firmly established by the first decade of the twentieth
century. After 1900, rich non-nobles not only far outnumbered the old
families within the ranks of the very wealthy, but also they accounted
for most of the total value of large-scale wealth and the bulk of the
largest fortunes in probate.

Still the increasingly bourgeois background of large-scale wealth
holders did not mean that the old nobility succumbed to financial ruin

---

[2] For a full discussion of the probate records in Turin, see the Bibliography. As far as
the luxury tax records, I have consulted the ACT, Ruolo tasse vetture private and the
Ruolo tasse domestici for the years 1899, 1906, 1912, and 1913. Data on landownership came from the AST, Sez. Riunite, Catasto Rabbini, Provincia di Torino
and Provincia di Novara. I have relied primarily on the twenty-six volumes of
Manno, Il patriziato subalpino for additional genealogical information on Piedmontese
aristocratic families.

[3] See Bulferetti, "I piemontesi più ricchi," pp. 77–79.

Table 3.1 *Hierarchy of wealth: aristocracy versus bourgeoisie*

Estate size	1862–1873 (%)	1874–1885 (%)	1901–1912 (%)
L. 250,000–500,000			
Aristocracy	52 (41)	52 (27)	32 (14)
Bourgeoisie	74 (59)	141 (73)	190 (86)
L. 500,001–750,000			
Aristocracy	19 (45)	21 (31)	10 (14)
Bourgeoisie	23 (55)	48 (69)	61 (86)
L. 750,001–1,000,000			
Aristocracy	7 (41)	6 (30)	5 (31)
Bourgeoisie	10 (59)	14 (70)	11 (69)
L. 1,000,001–2,000,000			
Aristocracy	12 (63)	12 (30)	14 (30)
Bourgeoisie	7 (37)	28 (70)	32 (70)
More than L. 2,000,000			
Aristocracy	8 (73)	5 (38)	5 (29)
Bourgeoisie	3 (27)	8 (62)	12 (71)

Table 3.2 *Distribution of wealth: aristocracy versus bourgeoisie (>L.750,000)*

Category	1862–1873 (%)	1874–1885 (%)	1901–1912 (%)
Numbers			
Aristocracy	27 (57)	23 (32)	24 (30)
Bourgeois	20 (43)	50 (68)	55 (70)
Total value			
Aristocracy	L. 49,551,307	L. 41,591,572	L. 41,004,246
Bourgeois	L. 27,919,290	L. 73,583,296	L. 105,464,438
Percentage of total	(%)	(%)	(%)
Aristocracy	64	36	28
Bourgeois	36	64	72

and disappeared from the scene in the last decades of the nineteenth century. On the contrary, aristocratic families continued to contribute a disproportionately large share of the local rich at least up to 1914. They certainly maintained a much stronger presence within Turin's elite of wealth than their titled colleagues managed to do in Paris or Naples in the last decade and a half before World War I. At a time when Piedmontese aristocrats continued to account for nearly a third of the individuals in the city who left estates over L. 750,000 and more than a quarter of their wealth, nobles were largely absent from the ranks of the wealthy in Naples, while less than 1 percent of the fortunes in Paris above 1 million francs still belonged to nobles.[4]

THE DISTRIBUTION OF WEALTH WITHIN THE NOBILITY

Those aristocrats who left estates over L. 750,000 constituted a small and exclusive elite at the summit of a much larger and more diverse class of nobles. The custom of primogeniture, together with the practice of ascribing aristocratic status to cadets and the inevitable variations in family fortunes over time, had long ensured that the second estate was not simply a collection of wealthy families, but rather a heterogeneous body whose ranks included both rich landed magnates as well as people of comparatively modest means. Probate returns confirm the existence of substantial disparities of wealth within the Piedmontese nobility in the late nineteenth and early twentieth centuries. At the same time, they also show that the nobility remained, on the whole, a decidedly affluent and economically privileged segment of Italian society up to the Great War.

These figures show that not all nobles who resided in Turin enjoyed great wealth, but that the vast majority of them were considerably more prosperous than the rest of the local population. In fact, over half of the nobles ranked in the top 1 percent of wealth-holders in Turin, while all but a few of them were well-to-do by the standards of smaller provinces such as Piacenza and Lucca. As a group, Piedmontese noble families conformed to an "aristocratic distribution" pattern, characterized by few very low values, a relatively high frequency of big estates, and a disproportionately large number of intermediate fortunes.[5]

In broad terms, the nobles who passed through probate in the decades after 1862 fit into one of four categories: (1) a poor nobility with less than L. 100,000 in assessed value; (2) a middling or respectable nobility whose estates ranged from L. 100,000 to 500,000; (3) an affluent nobility, with between L. 500,000 and 999,999 in assessed value; (4) a

---

[4] For statistics on Paris, see Daumard, "Wealth and Affluence in Paris," p. 105. In Macry's survey of the probate records of Naples in 1900, he found only one noble among the individuals who left estates over L. 100,000. See Macry, *Ottocento*, pp. xxiv–xxv. The nobility in Piacenza appear to have fared even better than the Piedmontese titled elite. In the years 1902–1905, they accounted for 34.4 percent of the estates over L. 20,000 and 39 percent of the total value, while the mean value of their fortunes continued to exceed that of the bourgeois elite. See Banti, *Terra e denaro*, pp. 29–32.

[5] See Daumard, "Wealth and Affluence," pp. 98–101. For data on wealthy elites in Piacenza and Lucca, see Banti, *Terra e denaro*, pp. 29–30 and "Ricchezza e potere," pp. 385–432.

Table 3.3 *Wealth distribution: general population versus aristocracy (percent)*

Total value	Gen. Pop.	Aristocracy
Less than 1,000	44	1
1,001–2,000	16	1
2,001–5,000	17	2
5,001–10,000	14	2
10,001–20,000		4
20,001–50,000	8	14
50,001–100,000	1	17
Less than 100,000 (sub-total)	99	41
100,001–250,000		28
250,001–500,000		16
500,001–750,000	1	6
750,001–1,000,000		2
1,000,001–2,000,000		5
More than 2,000,000	0.05	2
Total	100.05	100

Note: The figures on the wealth of the general population of Turin are based on statistics compiled by F. S. Nitti for the years from 1900–1901 to 1902–1903. See Nitti, *Scritti di economia e finanza*, I, p. 280. The data on the aristocracy refer to the entire period covered by the survey, namely the periods 1862–1885 and 1901–1912.

wealthy nobility of millionaires and multi-millionaires. Table 3.4 shows the pattern of distribution when the probate returns of the nobility are grouped according to these categories.

At the bottom of this hierarchy of wealth was a substantial group of individuals who seem to lend credence to the standard view that Italy, and Piedmont in particular, were territories over-run by impoverished or modestly endowed title-holders.[6] These "poor" nobles were poor to the extent that their assets at the time of their death were below the L. 100,000 minimum which the House of Savoy considered necessary to maintain "the dignity" of a noble title in the nineteenth century.[7] Although they accounted for two-fifths of all nobles in the survey, they held collectively a minuscule portion of the total aristocratic wealth that passed through probate. They did not possess, in their own right, the luxuries and material amenities traditionally associated with the aristocracy such as substantial landholdings, country houses, urban palaces, large staffs of servants, and splendid carriages. In fact, three-fifths of

[6] See Bush, *Rich Noble, Poor Noble*, p. 39.
[7] From the documents in AST, Prima Sezione, Titoli di Nobiltà, it is evident that the government in the first half of the nineteenth century required that individuals who aspired to the lowest level of nobility possess a patrimony of L. 100,000.

Table 3.4 *Aristocratic wealth distribution (1862–1885; 1901–1912)*

Category	Number	(%)	Share (%)
Poor	345	41	5.3
Respectable	368	44	29.7
Affluent	68	8	15.5
Wealthy	56	7	49.5
Total	837	100.0	100.0

them were completely landless; less than 7 percent possessed any urban real estate. In the majority of cases, paper assets supplied more than three-quarters of the assessed value of the estate, with private credits being the single most important factor.

The poverty of this group of nobles should not be exaggerated, however. To begin with, most of the poor nobles were comparatively well off by the standards of the rest of society. A mere 85 titled individuals, for instance, or about a tenth of the entire survey, fell below the L. 20,000 in patrimony considered necessary for inclusion in the provincial elites of Lucca and Piacenza. Nor did many of these nobles appear to be over burdened with debts. In only 41 out of 345 estates did liabilities amount to more than three-quarters of the gross assets.

More importantly, poor nobles were often sustained, in various ways, by the collective wealth of their families. As a result, many of them were able to enjoy a standard of living far higher than their modest personal patrimonies would ordinarily have allowed. In practical terms, this meant that they had access to financial assistance from their wealthier relatives, resided in comfortable suites or apartments in their family's urban palace and country house, enjoyed the services of the staff of servants in residence, and generally shared in a luxurious way of life that was subsidized by the head of the family.

The middling or respectable nobility constituted the largest single group of aristocrats in probate with 43 percent of the total, although they contributed less than a third of the value. They were not as dependent as the titled poor on the kindness and generosity of relatives, since they possessed sufficient wealth in their own right to maintain a style of life that was, if not extravagant, at least quite comfortable and consonant with their social positions. Like their poorer brethren, most respectable nobles (68 percent) did not own any urban real estate in Turin though they might have a villa in the provinces. But nearly three-quarters of them (70 percent) had some landed property and they were considerably less likely to leave estates heavily burdened with debt; only eight respectable nobles had liabilities that exceeded 75 percent of the value of their assets. They enjoyed an unearned income that, if well managed, allowed them to devote themselves to such traditional aristocratic pursuits as state service, politics, sports, and charitable works without having to worry about making a living.

The material resources available to the respectable or middling nobility paled, however, in comparison to those in the possession of affluent and wealthy titled families who together constituted the real aristocratic elite of Piedmont. Indeed, throughout most of the nineteenth century, these families furnished most of the region's greatest landowners, its richest magnates, and its most prominent public figures. Thus, Cavour, Alfieri di Sostegno, d'Azeglio, Thaon di Revel, and Solaro della Margarita – to mention only the best known statesmen and political leaders – fell into one of these two top categories of wealth.

By themselves, the affluent nobility supplied just 8 percent of the aristocratic estates in probate, but accounted for 16 percent of the total value or nearly three times as much as the poor nobility. Virtually all (91 percent) of the individuals in this category had rural properties that often included a country house. A majority of them owned substantial acreage, with landed estates in the countryside representing more than half of the assessed value of their wealth.[8] In contrast their less-well-endowed fellow nobles, they were also more likely to own a residence in Turin; a solid majority of them (63 percent) held urban real estate in the regional capital. Finally, the estates of the affluent nobility tended to have relatively low levels of debt. In only two cases did liabilities consume more than 75 percent of the gross value.

At the summit of the aristocratic pyramid of wealth was a small and exclusive group of individuals with very large fortunes valued at over L. 1 million. Although this "wealthy" nobility represented a modest percentage of the nobles in the survey (7 percent), their estates collectively contributed half of the total value of all aristocratic assets in probate. At least until the 1880s, they were the richest individuals in

---

[8] The relative importance of rural properties as a proportion of the gross value of estates among the affluent can be seen in this table:

Percentage value	Number	%
0	6	8.8
0.01–25	7	10.2
25.01–50	19	27.9
50.01–75	21	30.9
75.01–high	15	22.2
Total	68	100.0

Piedmontese society. In fact, their ranks contributed slightly less than half (45 percent) of all the millionaires as well as seven of the ten largest fortunes to pass through Turin's probate office in the first two and a half decades after unification.[9]

How wealthy were these "wealthy" aristocrats? In an era when the salaries of the most successful managers in the cotton industry ranged from L. 4,000 to L. 10,000 a year and an annual income of L. 2,500 was sufficient to be considered "bourgeois," they were certainly well-off. Nonetheless, it has long been a commonplace to insist on the modesty of the material resources possessed by the Piedmontese nobility, especially in comparison with those of the other regional nobilities on the Italian peninsula.[10] The paucity of information on aristocratic wealth holding elsewhere in Italy makes it rather difficult to test this claim.

On the one hand, the Piedmontese nobility lacked the enormous concentrations of wealth found in some other regions in the nineteenth century. No aristocrat in Turin, for instance, possessed a fortune even remotely comparable to that of Prince Tommaso Corsini with a total value of over L. 22 million in 1856, let alone that left by Genoese financier, Raffaele De Ferrari, Duke of Galliera, which was estimated at L. 140 million in 1876. The largest estate bequeathed by a noble in Turin belonged to Marchesa Giulia Falletti di Barolo; it amounted to slightly under L. 6.4 million in 1864.[11]

On the other hand, both the number and the size of the fortunes left by the top titled wealth holders in Turin in the first decades after Italian

---

[9] I have located eighty-three estates valued at over L. 1 million in the period prior to 1885; thirty-seven were left by nobles, forty-six by non-nobles. The ten largest fortunes were:
  1. Marchesa Giulia Falletti di Barolo – L. 6,390,781
  2. Giovanni Priotti – L. 4,955,696
  3. Marchese Paolo Solaroli di Briona – L. 4,709,790
  4. Prince Emanuele Dal Pozzo della Cisterna – L. 4,660,933
  5. Marchese Aynardo Benso di Cavour – L. 4,346,087
  6. Marchese Lodovico Pallavicino-Mossi – L. 4,283,649
  7. Princess Beatrice Dal Pozzo di Cisterna – L. 3,999,034
  8. Count Carlo Costa della Trinità – L. 3,452,490
  9. Vittorio Lanza – L. 3,450,506
  10. Carlo Ogliani – L. 3,112,724

[10] See Woolf, "Studi sulla nobiltà piemontese," p. 138; Cognasso, "Nobiltà e borghesia," p. 230. On the annual salaries of managers, see Romano, L'industria cotoniera lombarda, pp. 438–439; for the bourgeois minimum, see Ellero, La tirannide borghese, pp. 29–30.

[11] For information on the fortunes of De Ferrari and Corsini, see Massa Piergiovanni, "Eredità, acquisti e rendite," vol. 1, pp. 398–400 and Moroni, "Le ricchezze dei Corsini," pp. 284.

unification were considerably greater than those found in smaller provincial centers and compared favorably with those of the richest Florentine patricians, although they lagged somewhat behind those of the Milanese nobility. Thus, the combined value of the three largest aristocratic estates in probate in the late 1870s easily surpassed that left by the entire Piacentine elite and more than doubled that of the Lucchese elite in these years.[12] In the years from 1862 to 1875 the probate office in Florence registered nine estates over L. 1 million left by patricians, with the largest being that of the banker Emanuelle Fenzi whose estate was valued at L. 4,583,494. During the same period, Marchesa Falletti di Barolo topped a list of twenty titled Piedmontese millionaires and multi-millionaires in probate.[13] On the other hand, seven aristocrats in Milan left estates valued at over L. 5 million in the three decades after unification, four of which were larger than that of the Marchesa di Barolo. Likewise, the mean value of the estates of nobles in Turin between 1874 and 1885 was 23 percent less than that of their Milanese patrician neighbors which averaged L. 385,119 in the early 1880s.[14]

Regardless of their comparative dimensions, such material resources permitted wealthy aristocrats in Piedmont to lead a very luxurious way of life that separated them from the vast majority of their fellow nobles. As a rule, this entailed dual residences with a palace in Turin and a number of country houses, extensive foreign travel, the attentions of a large staff of servants, elegant carriages, and many other amenities that were beyond the means of most nobles. When Prince Emanuele Dal

[12] The three largest fortunes that changed hands by inheritance in Turin between 1876 and 1879 were those of Marchese Giuseppe Pallavicino-Mossi, Marchese Paolo Solaroli di Briona, and Marchese Aynardo Benso di Cavour; their total value was L. 13,813,525. The total values of all inheritance over L. 20,000 in Lucca and Piacenza during this period were respectively L. 5,973,694 and L. 11,542,429. See the two studies by Banti, "Ricchezza e potere," pp. 385–432 and Terra e denaro, pp. 59–60.

[13] Professor Raffaele Romanelli was kind enough to allow me to see his raw data, from which I compiled a list of nobles with estates valued at over L. 1 million for the period prior to 1875. Romanelli has subsequently continued his exploration of the probate records in Florence up to 1904. See Romanelli, "Urban patricians and 'bourgeois' society," pp. 3–21.

[14] Between 1862 and 1890, 70 aristocrats left estates over L. 1 million. The top titled wealth holders in probate were: Raimondo Visconti di Modrone (L. 9,541,597), Antonio Busca Arconati Visconti (L. 9,126,774), Antonio Litta Visconti Arese (L. 7,805,859), Vitaliano Borromeo (L. 7,705,425), Lodovico Melzi d'Eril (L. 6,338,234), Cesare Massimiliano Stampa Soncino (L. 6,355,397), Francesco Arese (L. 5,830,578), and Filippo Ala Ponzoni (L. 5,469,110). For data on wealth holding in Milan, see Licini's Milano nell'800, pp. 61–62, as well as her "Entità e composizione delle fortune ambrosiane secondo le dichiarazioni di successione degli anni 1871 e 1881" (unpublished typescript, 1992).

Pozzo della Cisterna died in 1864, he left legacies to a staff of thirty-
three servants. During the same decade Marchese Lodovico Pallavicino-
Mossi maintained a fleet of five two-horse carriages and enjoyed the
attentions of a staff of a dozen servants in his palace in Turin that
included five men in livery.[15] Predictably, the names of rich aristocrats
like Count Ferdinando Avogadro di Collobiano, Count Cesare Valperga di Masino, Count Ernesto Balbo Bertone di Sambuy, and
Marchese Emanuele Coardi di Bagnasco featured prominently on the
luxury tax rolls. At the end of the nineteenth century, for example, all
but six of the thirty-seven largest contributors on the servant tax rolls in
Turin were from noble families. The same titled elite also accounted for
twenty-six of the thirty-four top contributors to the carriage tax in
1899.[16]

The distribution of wealth within the Piedmontese nobility clearly
recapitulated the values of patriarchy, primogeniture, and pedigree. Not
surprisingly, men and women did not share equally in the material assets
possessed by titled families, as Table 3.5 reveals. While fewer than a
third of the noblemen left estates of less than L. 100,000 in the decades
after 1861, half of all aristocratic women who passed through probate
were below this benchmark and thus fit the profile of the poor noble. In
fact, they accounted for a majority of all poor nobles in the survey.
Even these statistics over-estimate the real material resources of such
women, since often their wealth existed mostly on paper in the form of
claims on the estates of their fathers, brothers, and husbands. Still, such
arrangements probably meant dependence rather than real poverty for
most "poor" noble women who shared the high standard of living
enjoyed by most titled families.

At the same time, this unequal distribution of wealth also left nearly
half of the women from titled families financially well-off and in a
decidedly privileged position vis-à-vis the rest of the population. They
clearly benefited from new inheritance laws modeled on those of the
Napoleonic Code which guaranteed that all legitimate heirs, including
women, received a share in the legacy. Given the wealth of the nobility,
the shares of titled women were often fairly substantial.[17] Over two-
fifths of the aristocratic women in probate were "respectable" in so far
as they possessed personal fortunes of between L. 100,000 and
L. 500,000 which placed them among the top 1.5 percent of wealth

---

[15] See the copy of Dal Pozzo's will in *Ufficio di Registro di Successioni di Torino* (hereafter
cited as *URST*) 1864, 5–v5, f. 346. On the staff and carriages of Marchese Lodovico,
see AST, Sez. Riunite, Archivio Pallavicino-Mossi, b. 17.

[16] See ACT, Ruolo tasse vetture private, 1899; Ruolo tasse domestici 1900.

[17] See Banti, "Una fonte per lo studio delle elites," 86–87.

Table 3.5 *Wealth distribution: aristocratic women compared with men*
(1862–1885, 1901–1912)

Category	Women (%)	Men (%)
Poor	51	32
Respectable	43	44
Affluent	3	12
Wealthy	3	12
Totals	100.0	100.0

holders in Turin. Moreover, the wealth of these women was seldom just paper assets, as the case of Marchesa Cristina Sant'Amour de Chanaz illustrates. In 1863, the Marchesa died at the age of 72, leaving an estate valued at L. 322,844. While claims on her husband's patrimony for her dowry amounted to L. 59,125, most (81 percent) of the estate's value derived from a building she owned in Turin and two farms in the rural commune of Cherasco.[18]

Daughters, wives, and sisters were much less likely to possess large fortunes in their own right. Only fourteen aristocratic women in the thirty-three years covered by my survey left estates worth over L. 1 million. As the cases of the three top female wealth holders attest, these dowagers owed their fortunes to the absence of a male heir. Marchesa Giulia Falletti di Barolo, the single richest titled individual to pass through probate, was a childless widow. She came into her fortune in 1838 when she inherited all of the vast possessions of her late husband, Marchese Tancredi, who was himself a second generation only child without any close male relatives. Marchesa Giulia lived for another quarter century and was therefore able to exercise genuine control over her vast wealth.[19]

On other occasions, women served more as legal conduits for the transfer of wealth within the family. The second largest estate held by a noble woman belonged, on paper, to Beatrice Dal Pozzo della Cisterna, one of two daughters, who were the only off-spring of the third richest aristocrat in the survey, Prince Emanuele Dal Pozzo della Cisterna.

---

[18] See *URST*, 1863, vol. 3, n. 368.
[19] See Archivio Opera Pia Barolo, b. 1 for the conditions of the Falletti di Barolo estate in the nineteenth century. On the genealogical background of the family see, Manno, *Il patriziato subalpino*.

Beatrice was in fact a teenager who died shortly after she inherited nearly L. 4 million from her father and, as a consequence, never really controlled the fortune that technically belonged to her.[20] The third female multi-millionaire, owed her great wealth to even more unusual circumstances. According to the probate office, Olimpia d'Harcourt possessed a personal fortune of over L. 2.3 million at the time of her death in 1876. In reality, she was the spinster sister of Count Giuseppe d'Harcourt, the fourth wealthiest noble in the survey, who exercised total control over her finances. A subsequent judicial inquiry concluded that Count Giuseppe had used her estate to conceal part of his own enormous assets in a scheme to avoid inheritance taxes.[21] Even in the case of rich heiresses then, great wealth often remained an essentially male preserve in the patriarchal world of the Piedmontese nobility.

Despite their subordinate position to the men in their families, aristocratic women were still more likely to be well off than their bourgeois counterparts. While titled families contributed only slightly more than a third (37 percent) of the estates in probate over L. 750,000, they accounted for nearly half of all the women with fortunes on this scale (see Table 3.6). As these statistics attest, aristocratic dowagers out paced rich women from non-noble families in virtually all major categories of wealth holding. They owned more real estate, their investment portfolios were thicker, and the average value of their estates was substantially larger.

The unequal sexual division of wealth within the titled families of Piedmont did not benefit all men the same, as Table 3.7 reveals. The steadfast observance of the traditions of primogeniture and lineal continuity ensured that first sons possessed the lion's share of the family wealth. In fact, they accounted for nearly three-quarters of the largest aristocratic fortunes in probate and over 90 percent of those in the hands of men.[22] Their importance as key links in a family line was evident not just in the scale of their wealth. It also found expression in the composition of their estates which almost invariably included the

---

[20] See *URST*, 1864, 6–v.5, f. 401. Beatrice passed away at the age of 13, later in the same year as her father.

[21] For the circumstances surrounding the estate of Olimpia D'Harcourt, see AST, Sez. Riunite, Archivio D'Harcourt, Atto di rinuncia ad eredità, November 29, 1892.

[22] Within the category of wealthy nobles, the distribution by family position was:

Family position	Number	%
First sons	50	90.9
Cadets	5	9.1

Table 3.6 *Wealthy women: aristocrats versus bourgeois*
(1862–1885, 1901–1912)

Category	Aristocracy	Bourgeoisie
Number	15 (48)	16 (52)
Total estate	26,989,132	21,285,649
Total property	17,181,839	11,043,194
Personalty	8,095,328	6,828,384
Average estate	1,799,275	1,330,353
Average property	1,145,456	690,200
Average personalty	539,689	426,774

Note: The category, "Total estate," includes all assets; "Property" refers to both urban and rural buildings as well as landholdings; "Personalty" includes all mobile assets such as stocks, bonds, credits, and savings.

Table 3.7 *Aristocratic men: first sons versus cadets (1862–1885, 1901–1912)*

Category	First sons (%)	Cadets (%)
Poor	23	43
Respectable	42	48
Affluent	17	6
Wealthy	17	3
Totals	100	100

ancestral villa or castle in the countryside as well as the most important family heirlooms and archives.

Only in exceptional circumstances did younger sons control great patrimonies. A mere five cadets left fortunes valued at over L. 1 million. Marchese Federico Asinari di San Marzano, for instance, became the principal heir to his family's substantial estate as a result of his older brother's premature death from cholera during the Crimean War. The even more fortunate Count Filiberto Avogadro di Collobiano was the last of five sons, but three of his older brothers never married, while the one who did died childless. As a result, the vast possessions of his family were concentrated in his hands and he died a multi-millionaire in 1868. In the case of another cadet, Marchese Alessandro Dalla Valle di Pomaro, who inherited virtually all of his family's sizeable landholdings in 1891, preference for a younger son seems to have been the result of a paternal decision to protect the position of the family patrimony by keeping it out of the hands of a less competent first son.[23] But whenever possible, these wealthy titled cadets themselves returned to the practice of primogeniture. Accordingly, Count Filiberto Avogadro di Collobiano ensured in his will that the bulk of his fortune passed to his first son, Count Ferdinando, who in turn gave similar preference to his third child, but only surviving male heir, Count Augusto.[24]

The concern for family continuity was understandable, since most of Turin's wealthiest aristocrats were also distinguished by their ancient lineage. Old "thoroughbred" families who traced their titles to the medieval or early modern period – rather than newly ennobled civil servants, bankers, and businessmen – continued to furnish the great majority of the richest nobles in Turin before World War I (see Table 3.8).

There were, of course, remarkable success stories of men like Marchese Paolo Solaroli di Briona who rose rapidly to fame and fortune. Born in 1796 into a humble family from Novara and with little formal education, Solaroli had an extraordinary career that took him from mercenary soldiering in India to the highest ranks of the Piedmontese army, the inner circles of court, and the world of high finance. Ennobled in the 1840s by Carlo Alberto, he was elevated to the title of Marchese of Briona by Vittorio Emanuele II in the 1860s. When he died in 1878, Solaroli left an estate of over L. 4.7 million, the seventh largest in the entire probate survey.[25] Conversely, there were instances of once wealthy old families like the Della Chiesa di Cinzano and the Ferrero della Marmora who had lost most, if not all, of their patrimonies by the end of the nineteenth century.[26]

---

[23] Marchese Alessandro Dalla Valle di Pomaro left an estate in 1905 with a gross value of L. 1,658,150.72. See URST, b. 694, f. 5, for a copy of his father's will, which specifically designated him as the principal heir, despite the fact that he was still a bachelor at the time, while his older brother Luigi was already married. For the estates of Marchese Federico Asinari and Count Avogadro di Collobiano, see URST, b. 1–2 f. 38 and b. 8 f. 36 respectively.

[24] See URST, b. 655, f. 38, for the probate records pertaining to the estate of Count Ferdinando Avogadro di Collobiano. The oldest of four sons and a daughter, he left one of the two largest aristocratic fortunes in probate during the last decade before World War I, one estimated at L. 3.9 million. While his daughter received L. 900,000, the rest went to his son and included 2,041 hectares of prime farm land in Vercelli.

[25] Information on the life of Marchese Paolo Solaroli di Briona comes from a privately published pamphlet in the possession of the family. I am grateful to Mrs. Flavia Adami (nee Solaroli di Briona) for access to the pamphlet. Dr. Alessandro Polsi has kindly furnished me with material on Solaroli's role in the banking world from his own research on the major stockholders in the joint-stock banks from 1853 to 1878.

[26] Marchese Lodovico Della Chiesa di Cinzano and Marchese Tommaso Ferrero della Marmora were scions of distinguished old aristocratic families in economic decline.

Table 3.8 *Top aristocratic wealth holders: family lineage (>L. 750,000)*
(1862–1885, 1901–1912)

Titled Lineage	Wealth-holder (%)	Spouse (%)
Pre-1722 nobility	77	64
Post-1722 nobility	8	3
Restoration nobility	7	0
Post-1861 nobility	8	2
Non-Pied. nobility	–	23
Bourgeois	–	8

Such cases of rapid upward and downward mobility stand out, however, precisely because they were so exceptional. New families ennobled after 1815 like the Solaroli and the Rignon accounted for only a tiny fraction of the wealthy nobility.[27] The prominence of the oldest families is most striking at the highest levels of wealth, which were monopolized by the bearers of the most venerated names of the *ancien régime* nobility like Solaro, Avogadro, Arborio, Alfieri, Balbo, Provana, Falletti, and Dal Pozzo whose fortunes predated the French Revolution.[28] Such a strong correlation between antiquity of noble title and large-scale wealth contrasts with the supposedly more "traditional" situation in the south where some of the richest nobles were comparatively new men like Barracco, Torlonia, or Pavoncelli, who amassed enormous fortunes and acquired their titles after the Napoleonic Era.[29] The enduring presence of the same names at the top of the aristocratic pyramid of wealth over the course of a century that witnessed the destruction of the *ancien régime* and the loss of hereditary

The Della Chiesa had been among the ten wealthiest in 1799; Marchese Lodovico left only debts to his heirs. Similarly, while Ferrero della Marmora's father had been one of the largest landowners in the province of Turin during the first half of the nineteenth century, Marchese Tommaso possessed landed assets valued at a mere L. 1800 at his death in 1901. See AST, Sez. Riunite, Insinuazioni, 221854, libro 7, vol. 1, pp. 381–490; *URST*, 1901, vol. 557, n. 24.

[27] Count Felice Rignon, whose father had been ennobled in 1826, left the fourth largest estate in the survey, L. 5,523, 647.

[28] Thirteen of the eighteen titled families designated as the richest in Piedmont by French authorities in 1799 were still among the elite of wealth in the second half of the nineteenth century. See Bulferetti, "I piemontese più ricchi," pp. 77–79.

[29] On the Baracco family, see Petrusewicz, *Latifondo*; for the case of the Pavoncelli, see Snowden, "The City of the Sun," p. 202. The *Rivista Araldica*, vol. x, November 1912 provides a brief summary of the rise of the Torlonia family.

privileges offers eloquent testimony to the economic strength and stability of the Piedmontese nobility's inner core of old-line "feudal"
families.

Two main conclusions can be drawn from probate data on the distribution of wealth within the Piedmontese nobility in the second half of
the nineteenth and early twentieth centuries. First, old-line titled
families remained a large, if no longer dominant, component of Turin's
wealthy upper classes at least up to World War I. Such wealth provided
the financial resources and leisure to maintain their status and to play a
prominent and highly visible role as patrons and leaders in local public
life. Second, the data belie the stereotype of a nobility polarized
between a small elite of very rich magnates and a large mass of impoverished nobles. While differences in wealth did exist, there was little
abject poverty and a majority of nobles possessed the material assets
necessary to live in conformity with the standards of their class. The
absence of extremes of rich and poor contributed in turn to the group
cohesion within the nobility.

THE STRUCTURE OF ARISTOCRATIC WEALTH

The wealth of aristocratic families in nineteenth-century Piedmont was
distinguished not only by its size, but also by its composition. Although
the estates of the nobility as a whole included every imaginable type of
real and personal asset, the estates of rich aristocrats (those with more
than L. 750,000 in assets) were typically quite different from those left
by rich non-nobles and helped to mark them as a separate and distinct
elite in Piedmontese society. Above all, the wealthy aristocrats continued in the decades after 1862 to follow traditional avenues of wealth
holding and investment, while largely avoiding the commercial and
industrial activities that produced a host of new bourgeois millionaires
in this period.

The distinctiveness of aristocratic patterns of wealth and investment
emerges clearly from a comparison of the structure of estates left by rich
nobles and non-nobles after 1861 (see Table 3.9). To begin with, these
figures show how real estate remained considerably more important in
aristocratic fortunes than personal assets, with landed wealth, the age-
old marker of noble status, constituting the largest single factor. Only
two rich aristocrats in the entire survey left estates in which rural property amounted to less than L. 100,000; one-third of them possessed
landholdings valued at more than L. 1 million. This characteristic
sharply distinguished their patrimonies from those of wealthy non-

Table 3.9 *Structure of wealth – nobles versus non-nobles (>L. 750,000)*
(1862–1885, 1901–1912)

Category	Noble	Non–noble	Noble % of Total
Real property	74%	43%	52
Rural property	56	16	68
Urban property	18	27	29
Personal property	19	50	20
Stocks	7	19	
Bonds	5	12	
Bank deposits	2	2	
Farm equipment	1	0	
Credits	5	13	
Cash	0	1	
Inter vivos gifts	4	5	
Other	3	2	
Total	100	100	40

nobles, for whom rural property assumed only secondary importance. In fact, nearly a third (32 percent) of the untitled rich left less than L. 1,000 in landholdings, while only 8 of the 125 wealthiest non-nobles in probate were great landowners with properties in the countryside worth more than L. 1 million.[30]

Such a pronounced preference for rural property ensured that large-scale landownership remained a predominantly aristocratic phenomenon in the Piedmontese countryside before World War I. Rich bourgeois rentiers, businessmen, and professional people represented only a small minority of the "large landowners" – those individuals whose rural properties had a capital value of more than L. 400,000 or measured over 300 hectares at the time of their death. Both the probate records and land registries of the nineteenth century confirm this reality. Of the eighty-six largest landowners whose estates went through probate between 1862 and 1885, sixty-seven or 78 percent came from the ranks of the titled aristocracy. Even after the agricultural depression of the late nineteenth century, the situation had not changed dramatically. In the

[30] At least two of the non-nobles with substantial wealth in rural property, Alessandro Martini and Giovanni Battista Biglia, hardly qualified as landed gentlemen. For the most part, their properties in the countryside were part of their industrial activities – liquor processing in the case of Martini and the construction of aqueducts in the case of Biglia.

first decade of the twentieth century, titled families still accounted for
two-thirds of the large landed estates.[31]

Aristocratic predominance was even more striking at the very highest
levels of landownership. The twenty-three greatest landed magnates,
with estates of over 1,000 hectares, were all nobles; I have not been able
to locate a single bourgeois landowner who owned more than 900 hectares before 1914. The data from the mid-nineteenth century land
survey, the *Catasto Rabbini*, show a similar pattern. In the province of
Turin, for instance, all of the landed estates over 300 hectares in the
richest communes of the plains belonged to titled families like the Ferrero
Fieschi della Marmora, Beraudo di Pralormo, and Thaon di St. Andrè,
while nobles accounted for two-thirds of the remaining properties
between 100 and 300 hectares. Likewise, in the plains of Novara, aristocratic landowners owned seven of the nine largest rural estates in 1850s.[32]

Geographically, the biggest properties were concentrated in the rich
plains of Vercelli and Novara. It was not uncommon for the major landowning families to have estates in more than one province; Marchesa
Falletti di Barolo, for instance, owned properties in the provinces of Vercelli, Turin, and Cuneo.[33] Conversely, Piedmontese landed aristocrats
rarely had property outside of the region. Those who did either possessed
estates in areas that immediately bordered on Piedmont like Marchese
Alessandro Dalla Valle di Pomaro (Lombardy) and Marchese Domenico
Del Carretto di Balestrino (Liguria) or else had acquired them late in the
nineteenth century as in the case of Count Giuseppe d'Harcourt's properties in the province of Ferrara.[34] In this respect, they differed from the
great titled families of Florence and Rome such as the Corsini, Borghese,
and Torlonia who had estates scattered across the peninsula.

By the standards of the British peerage or the Prussian Junkers, the
landed estates of even the wealthiest Piedmontese nobles were rather
modest in scale. Only twenty-three old-line families in the region had

[31] The group of individuals in probate who left rural property valued at over L. 400,000
had the following social composition:

Period	Aristocracy	Bourgeoisie	Total
1862–1873	42	8	50
1874–1885	25	11	36
1901–1912	25	13	38

[32] See note 2.
[33] See Archivio Falletti di Barolo, Opera Pia Barolo, b. 51, f. 1, Beni stabili 1864.
[34] D'Harcourt came into the possession of some 1550 hectares in the province of
Ferrara in the 1880s as a result of the default on a loan. See AST, Archivo D'Harcourt, b. 165, f. 10–11. For the properties of Dalla Valle di Pomaro and Del Carretto
di Balestrino, see *URST*, b. 694, f. 5, 1905 and b. 179, f. 110, 1869.

sufficient acreage to have been included in the ranks of the "greater gentry" of British landed society; none were anywhere near the peerage. Likewise, landed estates between 950 and 1,500 acres, which were the norm among the Prussian Junkers, were the exception in the Piedmontese plains.[35] The rural properties of the richest Piedmontese nobles were also considerably smaller than those of the great southern latifondisti and Roman princes. I have located only four titled families in nineteenth-century Piedmont whose rural estates measured over 2,000 hectares – Falletti di Barolo, Asinari di San Marzano, Dal Pozzo della Cisterna, and Avogadro di Collobiano – and none above 5,000.[36] Baron Alfonso Barracco, probably the biggest landlord in southern Italy in the nineteenth century, owned a latifondo that spread over some 30,000 hectares in Calabria, while the greatest landed family of Rome, the Borghese, possessed more than 23,000 hectares in central Italy. In Piedmont, only the royal family could claim comparable landholdings.[37]

But estate size was not always the best guide to its real worth. When capital values and income figures are substituted for acreage, the economic gap between wealthy Piedmontese aristocrats and their Roman or Southern counterparts narrows considerably. Although the estates of the princely Chigi family in Lazio were more than three times the size of those held by Falletti di Barolo, their capital value was only 10 percent greater. Similarly, Baron Barracco's huge latifondo generated annual revenues in the 1860s that were just slightly superior to those yielded by Marchesa Falletti di Barolo's properties.[38]

---

[35] For the size of aristocratic landed estates in England and Prussia, see Beckett, *The Aristocracy of England*, pp. 50–51 and Berdahl, *The Politics of the Prussian Nobility*, p. 15.

[36] At the time of her death in 1864, Marchesa Giulia Falletti di Barolo's estates measure 4,210 hectares; see Archivio Opera Pia Barolo, b.51, f.1. In 1829, Marchese Antonio Maria Filippo Asinari di San Marzano left landed estates that amounted to 2,511 hectares (AST, Prima Sezione, Archivio Asinari di S. Marzano, b. 30, "Inventario della eredita . . ."). The estate of Prince Emanuele Dal Pozzo della Cisterna included 2,147 hectares of land, concentrated for the most part in the plains of Vercelli. Count Ferdinando Avogadro di Collobiano left 2,040 hectares to his son in 1904 (*URST*, 1904, b. 655, f. 38).

[37] In 1815, the royal patrimony was measured at 23,254 hectares: see AST, Prima Sezione, "Carta geografica di una parte degli stati di Sua Maestà dove si trovano i beni componenti attualmente il Regio Patrimonio." For the Barracco and Borghese family properties, see Petrusewicz, *Latifondo*, p. 63 and Pescosolido, *Terra e nobiltà*, pp. 13–15 as well as Villani, "Ricerche sulla proprietà e sul regime fondiario nel Lazio," pp. 240–241.

[38] Throughout most of the nineteenth century, the Chigi princes owned roughly 15,000 hectares of land. The capital value of their properties in 1885 was estimated at L. 6,382,753.7; the estimated value of Falletti di Barolo's rural estates in 1864 was L. 5,704,280. The annual revenues of the Barracco latifondo in 1868 were 68,499.7

These comparisons reflect the relative success of Piedmontese nobles in exploiting economically their rural properties. As their comparatively high annual yields and incomes suggest, they tended to supervise their estates with great care and attention. Much like their British counterparts, Piedmontese noble landowners played a role which John Beckett has aptly likened to that of a corporate director, making vital decisions on crop selection, appointing and overseeing the management team, assessing grievances, and smoothing over relationships on the estates.[39]

The productivity of their estates reflected, in turn, the ongoing involvement of aristocratic landowners in commercial agricultural activities. Building on practices that had begun in the eighteenth century, titled families continued in the decades after 1815 to provide much of the leadership for the two most important agricultural improvement societies, the Royal Academy of Agriculture and the Subalpine Agrarian Association. More concretely, they were the major investors in canal building projects and crop and livestock experimentation.[40] Count Camillo Benso di Cavour has long enjoyed a deserved reputation as the most prominent aristocratic agricultural entrepreneur, but he was certainly not an isolated figure within the nobility. Already at the beginning of the nineteenth century, for instance, other titled families like the Tornielli and Leonardi played a key role in the construction of huge irrigation reservoirs in the plains of Novara that dramatically increased yields and rental incomes. In a similar fashion, two of the leading landed families in the province of Turin, the Beraudo di Pralormo and the Ferrero della Marmora, made a major capital investment in the 1820s, jointly financing the construction of a large reservoir that permitted the irrigation of over 700 acres in the commune of Pralormo.[41]

Support for agricultural improvements of this sort helped to transform the estates of wealthy nobles into some of the most valuable and productive farm land in the entire country in the third quarter of the nineteenth century. The financial rewards were significant. These years

ducati or L. 291,125. In 1864, the revenues of the Falletti di Barolo were L. 285,214. See Girelli, Le terre dei Chigi, p. 11; Petrusewicz, Latifondo, p. 58; Archivio Opera Pia Barolo, b. 51, f. 1.

[39] See Beckett, The Aristocracy in England, p. 6.

[40] See Donna d'Oldenico, L'Accademia di Agricoltura di Torino, pp. 15–18, 36–37, 44–89; Prato, Fatti e dottrine economiche. For the commercial agricultural activities of the nobles in the previous century, see Chapter 1.

[41] Donna d'Oldenico, L'Accademia di Agricoltura, pp. 166–170. The Beraudo di Pralormo and the Ferrero della Marmora together owned 48 percent of the land in the commune of Pralormo; see AST, Sez. Riunite, Catasto Rabbini, f. 95. On Cavour's numerous initiatives in the area of agricultural modernization, see Romeo, Cavour e il suo tempo, vol. I, pp. 607–707 and vol. II, pp. 117–191.

represented something of a golden age for Piedmontese agriculture as prices for virtually all the cereals soared. Rising farm prices in turn drove up both land values and rental rates which reached unparalleled heights in the 1860s and 1870s.[42]

Landed nobles clearly shared in the prosperity of this period, especially those who owned farm properties in the plains of Vercelli. Count Emiliano Avogadro della Motta, for example, was able to raise the lease rate on his 800 acre estate in Collobiano from L. 28,000 per year in the 1830s to L. 60,000 per year in the late 1860s. Similarly, Marchese Lodovico Pallavicino-Mossi saw the annual income from the largest of his three estates in the province of Vercelli rise from L. 36,154 in the first half of the 1840s to L. 93,847 per year in the second half of the 1860s.[43] As their experiences suggest, the growth of commercial agriculture in the Piedmontese plains hardly came at the expense of the wealthy old nobility which only became richer as a consequence. Much as the British landed elite, families like the Pallavicino-Mossi and Avogadro della Motta managed to enjoy the best of both worlds, combining the profits of agricultural businessmen and the prestige of aristocrats.[44]

Like other landowners, Piedmontese aristocrats were certainly not exempt from the effects of the world-wide agricultural crisis of the late nineteenth century. Its length and duration made it difficult for the families who lived exclusively on the rents from their estates.[45] But, on the whole, titled nobles do not appear to have suffered catastrophic losses as a consequence of falling farm prices. Above all, the depression did not provoke any immediate or massive flight of the nobility from the countryside comparable to what took place in certain provinces of Emilia-Romagna where the average size of aristocratic landholdings fell sharply.[46] The value of aristocratic rural property in probate, which had averaged around L. 235,000 in the period from 1874 to 1885, declined a

---

[42] Wheat prices, for instance, which had averaged around L. 20.8 per hectoliter in the 1860s, jumped to L. 24.49 in the years between 1871 and 1875. Similarly, the price of rice in the 1870s reached a level unmatched since the first years of the century, while productivity rose dramatically. See Pugliese, *Due secoli di vita agricola*, pp. 131, 177–178.

[43] See AST, Sez. Riunite, Archivio Avogadro di Collobiano e della Motta, b. 69 and 70, affittamenti-Collobiano, 1837–1868; Archivio Pallavicino-Mossi, b. 29, Saletta Granaglia, 1841–1869.

[44] For the case of England, see Stone and Fawtier Stone, *An Open Elite?*, p. 190.

[45] For a fuller discussion of the agricultural depression and its impact in Piedmont, see Chapter 6.

[46] In the province of Ravenna, for instance, the average size of their properties dropped from 474 hectares in 1835 to 224 in the years 1898–1900. Titled nobles saw their land holdings contract even more dramatically in the province of Piacenza, where they went from an average of 171 hectares before the crisis to a mere 71 at the

Table 3.10 *Aristocratic urban property, 1862–1885*
(fortunes >L. 750,000)

Value urban property	1862–1873	1874–1885
Less than L. 100,000	7	8
L. 100,001–200,000	5	3
L. 200,001–300,000	5	4
L. 300,001–400,000	3	3
L. 400,001–500,000	2	0
More than L. 500,000	5	5
Totals	27	23

mere 5 percent to L. 224,500 in the first decade of the new century. For wealthy nobles, land remained far and away the most important asset in their estates prior to World War I.

Urban real estate played a more modest role than rural property in fortunes left by wealthy nobles (see Table 3.10) Only four of the twenty-seven nobles with fortunes over L. 750,000 in probate during the quarter century after unification had more than half of their wealth in palaces and other buildings in Turin. Only a fifth of the wealthy aristocrats owned substantial urban properties (over L. 500,000), and for most of those who did, such assets still accounted for under half the total worth of their fortunes. Even the second largest titled urban proprietor in probate, Prince Emanuele Dal Pozzo della Cisterna, who possessed buildings worth over L. 1 million at the time of his death in 1864, derived the bulk of his great fortune from the 5,500 acres of rich farm land he owned in the Vercellese plains, which was valued at more than L. 3 million. Much the same could be said for the fortunes of the other top noble landlords in the city, the Falletti di Barolo and the Benso di Cavour.[47]

The subordinate place of urban real estate as a component of aristocratic wealth did not prevent a few very prominent old families from

beginning of the twentieth century. See Banti, "I proprietari terrieri nell'Italia centro-settentrionale," p. 14.

[47] See *URST*, 1864, b. 2, fasc. 346 for the probate file of Dal Pozzo della Cisterna. Marchesa Falletti di Barolo owned some ten dwellings in Turin, including an historical palace, valued at L. 656,990 when she died in 1864; her rural properties had an estimated value of over L. 5 million. The last surviving male in the Benso di Cavour family left a palace worth some L. 350,000 at the time of his death in 1876; his rural properties were estimated at nearly L. 3 million. See Archivio Opera Pia Barolo, b. 51, f. 1 and *URST*, 1876, b. 174, n.2.

being major property owners in Turin during the middle decades of the nineteenth century.[48] Many of the same families also benefited from the wave of real estate development that swept the city in the early 1860s. The big aristocratic landlords saw their buildings appreciate as a result of the general increase in urban rents and property values. The annual net income the Pallavicino-Mossi family derived from their palace in via Santa Teresa, for instance, rose from L. 18,291 per year in 1850 to L. 26,495 in 1880; the capital value of the building climbed from L. 350,000 to an estimated L. 588,788, a 68 percent increase.[49]

These gains, however, did not keep pace with the urban real estate investments of wealthy bourgeois proprietors in the second half of the nineteenth century. In contrast to the situation in the countryside, the urban propertied elite in Turin had already become much less aristocratic after the mid-1870s. Indeed, property in the city contributed much of the realty held by rich non-nobles and was the single largest component of their total wealth in probate between 1874 and 1885.[50]

The core of large-scale aristocratic properties in the city followed a pattern established in the late seventeenth century when political centralization and the attractions of court life triggered competition among nobles for the construction of very expensive palaces. From the outset, the palaces in Turin were designed to give their owners both profits and social prestige. Typically, the aristocratic family occupied the grand *piano nobile*, while the apartments on the upper floors and the shop and office spaces on the ground floor were rented out. In the 1850s, most of the important baroque palaces remained in the hands of nobles, in many cases (the Cavour, Asinari di San Marzano, Valperga di Masino, and Saluzzo di Paesana palaces) the same families who had them built still owned them.[51] Other substantial aristocratic properties arose in the decades after 1815 when a number of titled families moved to an area

[48] See Mantegazza, *Guida alle case della città*, pp. 127–259 provides a complete list of all owners of buildings in the city in that period. At that time the biggest landlords were: Luserna di Rorà (13), Balbo Bertone di Sambuy (12), Falletti di Barolo (11), Benso di Cavour (10), Saluzzo di Paesana (10), Natta d'Alfiano (9), and D'Harcourt (8). During the same period, the Gromis di Trana, Francesetti di Hautecour, and the recently ennobled Rignon family were among the six largest landowners in the commune of Turin, each possessing over 250 acres there. See AST, Sez. Riunite, Catasto Rabbini, f. 118.

[49] AST, Sezione Riunite, Archivio Pallavicino-Mossi, b. 15, Palazzo: Via S. Teresa, 11.

[50] For a fuller discussion of urban real estate in Turin, see Cardoza, "Elites patrimoniali e proprietà urbana."

[51] See Boggio, *Lo sviluppo edilizio di Torino*, pp. 19–29 for a list of the major baroque palaces, their original owners, and those in possession of them in 1909. On the construction of the palaces in the late seventeenth and early eighteenth centuries, see Woolf, "Some notes on the cost of palace building," pp. 299–306.

closer to the Po River along streets like via della Rocca where they built
neo-classical rental palaces. Although these edifices were not as sumptuous as their baroque counterparts, they were often linked to adjoining
apartment buildings to constitute large mixed residential-commercial
complexes that occasionally occupied a city block.[52]

The semi-commercial character of most palaces in Turin assured top
proprietors a comfortable rental income from their buildings, but one
that seldom did more than supplement the much larger revenues from
their rural estates. Family account books indicate that few of them
received a substantial share of their income from urban rents. During
the 1850s, for instance, Count Carlo Costa della Trinità, scion of a
prominent old-line family, averaged L. 32,881 in gross rental revenues
from his palace and two adjoining buildings, which together absorbed
most of an entire block in a fashionable area of the city. The actual net
income from this substantial urban property was considerably less, about
L. 16,629, after taxes and maintenance expenses had been deducted.
Sizeable as this sum was, it paled in comparison to the annual income
from the vast landed estates of the Costa della Trinità which netted
some L. 100,000 a year in the 1850s.[53] During the same period, another
prominent aristocratic landlord, Marchese Lodovico Pallavicino-Mossi,
owned a large palace in the center of the city with 4 courtyards and 194
rooms. Pallavicino-Mossi leased out a total of 155 of the rooms to 47
tenants, including the Banca di Sconto and the Banca di Sete, who collectively paid a rent of between L. 15,000 and L. 20,000 per year or
slightly more than a tenth of his total annual revenues in the 1860s.[54]

Count Costa della Trinità and Marchese Pallavicino-Mossi do not
appear to have been unique figures within the Piedmontese titled elite.
Marchesa Falletti di Barolo, for example, owned several buildings in
Turin in the early 1860s, but rented only one of them at L. 10,530 per
year, a sum that amounted to less than 4 percent of her total annual
income. Most of the other buildings she leased, rent-free, to various
institutions of the Catholic Church. Similarly, the revenue from the
enormous palace built by the Asinari di San Marzano in the 1680s
contributed no more than about 7 percent of the family's yearly income
in the middle decades of the nineteenth century.[55] Count Giuseppe
d'Harcourt was probably a more unusual figure. His rural properties

[52] Boggio, Lo sviluppo edilizio di Torino, pp. 29–30.
[53] See AST, Sez. Riunite, Archivio Costa di Polonghera, b. 12.
[54] AST, Sez. Riunite, Archivio Pallavicino-Mossi, b. 15, 17, and 19.
[55] See Archivio Opera Pia Barolo, b. 51, f. 1, "Beni stabili, 1864"; AST, Prima Sez.,
Archivio Asinari di San Marzano, b. 31. On the construction of the Asinari di San
Marzano palace, see Woolf, "Some notes on the cost of palace building," p. 303.

were relatively modest by the standards of the old nobility, so he had to rely on the residential dwellings he owned in Turin for a larger portion of his income. Still, even d'Harcourt received only about two-fifths of his annual revenues from urban rents in the late 1860s.[56]

The estates of wealthy Piedmontese nobles were further distinguished by the paucity of their personal assets – stocks, bonds, credits, and bank deposits. While virtually all nobles (96 percent) in the survey possessed at least some personalty, they contributed, on average, less than a fifth of the total value of big aristocratic fortunes in probate as compared to nearly half of the value of those left by rich non-nobles. Among these assets, stocks and bonds, in particular – the forms of wealth most closely associated with industrial development and the growth of the state – occupied a decidedly inferior place in the composition of bigger aristocratic fortunes. On average, they contributed together about 10 percent of the total value of the estates left by wealthy nobles as opposed to about 28 percent in the case of the untitled rich. Moreover, their contribution to aristocratic wealth actually seemed to decrease among the largest patrimonies. Thus, of the fifty-nine greatest noble estates that passed through probate between 1862 and 1885, forty-four contained no stock portfolios at all.

Not surprisingly then, the nobility accounted for only 16 percent of the estates with personal assets valued at over L. 400,000. Those few large aristocratic fortunes that did rest primarily upon non-landed investments tended to be the result of exceptional circumstances. General Alfonso Ferrero della Marmora, a major protagonist of the Risorgimento, represents a clear case in point. General Alfonso left a sizeable fortune estimated at L. 1,692,479 in 1878, but one that contained no rural or urban real estate. As the seventh of the eight sons in a family that also numbered five daughters, he did not owe his substantial wealth to his own aristocratic lineage. Unlike his oldest brother who had come into the bulk of the family's wealth in his teens upon the death of their father, General Alfonso became a rich man in his own right very late in life and only as a result of the death of his English wife, Bertie Matthews, whose portfolio of stocks and bonds he inherited in its entirety in 1876.[57]

The marginal importance of personal assets in the structure of aristocratic patrimonies was also evident in the way they were distributed

[56] AST, Sez. Riunite, Archivio D'Harcourt, b. 74, f. 13, "Consegna dei redditi, 1867."
[57] For the estate left by Marchese C. E. Ferrero della Marmora, see AST, Insinuazioni, 1854, libro 7, vol. 1, pp. 381–490. Raffaele Romanelli has provided me with information on the estate of Bertie Matthews which was probated in Florence; a copy of Alfonso Lamarmora's probate return can be found in URST, 1878, b.136, f.3.

within titled families. As a rule, the heads of noble households preferred
to use these more mobile forms of wealth rather than real property to
pay daughters' dowries and to satisfy the claims of their sisters, younger
brothers and sons to portions of the family patrimony. This practice
clearly shaped the structure of their estates. A majority of cadets from
noble families (55 percent) left patrimonies, in which personal assets
accounted for from a quarter to a half of the total value, while 28
percent of them had over three-quarters of their wealth in this form.
This pattern was even more pronounced in the case of aristocratic
wives, sisters, and daughters. Of the 371 women from titled families
who passed through probate, 229 or 62 percent had more than half their
wealth in personalty; for 186 of them, such assets furnished more than
75 percent of the total value of their estates. Two-thirds (67 percent) of
the first born, on the other hand, had less than a quarter of the value of
their holdings in personal assets.

In general, analysis of the probate returns for the second half of the
nineteenth century reveals a structure of wealth among noble families
that remained considerably more traditional than that of the prosperous
bourgeoisie in Turin. On the one hand, Piedmont's titled rich continued to be overwhelmingly a landed aristocracy. Rural property occupied far and away the most important place in the composition of big
aristocratic fortunes in a period when it was becoming a factor of steadily decreasing significance in the patrimonies of rich non-nobles. On
the other hand, the patrimonies of wealthy nobles contained relatively
modest personal assets in general, and of stocks and bonds in particular.
Neither the agricultural crisis of the late nineteenth century nor the
industrial take-off after 1896 fundamentally altered this pattern.
Although they resided in one of the centers of Italy's industrial triangle,
prominent old-line nobles were slow to invest in those newer, more
mobile forms of wealth that were fueling the enterprising business
milieu of Piedmont. To a certain extent, the composition of the wealth
possessed by titled families was the result of the ways it had been
acquired and thus reflected its origins, transmission, and strategies of
preservation.

THE PRESERVATION AND TRANSFER OF ARISTOCRATIC WEALTH

Piedmont's most renowned aristocrat in the nineteenth century, Count
Camillo Benso di Cavour, came from an old feudal family that had lost
much of its patrimony in the wake of the French occupation during the
late 1790s. During the Napoleonic era, the Benso di Cavour began a
remarkable recovery that continued into the Restoration, when they

amassed a vast new landed fortune that put them solidly among the country's elite of wealth by the second half of the century. Indeed, the estate left by the last male member of the family, Count Camillo's nephew Marchese Aynardo, was the twelfth largest fortune to pass through probate. The Benso di Cavour owed much of their new-found wealth to their ability to act as aggressive, risk-taking, agricultural entrepreneurs who invested heavily in the purchase and modernization of farm land in the plains of Vercelli.[58]

The great aristocratic fortunes in the second half of the nineteenth century and the first decades of the twentieth, however, were rarely the result of such active entrepreneurial endeavors or major purchases of property. On the contrary, most rich aristocrats continued in the nineteenth century to acquire their wealth the old-fashioned way: they inherited it. As we have already seen, many of their fortunes were in place before the French Revolution. Most were the product of a combination of circumstances that included not only outright purchases of property, but also various forms of inheritance, fortunate marriages, royal favors, as well as careful planning and good luck.

In some cases, these fortunes consisted of palaces and rural properties that had been transferred in a regular sequence from father to first son for generations. Such continuity of ownership found expression in the number of wealthy nobles who carried the same name as the areas where their estates were located. The vast patrimony of the Costa della Trinità, for instance, still included in the 1890s what had once been their fiefs of Polonghera, Trinità, Carru, and Arignano – possessions that had been in the hands of the family since the end of the fifteenth century.[59] Similarly, in the first half of the nineteenth century, the Avogadro di Quinto, Avogadro di Casanova, Caresana di Carisio, Beraudo di Pralormo, Coardi di Carpeneto, Mazzetti di Saluggia, Della Villa di Villastellone, and Provana di Collegno still had their principal estates in the communes that had once been their fiefs.[60]

While direct transfers from fathers to first sons represented the ideal, more complex forms of intra- and inter-family inheritance also could

---

[58] Romeo, *Cavour e il suo tempo*, vol. I, pp. 46–53, 130–179, 607–692. For the estate left by Marchese Aynardo, see *URST*, 1876, b.174, f.2.

[59] See AST, Sez. Riunite, Archivio Costa della Trinità, b.31, petition of Countess Ernestina Costa della Trinità to the Consulta Araldica Reale, 1879.

[60] See AST, Catasto Francese, Mandamento di Santhià, Commune di Carisio, f. 443; Mandamento di Vercelli, Commune di Quinto, f. 457; Mandamento di Livorno, Commune di Carpenetto, f. 437, Commune di Saluggia, f. 442.2; Mandamento di San Germano, Commune di Casanova, f. 448; Catasto Rabbini, Province di Torino, Commune di Pralormo, f. 95; Commune di Villastellone, f. 132; Commune di Collegno, f. 43.

play a crucial role in the acquisition of aristocratic wealth as the estates of Marchese Lodovico Pallavicino-Mossi, Marchese Emanuele Thaon di St. Andre, and Count Luigi Valperga di Masino – three of the wealthiest nobles in the late nineteenth century – graphically illustrate. All three men came from old titled families, but inherited the bulk of their patrimonies in the first half of the century. Pallavicino-Mossi came into his wealth in 1829 when he became the principal heir of his maternal cousin, Archbishop Vincenzo Mossi di Morano, the last member of one of the richest families in Piedmont in the eighteenth century. When he himself died in 1879, Marchese Lodovico passed on to his son and two daughters a patrimony valued at L. 4,560,000 – the eleventh largest in the entire survey.[61] Thaon di St. Andre, scion of one of the more distinguished families of the service nobility, acquired the centerpiece of his sizeable patrimony, the 2,500 acre estate of Ternavaso, only in 1849 when it was left to him by Vittoria De Sellon d'Allemand, Cavour's aunt and the childless widow of the previous owner Baron Luigi Blancardi Roero de la Turbie.[62] The Valperga di Masino were one of the oldest, wealthiest, and most prestigious families of the subalpine nobility, but the head of the family in the middle of the nineteenth century, Count Luigi, had been born into a modestly endowed collateral branch, the Valperga di Borgomasino. In 1845, the last of the principal line, Count Carlo Francesco Valperga di Masino, died without descendants. His wife and heir, Countess Eufrasia, then passed away four years later, leaving much of the land, the castle of Masino, and a palace in Turin as well as the family titles to Count Luigi who assumed the name Valperga di Masino.[63]

As a rule, marriage, however, remained the quickest and most important means employed by the nobility to amass great wealth. The richest titled family in nineteenth-century Piedmont, the Falletti di Barolo, for instance, could trace a large portion of their tremendous fortune to the marital alliance forged by their ancestor Gerolamo IV to the last descendant of the Provana di Druent, one of the greatest landed families in the realm at the beginning of the eighteenth century. As a result of this alliance, they acquired in the 1720s the bulk of an estate that included a magnificent palace in the capital city and nearly 5,000 hectares in the

---

[61] See Manno, *Il patriziato subalpino*, vol. XVII, pp. 484–486. Marchese Tommaso Mossi di Morano, the older brother of the archbishop, possessed a patrimony valued at L. 1,345,553, the tenth largest in Piedmont in 1799; see Bulferetti, "I piemontesi più ricchi," p. 77–79. For estimates of Marchese Lodovico's fortune, see AST, Sez. Riunite, Archivio Pallavicino-Mossi, b. 17.

[62] *Ibid.*, vol. II, pp. 319–320.   [63] See Spreti, vol. VI, pp. 800–801.

provinces of Turin and Vercelli.[64] Likewise, Marchese Maurizio Luserna di Rorà more than doubled the patrimony of his family thanks to his marriage in 1813 to Adelaide Oreglia di Novello. After her death in 1847 and that of her husband in 1854, their four children shared in a parental fortune worth nearly L. 7 million, of which about L. 3.7 million came from the mother's estate.[65] Even that family of aristocratic entrepreneurs par excellence, the Benso di Cavour, owed part of their rapid economic recovery in the early nineteenth century to a strategic marriage. In 1805, Camillo's father wed Adele de Sellon, whose large dowry lifted the Benso di Cavour out of the indebtedness into which they had sunk during the revolutionary period.[66]

In the case of the Balbo Bertone di Sambuy, lucrative marital alliances became something of a family tradition in the late eighteenth and nineteenth centuries. Count Carlo di Sambuy's marriage in 1791 to Marchesa Daria Ghilini proved to be a real financial windfall for the next generation. The last of a wealthy titled family from Alessandria, Daria divided an estate valued at L. 1,387,944 in 1836 among her four sons. While the largest portion of her estate, about two-fifths, went to the oldest son, Count Vittorio di Sambuy, who had already inherited the principal family seat, "San Salvà," upon the death of his father in 1828, the three cadets also received shares that assured them quite respectable rental incomes.[67] Count Vittorio, in turn, further enlarged his family's patrimony through his marriage in 1825 to Luisa, one of two daughters and the only heirs of Marchese Marco Adalberto Pallavicino delle Frabose. Though Luisa was nowhere near as wealthy as her mother-in-law, she still received a substantial inheritance from her father (L. 632,697), most of which she then passed on to her sole surviving son, Count Ernesto di Sambuy.[68] For his part, Count Ernesto, one of the last great aristocratic public figures in Turin, also married quite well. His wife, Bona de Ganay, was from a well-endowed French

---

[64] See Woolf, "Studi sulla nobiltà piemontese," pp. 188–191.

[65] See AST, Sez. Riunite, Archivio Costa della Trinità, b. 11. These patrimonial documents most likely found their way into this archive because one of the heirs, Costanza, married Count Paolo Remigio Costa della Trinità.

[66] See Romeo, *Cavour e il suo tempo*, vol. 1, pp. 23–24, 58–59.

[67] See *Archivio Balbo Bertone di Sambuy*, c. 96, 3, b. a., "Patrimonio della Contessa di Sambuy al 1 gennaio 1836." This archive is in the possession of retired Admiral Ernesto di Sambuy who kindly gave me permission to consult it. According to Bulferetti, Daria's father, Marchese A. Ghilini, had been one of the richest men in the province of Alessandria at the end of the eighteenth century. See "I piemontesi più ricchi," p. 79.

[68] Archivio Balbo Bertone di Sambuy, c. 96, 3, b. a., testament and patrimony of Countess Luigia di Sambuy (neé Pallavicino delle Frabose), 1846.

aristocratic family. In addition to an enormous dowry (L. 400,000), Bona brought into the di Sambuy family assets worth over L. 1.4 million by 1913 that included two palaces in Turin, sizeable agricultural properties in France, and a healthy portfolio of stocks and bonds.[69] The cumulative effects of three generations of such fortunate marriages was to make the last generation of di Sambuy born before World War I considerably wealthier than their eighteenth-century ancestors.

While marriage and other forms of inheritance remained the most important means of amassing large concentrations of aristocratic wealth, maintenance of such wealth in the nineteenth century required more than ever before considerable managerial skills, the cooperation of all family members, and a healthy dose of good luck. The great political upheavals of the late eighteenth century ushered in an era of change that swept away many of the traditional juridical safeguards that had provided rich nobles some protection from their own excesses and incompetence. During the Napoleonic era and then again on more permanent basis during the 1830s, legal reforms were introduced that prohibited the traditional noble practice of entailment, severely restricted the founding of binding primogenitures, and allowed for the sale of noble properties or their seizure in payment of debts. At the same time, a new inheritance law modeled on that of the Napoleonic Code guaranteed all heirs a share in the legacy. As a result, the property left to the first son and bearer of the family titles tended to diminish, since a legally designated portion of every noble estate now had to pass with each generation to the younger sons and daughters.[70]

In this less favorable juridical environment, those wealthy aristocratic families who were able to survive and flourish after 1815 did so by relying increasingly upon an unparalleled degree of voluntary cooperation and self-sacrifice by family members. On the whole, traditional kinship loyalties appear to have worked fairly effectively as substitutes for legal devices in the case of the subalpine nobility. Commenting on the situation of titled families in Piedmont in the 1850s, for instance, one Italian commentator observed how:

> The abolition of the law of primogeniture is only less ruinous to old houses in this country, owing to this instinct of union and concord. The eldest son steps into the place of the lamented parent, the rightful head of the family; his younger brothers affect a taste for celibacy, lest, by too

---

[69] *Ibid.*, Cart. xviii–C, bb., f. 5., "Beni della Contessa Bona di Sambuy-De Ganay, caduti in proprietà degli eredi . . . " February 1913.

[70] See Raumer, *Italy and the Italians*, pp. 250–252 for a description of some of the legal reforms of the 1830s in Piedmont. On the changes in inheritance laws, see Banti, "Un fonte per lo studio delle elites," pp. 86–87.

great an increase in the family, they should make too wide a breach in the common patrimony. The daughters are portioned off; the younger sons live in unconscious dependence, yielding, either from a feeling of love or from family pride, or from custom, to their eldest brother those privileges which the law allows to the first-born in aristocratic England and Germany.[71]

Much as in Spain, inheritance laws in Piedmont still allowed a great deal of freedom in drawing up the bequests. Thus, the first son could receive as much as three-quarters of the entire estate and all the rural property, provided that the lesser heirs were willing to accept their portions in non-landed forms of wealth, paid in installments spread out over a couple of decades. Baron Pietro Antonio Guidobono Cavalchini had precisely such a solution in mind when he urged his sons in his testament "to reduce their legal portion to a proportionate life-time pension by means of suitable contract with their first-born brother, my principal heir," assuring them that "they themselves would benefit by obtaining a larger net income that [was] secure and more suited to their station and career."[72] Accordingly, the rights of cadets could be satisfied without liquidating or fragmenting the family's primary propertied assets.

Demographic good fortune and an aristocratic tradition of state service clearly facilitated the success of this sort of strategy for the protection of large patrimonies. Not surprisingly, the families who had the greatest success produced a small number of male children, with the younger ones either remaining unmarried or dying without heirs. The family background of the titled multi-millionaires in probate underscores the crucial role played by fecundity in the preservation of great wealth within the nobility. Of the twelve men in this category who had inherited from their fathers, ten were the sole male heir, one had a single brother; only one came from a family where there were three or more sons.[73]

The case of the Avogadro della Motta illustrates how the most

---

[71] Gallenga, *Country Life in Piedmont*, pp. 47–48.

[72] AST, Sez. Riunite, Testamenti Pubblicati, vol. 42, p. 69, Testament of Baron Pietro Antonio Guidobono Cavalchini, July 24, 1848. For the situation in Spain, see Malafakis, *Agrarian Reform*, p. 68.

[73] The case of the latter, Count Filiberto Avogadro di Collobiano, has been discussed earlier in the chapter as an example of a wealthy cadet. The immense estate he left in 1868 as well as the even greater wealth of his sons could be traced in part to the fact that three of his older brothers were career officers in the army who never married, while the fourth, a diplomat, produced no heirs. As a result, they spent much of their lives away from the ancestral estates and their portions remained within the family and were passed down to the next generation, represented by Count Filiberto's sons, Ferdinando and Vittorio. See Manno, *Il patriziato subalpino*, vol. 1, pp. 123–125. On the estates left by Filiberto, Ferdinando, and Vittorio, see *URST*, 1868, vol. 8, f. 36; 1905, vol. 655, f. 38; and 1907, vol. 736, f. 46.

successful of the old titled families combined all these factors – inheritance, lucrative marital alliances, cooperation, careful management, judicious acquisitions, and luck – not only to maintain, but actually to increase their wealth in an era when they no longer enjoyed special privileges or legal protection. In the eighteenth century, the Avogadro della Motta were already long-established members of the titled nobility in Vercelli, with patrimony that included their palace in the provincial capital as well as an ancestral castle in Masazza surrounded by an estate which measured over 2,000 acres in 1748.[74]

The following 100 years saw the family add substantially to this patrimony which more than doubled in value by the 1860s. Count Ignazio Avogadro della Motta, the head of the family in the last decades of the *ancien régime*, began the process by developing the cultivation of rice on his estates. On the eve of the French invasion, he had become one of the principal growers of this lucrative crop in the province of Vercelli. Count Ignazio's commercial agricultural initiatives were favored by his marriage in the 1790s to Teresa Avogadro di Casanova, the daughter of one of the two largest rice growers, Giuseppe Maria Avogadro di Casanova.[75] This alliance entailed more than a handsome dowry; it also paved the way for profitable collaboration between Count Ignazio and his father-in-law under the Napoleonic regime. The devout Catholicism of the Avogadro della Motta did not prevent the two men from forming a partnership for the purchase of former church properties between 1801 and 1811, which then passed to the son-in-law after the death of Giuseppe Avogadro di Casanova. Count Ignazio continued to enlarge his property holdings in the Vercellese plains during the first decade of the Restoration by buying the Castle of Montemagno and the farm surrounding it.[76]

The chief beneficiary of these economic and marital initiatives was Count Emiliano Avogadro della Motta, Ignazio's first son and the primary heir of both his parents. Although the marriage produced six children, only Count Emiliano and his sister Agnese survived to adulthood. When their mother passed away in 1816, she settled two-thirds of an estate valued at L. 240,000 on Count Emiliano and the rest on

---

[74] See AST, Sez. Riunite, Archivio Avogadro di Collobiano e della Motta, b. 8, estate of Count Carlo Ignazio Avogadro della Motta, Oct. 26, 1748.

[75] See Davico, *"Peuple" et notables (1750–1816)*, pp. 112–113.

[76] AST, Sez. Riunite, Archivio Avogadro della Motta, b. 63, land purchases, Collobiano, 1801–1811; b. 141, land purchase, Viverone, 1801; b. 142, properties in Montemagno. The most important joint purchase was in the latter commune where the two men acquired over 600 acres. See Notario, *La vendita dei beni nazionali in Piemonte*, p. 530.

Agnese. Seventeen years later, when their father died, he also left the preponderance of his considerably larger estate to his first son, providing his daughter with a legacy of only L. 60,000. Agnese completed the process of concentrating the family wealth in the hands of Count Emiliano with her premature death in 1838. According to the terms of her will, Agnese's older brother became the principal heir to her estate, while her husband, Count Felice Avogadro di Quinto received only half of her dowry. Finally, the new head of the Avogadro della Motta family received an additional L. 75,000 upon the death of his aunt, Marianna, in 1845.[77]

Count Emiliano proved to be an extremely able administrator of the patrimony he had inherited. Not content simply to manage what he already possessed, he became an active participant in the Piedmontese land market after 1833, selling detached properties in order to realize capital for acquisitions closer to home. In the province of Vercelli, for instance, he sold off the castle and surrounding estate of Montemagno in 1841 for twice the price his father had paid in 1815. He used some of the profits to enlarge his ancestral estates in Collobiano with seven separate land purchases between 1837 and 1863 that made them the single most valuable family asset by the time of his death two years later.[78] At the same time, Count Emiliano also began to invest in rural property in the province of Turin, where the Provana di Collegno, the family of his wife and first cousin Teresa, were major landowners. Thus, in 1845 he bought from Count Ottavio Thaon di Revel the Tenimento dell'Isola, an estate of over 800 acres in the communes of Settimo Torinese and Gassino. Five years later, he purchased a villa surrounded by 21 acres in the foothills above the city of Turin.[79]

The estate left by Avogadro della Motta in 1865 eloquently testified to the success of his family's inheritance, marriage, and management strategies as well as to their good luck in the nineteenth century. The seventeenth largest aristocratic fortune to pass through probate in the decades after 1861, it was valued at L. 2,275,160 and included some 4,100 acres of rich farm land mostly in the plains of Vercelli or more than twice what his grandfather had inherited a century earlier.

[77] AST, Sez. Riunite, Archivio Avogadro della Motta, b. 8, Testament of Countess Teresa Iffigenia Avogadro di Casanova, 1816; Testament of Count Ignazio Avogadro della Motta, 1818; Testament of Countess Agnese Avogadro di Quinto (neé Avogadro della Motta), 1838; Estate of Marianna Avogadro della Motta, 1845.

[78] Ibid., b. 142, properties Montegmagno, 1815–1841; b. 63, land purchases Collobiano, 1801–1863.

[79] Ibid., b. 143, Tenimento dell'Isola, 1836–1851; b. 148b, villa in the foothills of Turin, 1850. Count Emiliano paid L. 46,091 for the villa and surrounding property.

Significantly, Count Emiliano and his father had expanded their family's wealth without altering its basic structure, which continued to reflect a traditional aristocratic preference for land over personal assets.[80] Moreover, they had not over-extended themselves financially in the process like some newer nobles such as Baron Vincenzo Bolmida who had to borrow heavily from banks to make their large purchases of rural property. As a result, the next generation of the Avogadro della Motta inherited a patrimony that was virtually free of any debt.[81]

ARISTOCRATIC WEALTH AND SYMBOLIC POWER

Quantitative analysis of the structure and composition of the estates left by nobles captures only part of the distinctive character of aristocratic wealth, in which economic and symbolic elements were inseparably linked. The patrimonies of old-line families provided more than handsome incomes. They also testified to the status of the family, its antiquity, and even its role in history. Aristocratic possessions often carried with them a prestige rooted in ancestral traditions of patronage and paternalism that could not be bought or sold, and thus gave those who possessed them a unique connection to particular territories and populations. In this respect, Piedmontese aristocrats were abundantly endowed with what Bourdieu has described as "a social power over time," namely the possession of "those things whose common feature is that they can only be acquired in the course of time . . . by inheritance or through dispositions which, like the taste for old things, are likewise only acquired with time and applied by those who can take their time."[82] It was these less tangible elements of aristocratic wealth that were critical both to the collective identity of the nobility and to their continued prominence in public life in the second half of the nineteenth century.

Above all, wealthy nobles derived great symbolic value from the

---

[80] AST, Sez. Riunite, Archivio Avogadro della Motta, b. 9, estate of Count Emilio. More than 90 percent of the value of the estate came from rural properties. Three-quarters of the landed assets were located in the Vercellese plains, with the remainder in the province of Turin.

[81] *Ibid.*, b. 9. The only liabilities in Count Emiliano's estate consisted of claims by his own children to legacies left by their mother and their great aunt Marianna, and the dowry of the one daughter, Assunta. Baron Vincenzo Bolmida, a banker and advisor to Cavour who received his title in 1861, owned 7,560 acres in the province of Modena which he had purchased after unification. By the time of his death, he still owed L. 919,640 to the seller as well as L. 1,134,283 to the Banca Nazionale, a burden of debt that far exceeded the total value of his estate (L. 1,235,902). See *URST*, 1877, vol. 74, f. 30.

[82] Bourdieu, *Distinction*, pp. 71–72.

possession of large rural estates with villas and lands carrying the family name. Unlike many of their newer bourgeois neighbors in the countryside, old noble families had a profound attachment to their property which was considerably more than a simple material possession. Most of them spent roughly four to six months each year on their rural estates which remained the primary physical embodiments of ancestral traditions, lineal antiquity, and continuity. Much like the country seats of the English gentry, their villas provided the site for the family residence, its memories, its heirlooms, and often its name. The legacy of the past was also evident in the *censi perpetui* still paid to titled families by municipalities that had once been their fiefs as well as in the exclusive fishing and hunting rights that continued to appear among their assets in probate into the twentieth century.

In his recollections of his childhood passed in a country house in the commune of Rocchetta di Tanaro before World War I, Marchese Mario Incisa della Rocchetta gave voice to the nobility's deeply felt sense of place:

> I was happy knowing that a part of our property was still called "the fief" . . . I was proud to know that when there used to be mills along the Tanaro [River], they were all ours, and that the right to fish in the river still belonged to us. This entire way of feeling and thinking had been maintained, coined, and stored up thanks to the physical surroundings in which I lived . . . For seven or eight months of the year, I lived in Rocchetta, cradle of our family and its seat for nine centuries.[83]

On estates like that of the Incisa di Rocchetta, old-line families were able to perpetuate symbolically an exceptional status that no longer existed in law. The aristocratic patriarch was known by the villagers who lived near his property, his presence was often required at festivals and other customary rituals that linked his family to the village. Predictably, their attachment to ancestral properties led most landed nobles to request in their last wills and testaments that they be buried on their family estates rather than in Turin.

Such stability and continuity on the land gave the old titled families a rather special relationship with the rural population in those districts where they remained the principal employers and patrons. Even in the absence of police and judicial powers, nobles could still exert social power of a traditional kind in the nineteenth century within a voluntary

---

[83] Mario Incisa dell Rocchetta, "Impressioni e ricordi di 'altri tempi'" (typescript, no date), pp. 27, 171–172. I would like to thank Incisa's sister, Maria Beraudo di Pralormo and his niece Gabriella Salvi del Pero for permission to quote from the manuscript.

framework of reciprocal rights and duties. Prominent aristocratic families like the Avogadro di Collobiano and Pallavicino-Mossi did more than help celebrate local holidays, assist the poor and the sick in their villages, and mediate disputes between villagers. They also took an active interest in the religious and moral education of the villagers by supporting country parishes, providing school houses, and subsidizing their operations. Paternalistic concern for the villages linked to ancestral estates continued even after death; aristocratic testaments invariably included charitable bequests to the "most needy" in their family's traditional rural enclaves.[84]

These activities, which conformed to an aristocratic ideal of noblesse oblige, seemed to bring some titled landowners a certain local popularity and deference. They found their most obvious expression in the frequent election of nobles as mayors in the communes where their estates were located. But they were also evident in less official ways, especially during important moments in the lives of aristocratic families such as the birth of the first son, weddings, and funerals which all became occasions for joyful celebration or seemingly genuine mourning in the local villages. When the daughter of Count Ferdinando Avogadro di Collobiano got married in 1896, for example, the people of Vigliano, where the family had one of its castles, collected a "substantial sum" by public subscription to provide the newly weds with a "splendid" bouquet of flowers as an expression of their "feelings of profound veneration for he who has given generously for so many years . . . " After the death of Count Ferdinando eight years later, his funeral procession from Vigliano to the family vault near Carisio included not only the mayors of half a dozen villages, but also "a very long file of tenant farmers, school children, and clergy."[85]

While country estates remained the symbolically most important component of aristocratic wealth, the urban properties also represented more than sources of income. In fact, considerations of prestige and family image often took precedence over those of profit in the way wealthy nobles treated their property in Turin. Most of the great titled families used their ancestral palaces, first and foremost, as prestigious residences near court and suitable settings for the exclusive dinner

[84] On the charitable activities of the Avogadro di Collobiano in the commune of Vigliano, for instance, see *La Tribuna Biellese*, February 23, 1896. Marchese Lodovico Pallavicino-Mossi founded and maintained at his own expense a school for girls in the commune of Frassineto-Po where he owned a large estate. See AST, Archivio Compans di Brichanteau, c. 4, ua.9, f. 5, funeral speech, July 22, 1879.

[85] See *La Tribuna Biellese*, February 23, 1896 and *La Gazzetta del Popolo*, October 10, 1904.

parties, balls, and fêtes that structured the rituals of Turinese high society.[86] For these purposes, the Pallavicino-Mossi family occupied thirty-nine rooms of their palace. Marchese Lodovico Pallavicino-Mossi's expenditures for a staff of a dozen servants and the maintenance of his carriages and stables alone absorbed 85 percent of the rental income from his palace. Count Carlo Costa della Trinità, for his part, dispensed with L. 8,200 a year in potential rental income from his urban properties by occupying the most spacious apartments in the main palace and by providing additional free lodging for the family priest, his personal secretary, and four doormen.[87]

The symbolic element in aristocratic wealth found expression not only in their possessions, but also in the size and distinctive form of their outstanding debts and liabilities. On the whole, the burdens on the fortunes of rich nobles were greater than on those of wealthy non-nobles. Although aristocrats made up only a third of the richest individuals in the probate survey, they contributed more than half (59 percent) of the total value of their liabilities. Especially in the first decades after unification, the greater debt burdens facing heirs of wealthy titled families resulted largely from their responsibility for generations of family charity and paternalism in the form of *legati pii, annualità perpetue,* and *pensioni vitalizie* provided to various religious institutions, relatives, and dependents.[88]

As the heavily symbolic character of aristocratic wealth suggests, the survival of the nobility as a separate, exclusive, and influential elite in Piedmontese society involved more than their being simply rich plutocrats. In purely monetary terms, old-line aristocratic families no longer monopolized the ranks of the richest individuals in probate by the last quarter of the nineteenth century. Rich nobles remained a large and important component of Turin's wealthy upper classes, but they were increasingly overshadowed by new men and new fortunes made in commerce and industry. The cohesion and collective identity of the nobility also required innovative strategies of social reproduction and reinvention in order to preserve and transmit distinctive customs and rituals as well as to maintain their distance from other segments of the propertied classes.

---

[86] See Ricci (ed.), *Memorie,* vol. I and Gerbore, *Dame e cavalieri del Re.*

[87] See AST, Sez. Riunite, Archivio Pallavicino-Mossi, b. 15 and 19; Archivio Costa di Polonghera, b. 12.

[88] The estate of Marchese Roberto Taparelli d'Azeglio, for example, included among its liabilities four *assegni perpetui* and nine *censi,* with many of them dating back to the seventeenth and eighteenth centuries. Similarly, the heirs of Marchese Federico Asinari di San Marzano were responsible for paying five *censi,* sixteen *legati,* anf fourteen *pensioni vitalizie.* For d'Azeglio, see URST, b. 1–v.2, f.92, 1863; for Asinari, *ibid.,* b. 1–v.2, f.38, 1863.

PERPETUATING AN ARISTOCRATIC SOCIAL ELITE

In the second half of the nineteenth century, Piedmontese aristocrats and their blue-blooded counterparts elsewhere on the Italian peninsula confronted a world in which many of the old social boundaries and barriers had been dismantled or blurred. With the disappearance of the absolute monarchy and the abolition of the last remnants of feudalism, nobles ceased to be members of a legally distinct order possessing any exclusive rights and prerogatives. Old-line families still had a legal right to sport their titles as symbols of their antiquity and to pass them from generation to generation, but these titles no longer afforded special privileges or significant economic advantages. Henceforth the prestige and influence of the nobility would have to rest chiefly on their status as a social elite.

The loss of privileges unavoidably raised, however, fundamental questions about what it now meant to be a noble and about the extent to which individual nobles still constituted a coherent group, separate from other elements of Piedmont's propertied classes. Once titles ceased to carry with them tangible and exclusive benefits, they also ceased to provide even the appearance of unity to an "estate" that, in fact, had always encompassed sizeable variations in wealth, origins, and family lineage. In the absence of shared privileges, there existed a natural tendency for the divisions between the nobility and bourgeoisie to disappear as the diverse interests and abilities of individual nobles drew them inexorably closer to other like-minded individuals across old class and caste boundaries.[1]

The extent to which aristocratic families in Piedmont managed to avoid or postpone this fate in the second half of the nineteenth century depended in large part on their ability to preserve and exploit not only

---

[1] This argument has been advanced recently in Harris and Thane, "British and European Bankers," pp. 215–219.

their inherited wealth, but also their enduring social distinctions. As I have argued at the end of the previous chapter, many old titled families possessed an abundance of social and symbolic resources in addition to their wealth. They still enjoyed, for instance, the prestige and renown attached to their family names. Likewise, they had powerful kinship connections and extensive networks of alliances and relationships that had been forged over several generations, as the case of the families linked to Marchese Carlo Compans di Brichanteau illustrates. These social resources, when accompanied by sufficient wealth, allowed a portion of the old nobility to reinvent a collective identity for themselves, an identity that helped to preserve their cohesion and exclusivity, and to legitimize their influential role in public life.

Aristocratic social reproduction in Piedmont after 1848 entailed a combination of conservation and innovation. Perhaps more than anywhere else in the country, titled families here reaffirmed in word and deed a set of ancestral values and customs. Accordingly, they steadfastly exalted loyalty to throne and altar, the honor of military service, and the importance of lineage, patriarchy, paternalism, and social exclusivity. The perpetuation of these traditions, however, took on a new meaning in the absence of legal privileges in the second half of nineteenth century. Now, for instance, they were intended to highlight continuities with an aristocratic past precisely because that past was inaccessible to those newer segments of the propertied classes who were beginning to overshadow titled families in the political arena and in the economic life. Recourse to old values and customs helped, in this fashion, to foster a sense of superiority in an era when the nobility, as such, did not possess any formal organization or constitute a separate class based on privilege or economic position.

Nobles also relied increasingly on newly founded private schools and gentlemen's clubs to inculcate traditional values and conventions of behavior, and to enhance their cohesion and exclusivity. While none of these institutions was purely aristocratic in its membership, they all tended to be dominated by blue-blooded families who set the tone for the rest. In any case, no one institution guaranteed prestige and acceptance. Rather it was the combination of pedigree, wealth, and shared associations that ensured high status and distinguished the aristocratic elite from the rest of the wealthy, propertied classes in the decades after 1848.

The same blend of traditional customs and modern institutional settings that helped to perpetuate aristocratic prestige and distinctiveness in Piedmont, also served to redraw social lines in new ways that excluded or marginalized segments of the pre-1848 nobility. More than ever before, hereditary titles were of little value to those families who lacked the wealth, pedigree, or inclination to maintain these customs and practices. To the extent that they were unable or unwilling to conform, such families tended to lose contact and drift away from the core of the elite – a small and closely integrated community bound together by shared experiences, acquaintances, and personal connections. In this respect, the internal hierarchies of the nobility can be compared to a series of concentric circles. At the center was the cultural ideal: the old, titled, affluent, landed family whose members divided their time between their urban palace in Turin and the ancestral estate in the country. Sons attended one of a few select private schools and served, like their fathers before them, in the regiments as well as in some honorary capacity at court; they were members of the Società del Whist and married a women from families of comparable wealth and lineage. Mothers and daughters, for their part, participated in the ceremonies of the House of Savoy, represented their families in the boxes at the Royal Theater and the pews of the more fashionable churches of Turin, and were active in Catholic charitable activities. While great wealth or ancient pedigree always permitted a certain degree of eccentricity, those individuals and families who strayed too far or for too long from this ideal-type and the code of conduct it embodied, tended to find themselves in the outer circles. The further they strayed, the less value their titles possessed and the more indistinguishable they became from other segments of the propertied classes.

THE CHARACTER AND DIMENSIONS OF THE ARISTOCRATIC FAMILY

Like the members of old elites elsewhere on the continent in the nineteenth century, the Piedmontese aristocrat's sense of identity and his ascriptive status were deeply rooted in his family, its past, and territorial base. Family membership remained the central social and cultural reality for most nobles, who tended to organize their world into meaningful categories on the basis of it. If anything, the loss of legally privileged status only accentuated the importance of the family as the primary vehicle of elite solidarity and social reproduction.

The memoirs of Piedmontese nobles clearly attest to a keen interest in the history of their families and great pride in their achievements. From their earliest years, children were steeped in the lore and traditions of their ancestors. In his recollections of his boyhood in the late 1790s and early 1800s, Count Clemente Solaro della Margarita, for instance, recalled how his "ancestors had collected a large number of memoirs and books about the Solaro, a great family from Asti, and I read them assiduously."[2] Similarly, Carlo Alberto Costa di Beauregard wrote how in his family the grandmothers passed "long winter evenings narrating the history of the lineage . . . and [their] good works became legendary in the minds of the children."[3]

The memories of Marchese Mario Incisa della Rocchetta of his childhood in the years before 1914 suggest that the dramatic changes that had taken place in the century following did not eroded the nobility's sense of connection to the past nor their pride in belonging to distinguished old lineages. As Marchese Mario recollected, "already when I was eight or ten years old, I thirsted for news of our ancestors."[4] Significantly, two of the Piedmontese nobility's most famous iconoclasts, Camillo Benso di Cavour and Massimo Taparelli d'Azeglio, were not immune to the appeal of family traditions. Despite their notorious impatience with the more stifling aspects of aristocratic society, both paid implicit homage to these traditions through their preference for their feudal appellations, Cavour and d'Azeglio.[5]

This cult of ancestors reinforced a vision of family or *casata* (house) that was both deep and broad in the sense that it linked members to a long chain going back in time as well as to a much broader kinship group. Aristocratic family archives, with their accounts of the past and their detailed genealogies familiarized children with their lineal past and helped to locate them among their peers in larger cousinhoods and social networks. Similarly, the material possessions that were transmitted from generation to generation – the homes, portraits, coats-of-arms, and other souvenirs – reinforced a consciousness of identity and social belonging among family members who lived in the same spaces and were surrounded by the same objects as their ancestors. Country houses, in particular, both linked the living family members to the past and provided settings for traditional reunions in the summer where relatives reassembled and family unity was reasserted.[6]

As marriage contracts and testaments show, the basic rites of passage in the lives of nineteenth-century nobles also continued to nourish a sense of family and of connection to the past. Thus, aristocratic marriages were presented as more than a coming together of two indi-

---

[2] See Archivio Solaro della Margarita, *Diario*, 1799, as cited in Lovera and Rinieri, *Clemente Solaro della Margarita*, vol. I, pp. 7–21.
[3] Costa di Beauregard, *Un uomo d'altri tempi*, pp. 12–13.
[4] Incisa della Rocchetta, "Impressioni e ricordi," p. 27.
[5] Cognasso, "Nobiltà e borghesia," p. 227.
[6] For an exploration of these characteristics within French noble families, see Mension-Rigau, *Aristocrates et grands bourgeois*.

viduals; they also explicitly linked two lineages and two patrimonies. When Count Cesare Valperga di Masino wed Cristina San Martino di San Germano in 1855, for example, the marriage contract drawn up by their parents not only defined economic arrangements between the bride and groom, but also emphasized how the two "illustrious houses [casati] . . . as an expression of their mutual esteem and cherished memories of ancient kinship, wished to see their bonds of friendship reconfirmed by new ties of kinship."[7] The press reinforced this emphasis on lineage in their accounts of aristocratic weddings. The announcement of the engagement of Marchese Giuseppe Pallavicino-Mossi to Countess Irene Avogadro di Collobiano in the winter of 1895–1896, for instance, inspired La Stampa to write of the impending marriage as a union of "the descendants of two illustrious families" and to note how the bride's family, in particular, was "related by marriage to the entire Piedmontese aristocracy so that the joy of the young countess Irene finds a sympathetic echo among our most eminent families."[8]

A similar preoccupation with the family line, past and future, typically informed the testaments of prominent nobles. Aristocratic scions continued throughout the century to reaffirm the custom of primogeniture in both the language and instructions of their wills in order to, in the words of Count Augusto Salino, "conserve for the . . . family and the name that represents it the bulk of its ancestral patrimony."[9] As Count Ernesto Balbo Bertone di Sambuy told his children, this practice meant not only that the first son received the lion's share of the wealth, but also that he assumed "the special duties that the status of head of the house imposes on the first born son." In recognition of his unique role, the first son's portion included the symbolically most important assets of the lineage: the ancestral home in the countryside and "all the papers and documents that constitute the family archives."[10] Decades later, Count Luigi Valperga di Masino's final testament stressed the importance of "safeguarding the continuity of the family line," and urged his only son and principal heir to follow "the traditions of your grandfather Cesare and of so many of our ancestors who have held high the honor and prestige of the House of the Valperga di Masino."[11] When possible,

---

[7] See URST, 1903, v. 601, f. 17, dowry contract between Cristina S. Martino di S. Germano and Count Cesare Valperga di Masino, 1855.

[8] See La Stampa, December 26, 1895 and February 9, 1896.

[9] URST, 1878, v. 86, f. 12, Testamento di Count Augusto Salino.

[10] URST, 1909, v. 788, f. 17, Testamento of Count Ernesto di Sambuy, November 2, 1889.

[11] URST, b. 1629, f. 26, Testament of Count Luigi Valperga di Masino, January 31, 1923.

Table 4.1 *Aristocratic lineage and family size (percent)*

Children	Old nobility (%)	1700–1800 (%)	1800–1900 (%)	New nobility (%)
None	21	24	21	20
One	21	17	16	10
2 to 4	43	44	46	45
>4	16	16	18	25
Totals	100	101	101	100

most nobles also sought to be buried with their ancestors, following the example of Count Luigi Seyssel d'Aix di Sommariva, who expressed his wish to be laid to rest "in the church of Santa Maria in Sommariva del Bosco, beside the other members of my family in the customary way and with the usual ceremonies."[12] Likewise, heirs were reminded to celebrate masses each year in memory of their ancestors and to carry on their family's longstanding traditions of charity in the form of *legati pii*, *annualità perpetue*, and *pensioni vitalizie* in favor of religious institutions, relatives, and dependents.[13]

Despite the importance attached to the family name and its antiquity, lineage did not have much impact on the actual size of noble families in the nineteenth century. Data on the number of surviving children of the titled individuals in probate show little variation between the families of old and new nobles. As the figures in Table 4.1 indicate, a majority of married couples of noble origins had from one to four children survive them, while very large families were comparatively rare. On the whole, the aristocratic couples who passed through probate had relatively small families. From a third to two-fifths of them had no more than one child, while at the other end, a mere three couples produced seven sons; in only one case was there a family with seven daughters. In sharp contrast, nearly one-sixth of the households in the eighteenth century had enormous families with eight or more children surviving to adulthood.[14]

The decline in the size of noble households, which suggests the

---

[12] *URST*, b. 115, f. 26, 1881, Testament of Count Luigi Seyssel d'Aix.

[13] See, for examples of this, Chapter 3, note 88.

[14] If anything, this figure errs on the conservative side. The information provided by Manno is, in many cases, not complete or somewhat sketchy. I have counted as surviving children only those for whom Manno indicates the years of birth and death of the child or else a description of their professional activities. See *Il patriziato subalpino*, vols. I–XXVII.

possibility of conscious family limitation, was, at least in part, a response to new inheritance laws that abolished primogeniture and fidecommessi and eroded respect for the social obligations governing the marriage customs of cadets and daughters. In the eighteenth century, large Piedmontese titled families had tended to follow a traditional aristocratic strategy practiced elsewhere on the peninsula and in Europe, a strategy that involved limitation of marriage in order to keep the patrimony intact and still preserve the lineage. Ideally, the first sons married and attempted to have at least one son to assure the continuity of the male line, while, for their part, younger sons and a portion of the daughters were expected to remain celibate so that as much as possible of the family inheritance passed through a single line.[15]

Much as in neighboring Lombardy, the introduction of partible inheritance laws with the arrival of the French in the late 1790s brought about gradual, but important changes in the marriage practices of the nobility in Piedmont.[16] The increased financial autonomy which these reforms provided to all heirs clearly weakened the authority of the aristocratic patriarch to impose the interests of the lineage on his progeny. In the absence of legal restrictions, the perpetuation of traditional dynastic strategies depended upon an unparalleled degree of voluntary cooperation and self-sacrifice by family members. Entrenched customs and abiding family loyalties reduced some of the impact of the reforms in the short run. At least this was the view of contemporary observers like Antonio Carlo Napoleone Gallenga.[17]

The statistical evidence provided by the probate records only partially supports Gallenga's impressions. It does indicate that cadets in the nine-

---

[15] For a fuller discussion of the aristocratic ideology of family in eighteenth-century Piedmont, see Marchisio, "Ideologia e problemi dell'economia familiare," pp. 67–130. A survey of 392 eighteenth-century nobles, for whom Manno has provided information, reflects this pattern, especially in regard to the male members of prominent old families:

Aristocratic celibacy – eighteenth century

Family position	Total number	% celibate
First sons	54	12
Cadets	117	68
Daughters	139	18

The high percentage of married first sons and celibate younger brothers clearly attests to the attention which titled families in Piedmont gave to dynastic considerations in determining matrimonial policies prior to the French Revolution.

[16] For the situation in Lombardy, see Zanetti, "The patriziato of Milan," pp. 745–760.

[17] See Gallenga, *Country Life in Piedmont*, pp. 47–48.

Table 4.2 *Aristocratic celibacy: nineteenth century*

Family position	Total numbers	(%) celibate
First son	264	12
Cadet	209	39
Daughter	371	13

teenth century were less inclined than their predecessors to renounce the pleasures of domestic life for the sake of the lineage. While most first sons still took their dynastic responsibilities seriously and continued to be much more likely than their younger brothers to marry, only a minority of aristocratic cadets remained celibate. As a result, the prospect of large numbers of younger branches and the consequent fragmentation of family wealth greatly increased. In this context, smaller households conformed to the logic of the lineage by reducing the number of heirs with whom the first born had to share the family patrimony.

Exclusive emphasis on parents and children, however, provides only a partial view of the reality of domestic life within the Piedmontese nobility. Memoirs and family papers reveal a considerably larger and more complex household that also might include grandparents, unmarried relatives, priests, governesses, tutors, and a wide variety of servants. Count Clemente Solaro della Margarita, for instance, spent the better part of his early years at home, but mostly in the company of his uncle Gasparo and the family priest Father Illuminato Salvaia.[18] Several decades later, the son of one of the signers of the *Statuto*, Count Carlo Broglia di Casalborgone and his wife, resided in a luxurious apartment in Turin along with their four children as well as the Count's widowed mother, his two younger brothers, a governess, two maids, and a man servant.[19] The considerably wealthier Marchese Lodovico Pallavicino-Mossi and his wife headed a domestic menage in the same period that included his three children, his mother-in-law, and a resident staff of four maids and nine man servants.[20] For his part, Count Giovanni Figarolo di Gropello recollected his childhood in a spacious residence of "Belle Epoque" Turin, which he, his parents, and two sisters shared

[18] See Lovera e Rinieri, *Clemente Solaro della Margarita*, vol. I, pp. 18–20; Barbagli, *Sotto lo stesso tetto*, pp. 310–311.

[19] AST, Sez. Riunite, Archivio Broglia di Castelborgone, b. 3, Census form, 1861 and b. 31, inventory of the family residence in via dei Mille 16, 1885.

[20] AST, Sez. Riunite, Archivio Pallavicino-Mossi, b. 17, lists of persone di servizio, 1867 and 1873.

with "the personnel (wet-nurses, nurse maids, and similar types) who
dealt exclusively with the children," as well as a valet, maid, cook,
apprentice cook, washerwoman, coachman and the family's French
governess, Mademoiselle Gillotte.[21]

In his memoirs, Marchese Mario Incisa della Rocchetta provides a
detailed description of the dimensions and dynamics of his parents'
household. Born at the end of the nineteenth century, Incisa della Rocchetta grew up in a sprawling family of six children whose needs were
met by a "well-supplied platoon of governesses, nurse maids, nurse
aides, 'trusted' persons and the 'old women of the house' . . . those
responsible for overseeing our well-being, upbringing, and the beginning of our education." The dominant figure among the latter was a
certain "Madama Cristina," the widow of a great uncle's agent, who
acted as a sort of housekeeper as well as confidante to the children's
mother. Another set of "internal" servants, "with whom it was important to maintain good relations," ran the rest of the household. They
included the Marchesa's personal maid, who remained with her mistress
for more than fifty years, a valet "in livery", a younger servant who
played with the children, and finally a cook and his assistant. Growing
up in the ancestral castle in La Rocchetta, the family also had need of an
"external" staff that included a gardener, an all-purpose repairman, a
grounds keeper, who had been the grandfather's orderly, and a
coachman.

As Marchese Mario recalled, the children considered both the internal and external staff as being very much a part of the family:

> All of them together constituted the "house staff": *familiari*, as they were
> called then, with a term that unfortunately no longer has meaning,
> having derived from the old "family", when the head of the house and
> the absolute despot was . . . the father. We were on very familiar terms
> with all the "internal and external" staff . . . and used to engage them in
> long conversations that we would never have been able to do with our
> parents and our other "elders". The "familiari" . . . listened to us and
> discussed things with us frankly and calmly; and we, instinctively, felt
> them to be our equals, "subordinates" like us and we understood them
> better than we did our own parents and their "betters".[22]

For his part, Figarolo di Gropello described a similar relationship
between children and servants in his parents' home in the early years of
the twentieth century. In particular, his mother's maid, who had fol-

---

[21] "Diario dell'Ammiraglio di Divisione, Conte Giovanni di Gropello," January to
June 1986, pp. 4–5.

[22] See Incisa della Rocchetta, "Impressioni e ricordi", pp. 36–41.

lowed her from her family, was especially attached to them, providing in the words of Count Giovanni, some "of the sweetest and dearest memories of our childhood and adolescence."[23]

The Piedmontese nobility may well have been less inclined to abandon a traditional model of parent–child relations than their titled colleagues elsewhere in northern Italy. It has been argued that the nineteenth century witnessed a profound transformation in the internal dynamics of aristocratic families. An older model of household relations based on deference, subordination, and fear entered into crisis with the generation of nobles who were born between 1821 and 1845. As a result, the cold and respectful formalism that had once governed relations between noble parents and children gave way to a new model characterized by greater intimacy and informality.[24]

Little of this intimacy and informality appears to have penetrated noble families in Piedmont, judging by the Incisa della Rocchetta household. On the whole, their father, Marchese don Enrico, remained aloof from his progeny, intervening only "when there were big problems or major domestic crises." Deference and fear dominated the sons' relations with their father. When he took them with him on horse rides to survey the family estate, for example, Marchese Mario recalled: "we knew that we must follow him at a distance of ten paces, in silence; it was out of the question to ask him anything, if only because we would have had to raise our voice and we would have never dared to do that." On those rare occasions when Marchese don Enrico went out of his way to please his sons, they were "astonished and deeply moved, but knowing him well, we avoided showing him our gratitude in words; he would have responded to us with a cold shower (*doccia fredda*)."[25] While Figarolo di Gropello's father, unlike Marchese don Enrico, was willing on occasion to display great affection toward his children, he was also prone, in the words of Count Giovanni, to "explosions of anger that terrified us"; their mother was more even tempered, but less inclined to "noisy displays of affection."[26]

The memoirs of both Incisa della Rocchetta and Figarolo di Gropello point then to the apparent survival of older hierarchies and patterns of subordination within aristocratic families long after the Restoration and the ostensible triumph of modern forms of conjugal domesticity. Such survivals did not mean that nothing had changed. Noble households in the nineteenth century tended to have fewer children than in the past,

[23] Figarolo di Gropello, *Diario*, p. 4.
[24] See Barbagli, *Sotto lo stesso tetto*, pp. 303–328, 339–342.
[25] Incisa della Rocchetta, "Impressioni e ricordi", pp. 32–33, 36, and 48.
[26] Figarolo di Gropello, *Diario*, p. 7.

while cadets displayed a new independence in their marital practices. Nonetheless, as both marital statistics and personal recollections indicate, the authority of the family patriarch and loyalty to the lineage remained strong and continued to exercise a powerful influence on young nobles well into an era when all were equal before the law. The family still acted as the first and most important instrument for the perpetuation of traditional values and modes of comportment within the Piedmontese nobility.

ARISTOCRATIC EDUCATION WITHIN THE FAMILY FORTRESS

The initial learning experiences of aristocratic children continued in the nineteenth century to take place within the relative social isolation of the family's ancestral palace and/or country estate. Such settings permitted parents, governesses, and tutors to instill early on in the children an awareness of belonging to a special group, separate and distinct from the rest of society. Marchese Mario Incisa della Rocchetta's recollections provide some insight into the rather secluded environment in which aristocratic children were raised:

> It would never have entered their minds [his parents] to have us attend the local public school; they would have been even less inclined to permit us to go about in the village by ourselves or take part in the games of the "ragazzacci" of Rocchetta. We crossed the village without stopping . . . During our early years, we used to spend the days at Rocchetta always in the house and the garden and always in the same way: for "logistical" reasons, because we "big" kids had to adapt to the needs of the "little ones." But what we always called the "garden" is basically a true park: small (about 4 hectares), but a "park" because it has all the characteristics of one: variety and sizes of trees, the absence of flowers and flower beds . . . ; namely an (artificial) appearance of "natural" scenery. Thus, we did not feel constrained as we would have been in a true garden.[27]

Social isolation, however, did not mean extravagant luxuries or indulgent treatment for the children of noble families. On the contrary, virtually all aristocratic commentators stressed the importance of severe discipline, strict obedience, and austerity in their upbringing. In his autobiography, for instance, Massimo d'Azeglio described the daily regimen of his childhood in the first years of the nineteenth century, a regimen designed to instill in him "the strength to make sacrifices and to learn how to suffer." D'Azeglio spelled out in some detail what his

---

[27] Incisa della Rocchetta, "Impressioni e ricordi," pp. 28–29.

parents' educational philosophy entailed. D'Azeglio himself remained an enthusiastic supporter of his father's "excellent authoritarian methods" which, he wished "could be the general rule throughout Italy."[28]

If the recollections of Marchese Mario Incisa della Rocchetta and Count Giovanni Figarolo di Gropello provide any indication, the approach to the early education of children in the d'Azeglio household remained popular with the families of the Piedmontese nobility a century later. Marchese Mario remembered how he and his brothers and sisters spent their childhood "in an authoritarian regime. That which happened to us, for us, and around us, was not debated: thus it had to be and thus it was. And that was enough."[29] In a similar vein, Figarolo di Gropello thanked "heaven and my parents" for the way he and his sisters had been "very strictly raised" in the opening decade of the twentieth century.[30]

An approach to child-rearing that unabashedly stressed hierarchy, discipline and obedience conformed perfectly to the traditional values that titled families sought to perpetuate and instill in their progeny: a rigorous sense of duty, unwavering obedience to the monarchy, and devotion to the Roman Catholic Church. The Alfieri di Sostegno and Taparelli d'Azeglio provided perhaps the most articulate exponents of this Piedmontese aristocratic ethos. Early in the century, for instance, Marchese Carlo Emanuele Alfieri di Sostegno instructed the younger generation: "Cherish your high birth, since it imposes duties; cherish your ancestors, since they are examples for you; but guard yourself from believing that nature has transmitted to you the glories [of the family] as an inheritance, which you have only to enjoy . . ."[31]

Similar concerns reappear in the letters and testimonials that other members of the two families directed toward their sons, nephews, and grandchildren in the decades prior to 1848. After the death of her husband, Marchese Cesare d'Azeglio in the 1830s, Cristina Morozzo della Rocca di Bianzè held him up to her sons as a model of what she considered the essence of nobility: "a sense of true honor, based on faith in God and loyalty to King, probity and loftiness of soul."[32] She urged her grandson, Marchese Emanuele d'Azeglio, to live up to the same standards, insisting that his "name, discrete patrimony, [and] uncommon intelligence" required him "to be useful to the fatherland" and to

[28] D'Azeglio, *Things I Remember*, pp. 34–37.
[29] Incisa della Rocchetta, "Impressioni e ricordi," p. 48.
[30] Figarolo di Gropello, *Diario*, p. 7.
[31] Quoted in Masi, *Asti e gli Alfieri*, pp. xiii–xiv.
[32] Quoted in d'Azeglio, *Things I Remember*, p. 6.

achieve a "good reputation [and] public esteem . . . "[33] Marchese Emanuele received similar admonitions from his father and his aunt, Marchesa Luisa Costa della Trinità. Marchese Roberto d'Azeglio wrote to his son in 1832 to express the hope that he would become a man "capable of occupying with the dignity of the nobility and the loftiness of its views that honorable place that his birth has designated for him in the state." For her part, Marchesa Luisa advised her nephew: "endeavor to be rigorous in the execution of your duties and those of your state, respect and care for our religion, serve your King with zeal and loyalty."[34]

Such values continued to find expression in the missives that prominent aristocrats directed to their children in the decades after national unification. Count Emiliano Avogadro della Motta implored his children in 1865 to consider his "faith," and not his vast wealth, as "the best inheritance that I can leave to you . . . "[35] Count Ernesto Balbo Bertone di Sambuy urged his oldest son Vittorio in the late 1880s to remember "in every moment our old motto, *Fair devoir*, so that all your actions will carry the imprint of the perfect gentleman." For their part, his younger sons were expected to honor the duty that "is incumbent upon all to serve their own country."[36] In the same period, Marchese Giuseppe Dalla Valle di Pomaro recommended to his two sons and one daughter "as a norm and secure guide in their lives, those religious principles that from infancy were diligently inculcated in them by their parents."[37]

Like their titled counterparts elsewhere on the peninsula, Piedmontese aristocrats attached a great deal of importance to the religious dimension of their progeny's education. Many of them maintained in residence a trusted priest who typically served as the children's first tutor. Massimo d'Azeglio recalled that when he was a child, "all noble families who were religious had to have their domestic chaplains."[38] Count Paolino Gazelli di Rossana, for example, invited his old curate in the Citadel of Turin in the 1820s to reside in the family's palace and en-

---

[33] Archivio Taparelli d'Azeglio, Saluzzo, carteggio private Marchese Emanuele, corrispondenza varia, 1828–1887, as cited in Maldini Chiarito, "Trasmissione di valori e educazione familiare," p. 51.

[34] Both letters are cited in *ibid.*, pp. 48–49.

[35] AST, Sez. Riunite, Archivio Avogadro di Collobiano e della Motta, b. 9, Testament of Count Emiliano Avogadro della Motta, n.d. 1865.

[36] URST, b. 788, f. 17, Testament of Count Ernesto Balbo Bertone di Sambuy, November 2, 1889.

[37] URST, b. 694, f. 5, 1905, testament of Marchese Giuseppe Dalla Valle di Pomaro, n.d., 1888.

[38] D'Azeglio, *Things I Remember*, p. 45.

trusted him with the classical education of his son Stanislao. The priest must have had a profound influence on Stanislao who at the age of thirteen chose to enter the priesthood.[39] Count Giuseppe Ignazio Avogadro della Motta provided his family's curate, Don Giacomo Toso, with a life-time pension as well as permanent board and lodging in the family's palace in recognition of what he had done "for the education of my son."[40] Of course, the efforts of clerical tutors could also backfire on them. Massimo d'Azeglio, for one, attributed his lack of respect for religious authority, in part, to "the limitations and misplaced zeal of my priest."[41]

Exclusive reliance on priests, nannies, and preceptors for the instruction of aristocratic children within the familiar confines of the country house or urban palace became more difficult in the nineteenth century. In an increasingly competitive society, nobles were under mounting pressure to provide at least their sons with the formal education that was becoming necessary to pass public examinations and gain access to positions of power and influence. Especially in the decades after 1848, titled families had to adapt their sons' educations to a world that was no longer based so much on birth and inherited privilege as on wealth, talent, and certain standards of culture and civilization.

PRIVATE SCHOOLS AND ARISTOCRATIC EDUCATION

A number of new or restructured educational institutions began to appear during the Restoration to meet those needs. These mostly private schools represented both a challenge and an opportunity for aristocratic families. In general, secondary schools represented, by their very nature, a threat to hereditary transmission of status and profession, since they "sought to replace the titles of nobility with others like the *laurea* or the diploma, which conferred privileges on those who acquired them."[42] At the same time, exclusive private schools also offered the hereditary nobility not only competitive skills, but also a much needed opportunity to strengthen group identity and cohesion and to inculcate traditional values and attitudes into the younger generations.

From the outset, the interaction among youths within these institutions reinforced and broadened alliances and connections already based on marriage, family contacts, and more casual encounters in urban

[39] di Robilant, *Un prete di ieri*, pp. 18–22.
[40] AST, Sez. Riunite, Archivio Avogadro di Collobiano e della Motta, Testament of Count Giuseppe Ignazio Avogadro della Motta, n.d., 1818.
[41] D'Azeglio, *Things I Remember*, pp. 50–53.
[42] Barbagli, *Educating for Unemployment*, p. 60.

palaces or country houses. Shared experiences and daily rituals in boarding school encouraged a web of friendships and camaraderie to develop among the students that often carried over into their adult lives. The structure, discipline, and curricula of these schools also served to glorify and promote the values of "Religion, Fatherland, Family,"[43] and, in this fashion, helped perpetuate and reaffirm the ideals and traditions that had long defined the aristocratic ethos in Piedmont.

This blend of new and old functions was clearly evident in the two most important elite educational institutions that appeared in the decades after the fall of Napoleon: the Royal Military Academy of Turin (1816) and the Royal Carlo Alberto College of Moncalieri (1838). Although the Academy was founded by the monarchy while the Barnabite religious order ran the College, both schools had their roots in the *ancien régime* and in shared ideals, goals, and methods that reaffirmed older models of aristocratic comportment. In fact, the new academy inherited the name and seat of the original Accademia Reale which had provided military training to young men from the Piedmontese nobility in the century preceding the French Revolution.[44] Similarly, the Royal Carlo Alberto College was the successor to an older educational institution, the Collegio dei nobili di Torino, which had been administered by the Jesuits before 1773 and then by the Barnabites in the 1790s.[45]

Despite these elements of continuity with the *ancien régime*, the two schools were also very much institutions of the nineteenth century that were designed by founders and sponsors to combat new threats to throne and altar. Thus, Vittorio Emanuele I and his army commanders conceived of the Academy not just as an institution of education in military science, but also as an instrument to inoculate young officers against the subversive and heretical ideas that had ostensibly flourished during "the long fifteen year dream" of French occupation.[46] A couple of decades later, the Royal Carl Albert College was founded with two primary objectives: first, to help insure the loyalty of the next generation of "boys of noble and refined status" to the crown and tradition after a number of officers had become involved in the Mazzinian uprisings of 1833 and, second, to prepare for an ambitious program of national unification.[47]

---

[43] *Il Real Collegio Carlo Alberto di Moncalieri. New LXXV anno*, p. 21.

[44] See Rogier, *La R. Accademia Militare*, vol. I, pp. 23–42.

[45] *Le scuole dei Barnabiti (1533–1933)* (Florence, 1933), p. 174.

[46] Quoted in Rogier, *La R. Accademia Militare*, vol. I, p. 48; on the larger ideological functions of the Academy after 1816, see also Barberis, *Le armi del principe*, pp. 286–87.

[47] See Tabboni, *Il Real Collegio Alberto*, p. 29.

In their daily rituals, the Royal Military Academy and the Royal Carlo Alberto College promoted the same traditional ideals and virtues that aristocratic families like the Taparelli d'Azeglio and Alfieri di Sostegno were already attempting to instill in their offspring. Not surprisingly, the two schools attached special importance to religious faith and practice. Cadets of the Academy, for instance, were told that among their duties, "those of religion are the first." Institutional regulations and constant exhortations from commanders called for monthly confessions, daily attendance at mass, and strict observance of all religious duties.[48] Similarly, prayers opened and closed every day as well as every activity of what had previously been the Convent of San Francisco of Moncalieri, while religious observances of the students were carefully prescribed and regulated down to the smallest detail.[49]

Devotion to the monarchy went hand in hand with religion in the educational agenda of both schools. From the outset, commanders of the Royal Military Academy encouraged cadets to view the monarch as the "venerated head of the military family" and to work hard and behave well in order to "deserve Royal Favors" and "the paternal tenderness of the King." To reinforce these sentiments, Vittorio Emanuele I made special trips to the Academy to inspect the cadets and show his interest in their progress.[50] For their part, the Barnabite superiors exalted their school's tradition of "Piedmontese discipline [and] loyalty to the House of Savoy," a tradition that found expression in everything from the portraits of members of the dynasty that graced the walls of school to the elaborate rituals surrounding the annual presentation of student awards by the king or other members of the royal family.[51]

Their shared devotion to throne and altar did not keep the two schools from pursuing different emphases in their respective curricula. The Military Academy initially made the study of Latin the base of its curriculum like other schools of the time, but from the outset a much greater emphasis was put on mathematics than the humanities. From 1839 onward, entering students had to be between the ages of 14 and 16, with a basic knowledge of Latin, Italian, arithmetic, elementary geometry, and the fundamental principles of the Catholic religion. The course of studies for students bound for service in the infantry and

[48] Rogier, *La R. Academia Militare*, vol. 1, pp. 48–49.

[49] *Il Real Collegio Alberto di Moncalieri, 1838–1938*, p. 103. For a fuller discussion of the role of religion in the educational experience of the college, see Tabboni, *Il Real Collegio Alberto*, pp. 89–90.

[50] Rogier, *La R. Accademia Militare*, vol. 1, pp. 50–51.

[51] See Vico d'Arisbo, *Quand'ero in Collegio* (Milan, 1928), p. x; *Il R. Collegio Carlo Alberto, 1838–1938*, p. 64.

cavalry lasted five years; for those headed to artillery, engineering, and the General Staff, six years. During the first two years, all students took the same set of courses, which included arithmetic, algebra, geometry, French language and grammar, Italian literature, design, and military regulations. In the succeeding years, both groups of students continued to study French and Italian, along with geography, history, and military regulations. Future infantry and cavalry officers studied advanced algebra, trigonometry, topography, statistics, physics, fortification, and other military-related courses. Students training for the more technically specialized branches also took these courses as well as more advanced courses in calculus, mechanics, chemistry, and cosmography.[52]

The Royal Carlo Alberto College, on the other hand, maintained a curriculum which was modeled after the Jesuit *ratio studiorum* and in conformity with the programs of the Ministry of Education. Accordingly, precedence was given to the humanities, Latin, Greek, and Italian over all other subjects. The program of studies began with four years of elementary school, followed by an external public examination for admission to the next level. The program of humanities occupied the next four years and included three years of grammar, two years of rhetoric, and two years of philosophy, or in its place a two year preparatory program for aspirants to the Military Academy.[53]

In general, the Military Academy and the Royal Carlo Alberto College were concerned not only with imparting a specific body of knowledge to their charges, but with shaping and molding their overall character. The two schools actively promoted a code of comportment that embodied the traditional ideals of the Piedmontese nobility. As one nineteenth-century critic later complained, the titled commanders of the Military Academy attempted "to instill in those tender young minds all the attitudes of that aristocratic intolerance and petulance which were reputed then to be inseparable from the nature of the gentleman."[54] The written orders constantly made implicit reference to the precept of *noblesse oblige* by emphasizing the special duties of cadets who were a "chosen youth" and belonged to a "most noble corps." Exemplary punishments awaited those cadets guilty of "behavior contrary to the dignity of well born youths" or lacking in "that level of honor which shapes the proper character and sentiments of a true military man . . . "[55] Likewise, the first program of the Royal Carlo Alberto College

[52] See Rogier, *La Real Accademia Militare*, vol. I, pp. 66–68, 90–91, 136–139, 154.

[53] See Tabboni, *Il Real Collegio Alberto*, pp. 52–55.

[54] See Pinelli, *Storia militare del Piemonte*, vol. II, Chap. 4, as cited in Rogier, *La R. Accademia Militare*, p. 54.

[55] *Ibid.*, pp. 54–55.

promised to provide "boys of noble and refined rank" with an education not only in the standard academic subjects, but also in piety and social sophistication (*urbanità sociale*) in order to prepare them for the admission to the Academy and a military career. Nearly a century later, the College's regulations still spoke of instilling in the "youths from select families . . . a noble demeanor, dignified and companionable, which is proper to persons of high rank."[56] In this fashion, the two schools reinforced in their students an awareness of belonging to an exclusive and distinguished elite that had special prerogatives and duties.

Commandants and headmasters paid more than lip-service to these goals. The social isolation, strict discipline, and austerity that characterized child-rearing practices within Piedmont's titled families also typified the educational philosophies of the Military Academy and the College of Moncalieri. Both institutions took virtually total control over the lives of their students whom they kept almost completely isolated from the outside world. One alumnus of the Carlo Alberto College recalled approvingly in his memoirs how the school "wanted to be a great family and . . . did not tolerate interruptions of any sort, considering them, not wrongly, as harmful." Even the reading of newspapers was rigorously forbidden. The schedule of the College until 1906 allowed students no overnight absences and only three lunches a year with their families so that some became "strangers in their homes and in their country"; the Academy, for its part did not provide for any official vacation time.[57]

From dawn to dusk, school authorities regimented every aspect of the students' daily lives and employed a variety of punishments for any misbehavior to encourage unwavering obedience and self-abnegation. Cesare Saluzzo di Monesiglio, commandant of the Academy in the 1820s and 1830s, imposed on them a spartan regimen that required boys as young as nine years of age to spend much of their time outdoors in all kinds of weather, drilling, marching, performing physical exercises, and engaging in aggressive, violent forms of sport. All this was intended, in the words of one alumnus, to "inculcate in those youths a masculine, soldierly character."[58]

The Barnabite superiors of the Royal Carlo Alberto College sought

[56] See *Il Real Collegio Carlo Alberto 1838–1938*, pp. 15–16; *Regolamento per i convittori* (Turin, 1929), p. 35.

[57] See *Il Real Collegio Carlo Alberto 1838–1938*, p. 16. For the comments of the former student, see L. Segàla to Vico d'Arisbo, in *Quand'ero in collegio*, p. 239. See Rogier, *La R. Accademia Militare*, vol. 1, pp. 58–61 who describes the strict regimen followed by the cadets.

[58] Rogier, *La R. Accademia Militare*, vol. 1, pp. 91–92.

to encourage in their charges the same military, ascetic virtues with a strict uniform code and a rigid schedule that allowed no privacy and structured virtually every minute of their day from 6 a.m. to bedtime at 8.45 p.m. Students were expected to remain in uniform away from the College, since as one father wrote to his son, it "distinguishes and honors you everywhere, in contrast to the bourgeois coat which fits well even on the shoulders of a scoundrel (*manigoldo*); the uniform of a student of the Barnabites is a guarantee of honesty."[59] Emphasis on discipline and duty extended even to time set aside for play which had, in the words of former students, "the appearance of a regulation to be observed, of a duty to be discharged. It was an obligation to enjoy oneself." The task of enforcing such regimentation fell to the rector and a hierarchy of prefects who required students to "accustom themselves to obey blindly."[60]

The ethos of the Royal Carlo Alberto College, in particular, also exalted careers that reflected the aristocratic ideals of honor and public leadership rather than the pursuit of production and profit. In the words of one history teacher, the school aspired to train students "to observe a constant love for their own country, to be inspired to fulfil all their duties and in this way to become perfect citizens who are truly of assistance, consolation, and glory to their own family and city, but even more to the great Italian Fatherland."[61] For their part, the Barnabite superiors proudly trumpeted their role in the formation of "thousands of illustrious citizens in the armed forces, diplomacy, courts, politics." Conversely, the worlds of commerce and industry were largely ignored. In 1913, the school's chroniclers, for instance, gave only passing reference to the graduates who achieved prominence in these sectors.[62]

The aristocratic ethos of the Military Academy and the Royal Carlo Alberto College was evident not only in their rituals and educational philosophy, but also in the social backgrounds of their students and, in the case of the Academy, the institutional leadership. In fact, all ten of its commandants between 1816 and 1859 came from old titled families like the Nicolis di Robilant, Saluzzo di Monesiglio and Faà di

---

[59] *Il Real Collegio Carlo Alberto, 1838–1938*, p. 15.

[60] See *ibid.*, p. 166. *Regolamento dei Prefetti* (Turin, 1884), p. 46, quoted in Tabboni, *Il R. Collegio Alberto*, p. 92.

[61] Declaration of a Barnabite history teacher from the school's program of 1897, quoted in Tabboni, *Il Real Collegio Alberto*, p. 61.

[62] Comments of Padre Semeria in the preface to V. d'Aristo, *Quando ero in collegio*, p. x. For indications of the lack of status which the school attributed to careers in business, see *Il Real Collegio Carlo Alberto di Moncalieri nel LXXV anno*, pp. 84–87 as well as Tabboni, *Il Real Collegio Alberto*, pp. 114–122.

Table 4.3 *Social origins of students (Royal Carlo Alberto College)*

Category	1838–1857 (%)	1858–1877 (%)	1878–1897 (%)	1898–1917 (%)
Nobility	52	49	29	22
Professions	9	13	16	21
Landowners	29	30	49	50
Commerce	2	7	3	1
Banking	6	–	–	–
Military	1	0.3	3	2
Industry	–	1	0.6	4
Bureaucracy	–	0.5	0.2	0.4

Source: Tabboni, *Il Real Collegio*, p. 75.

Bruno.[63] More importantly, the large number of young aristocrats who passed through their doors testifies eloquently to the importance which Piedmont's nobility attached to these elite schools in the nineteenth century. Roughly 90 percent of the first class of recruits to the Military Academy in 1816 came from the ranks of the aristocracy. Over 600 more blue-blooded youths followed suit in the decades up to 1870. Led by the Asinari di San Marzano, Morozzo della Rocca, and Galli della Loggia, a core group of some 20 titled families alone sent 102 sons to the Academy in these years.[64] Pressures to enlarge and professionalize the army, however, necessitated a much broader base of recruitment into the officer corps and thereby worked to erode gradually the social exclusivity of the Military Academy. Even before unification, the social makeup of the Academy had changed noticeably. Titled families, which had accounted for 66 percent of the recruits in the 1820s, were contributing only 30 percent of the total by the 1850s.[65]

The Royal Carlo Alberto College proved to be somewhat more resistant to bourgeois penetration. Indeed, the social composition of its student population remained predominantly aristocratic into the last quarter of the nineteenth century. From its founding in 1838 until 1917, the College took charge of the education of 846 young men from titled families. Table 4.3 provides some quantitative measure of how significant this aristocratic presence was. As these statistics show, boys from

---

[63] For a complete list of the commandants, see Accademia Militare, *Annuario per l'anno scolastico 1887–1888* (Turin, 1887).

[64] For a complete list of all cadets as well as brief biographical sketches, see Rogier, *La R. Accademia Militare*, vol. II, pp. 1–19, 413–439.

[65] Del Negro, *Esercito, stato, società*, pp. 63–64. On the modernization of the army, see Whittam, *The Politics of the Italian Army*, pp. 26–49.

noble families continued to make up far and away the largest single group within the college until the late 1870s; in the decades immediately preceding World War I, they were outnumbered only by the sons of non-noble landowners, a considerably larger and less close-knit segment of Piedmontese society.

The declining aristocratic presence in the Royal Carlo Alberto College in the last decades of the nineteenth century was due in part to increased competition from other private educational institutions in Turin such as the Jesuit Collegio dell'Istituto Sociale di Istruzione ed Educazione Privata and the Christian Brothers' Collegio San Giuseppe which also catered to the sons of prominent families. Although the former opened its doors only in 1881, its founding rector, Father Luigi Asinari di San Marzano, came from one of Piedmont's most prestigious old families; that plus the long tradition of upper-class, Jesuit education in the region going back to the seventeenth century ensured the Istituto Sociale immediate acceptance, especially in the more ultra-montane circles of the nobility.[66] While the 484 blue bloods who enrolled in the school before World War I represented less than a fifth of the total student population, their ranks included the sons of many of Piedmont's oldest and wealthiest aristocratic families. Indeed, the presence of names like Pallavicino-Mossi, San Martino di San Germano, and Cacherano di Bricherasio eloquently testified to the prestige and status the Istituto Sociale enjoyed within the nobility. Much like their counterparts in Moncalieri, these students had to wear uniforms at all times and received a strict Catholic education, but they were much less socially isolated. In contrast to the Royal Carlo Alberto College, the Istituto Sociale had a substantial number of day students and even those who boarded were allowed weekly visits with their families.[67]

Founded in 1867, the Collegio San Giuseppe ranked slightly below the Barnabite and Jesuit schools in the hierarchy of elite private institutions favored by Piedmont's titled families in the late nineteenth and early twentieth centuries. Like the other two, the Collegio San Giuseppe openly asserted its elitist character, promising "families of refined status" to cultivate in their sons "the forms of comportment that are appropriate to well-born young men."[68] Despite these claims, the regimen of the school was less all-encompassing and the student popu-

---

[66] See Istituto Sociale di Torino, *L'Istituto Sociale*, pp. 1–17, 40–42.

[67] See *ibid.*, pp. 86–133 for a list of the students who entered the school between 1881 and 1915. The school ceased to provide facilities for boarders in 1923.

[68] See AST, Sez. Riunite, Archivio Broglia di Casalborgone, b. 10, f. 1, "Collegio San Giuseppe con Semiconvitto per le scuole, elementari, ginnasiali e techniche (Torino, via S. Francesco da Paola, 23)" (Turin, 1895).

lation less socially exclusive than the Royal Carlo Alberto College. Most were day students and even the full-time boarders spend only nine months a year *in collegio*. While the names of some of the oldest titled families appear on the school's class rosters, young nobles represented a tiny minority of the students enrolled in the San Giuseppe. In the years from 1901 to 1915, for instance, they accounted for less than a tenth of the total enrollment which consisted predominantly of the sons of industrialists, merchants, and bankers.[69]

Aristocratic young women did not fare as well educationally as their brothers. Indeed, the virtual exclusion of women from public life in Liberal Italy reinforced the inclination of titled families to devote considerably less attention and resources to the education of their daughters. In this respect, they appear to have followed the advice of one of their own, Count Cesare Balbo, who had recommended earlier in the century that "the education of the girls . . . can and should be done in the home by the mothers."[70] Significantly, information on the formal schooling of aristocratic young women is almost completely absent from family papers and other available sources. The few indications that do emerge from the documents suggest that the nobility invested much less in their education. In the 1870s, for example, Marchese Lodovico Pallavicino-Mossi annually spent more than twice as much on his son's instructional expenses than on those of his two daughters.[71] When they chose to go beyond the teaching of good manners and comportment at

---

[69] Archivio del Collegio San Giuseppe, Elenco dei studenti, 1901–15. These handwritten lists not only provide the names of the students enrolled each year, but also the names and professions of the parents. The following table indicates the distribution of the students for whom the list offers information on the profession or status of their fathers:

Category	1901–1902	1905–1906	1910–1911	1914–1915
Nobility	30	24	35	19
Industry	28	50	53	45
Merchants	41	38	50	58
Proprietari	20	14	11	14
Administration	14	–	14	7
Military	8	14	8	9
Landlords	7	14	11	14
Finance	7	11	2	6

[70] Cesare Balbo, *Le speranze d'Italia* (Paris, 1844), cap. XI, "Come si possano aiutar tutti gli Italiani," quoted in Alighiero Manacorda, "Istruzione ed emancipazione della donna," p. 13.

[71] See AST, Sez. Riunite, Archivio Pallavicino-Mossi, b. 12, "Estratto generale dei redditi e delle spese" 1875, 1876, 1877, and 1878.

home, aristocratic families seem to have shared with other segments of the propertied classes a decided preference for private Catholic girls' schools that emphasized the traditional values of obedience and devotion to the family.[72]

It is easier to describe the aims and aspirations of the all-male elite private schools than to measure the results they achieved. How effective were they at instilling traditional aristocratic values and modes of comportment in the sons of noble families? Camillo Cavour's experiences in the Royal Military Academy suggest that, in some cases, they failed utterly in their ostensible mission.[73] Still, analysis of the career paths followed by the titled graduates of the Academy and the Royal Carlo Alberto College indicates that the example of Cavour was far from typical. In the 1830s and 1840s, for instance, 96 percent of all noble youths who entered the Academy received their officer's bars. Indeed, the nobility accounted for 65 percent of all the commissioned officers from the Academy in the 1830s and 55 percent in the 1840s. More than a quarter of the cadets from the core group of old aristocratic military families ended their careers at the rank of general.[74]

Most graduates of the Royal Carlo Alberto College also pursued a path in life that conformed to the ideals and traditions of the Piedmontese nobility, judging by a survey of 414 alumni the school's officials carried out in 1913. Their findings reveal the distribution of careers as shown in Table 4.4. Young men from the titled nobility, in particular, tended to fulfill the expectations of their families and Barnabite mentors once they entered the outside world. Although aristocratic students made up only 37 percent of the total enrollment in the College of Moncalieri between 1838 and 1913, in the survey they monopolized court offices and contributed 81 percent of the high ranking army officers, 79 percent of the diplomats, and two-thirds of the alumni in public administration and politics. Conversely, blue bloods were decidedly under-represented in those potentially more lucrative areas strongly associated with the middle classes: the professions and the business world. At a minimum, these figures strongly suggest that elite schools like the Royal Carlo Alberto, working in harmony with the old families, contributed significantly to the perpe-

---

[72] See Covato, "Educata ad educare," p. 135.

[73] See Romeo, *Cavour e il suo tempo*, vol. I, pp. 189–222.

[74] Of the 102 boys from the core group of 20 families who entered the Military Academy between 1816 and 1870, 29 attained the rank of lieutenant or major general. See Rogier, *La R. Accademia Militare*, vol. II, pp. 1–411. On the percentages of nobles who received their commissions, see Del Negro, *Esercito, stato, società*, pp. 61–64.

Table 4.4 *Career patterns of graduates (Royal Carlo Alberto College)*

Profession	All alumni	Aristocratic alumni
1. Army	156	–
a. Generals	25	20
b. Colonels	27	21
c. Majors	20	17
2. Diplomacy	33	26
3. Public Administration	31	21
4. Court Posts	6	6
5. Politics	30	20
6. Professions	65	12
7. Agriculture & Industry	21	6

Source: *R. Collegio Carlo Alberto, 1838–1913*, pp. 32–56.

tuation of traditional values and the reproduction of a distinctive aristocratic ethos in nineteenth-century Piedmont.

AN OFFICER AND A GENTLEMAN: ARISTOCRATIC CAREER PATTERNS

As the data on the graduates from the Royal Carl Albert College suggest, a significant part of the Piedmontese nobility's sense of their own enduring distinctiveness continued to derive from their socially conditioned choice of careers. Indeed, the loss of legal privileges greatly accentuated the importance of the officers corps in maintaining and revitalizing traditions critical to the nobility's social cohesion and sense of purpose in the nineteenth century.

Of course, the military establishment, which young men from Piedmontese titled families entered, changed from a "feudal" force to a modern "industrial" army during the century. Organizational expansion, technological innovation, and political change all combined to erode the nobility's traditional domination of the officer corps. As early as the 1830s, a serious shortage of officers created irresistible pressures on the House of Savoy to broaden the social bases of recruitment. At the same time, the increasing pace of technological change in Piedmont, especially with the spread of the railroads in the 1850s, favored the modernization of the army and the formation of an officer corps that viewed wars as "something more than the extension of hunting."[75] Efforts to enlarge and professionalize the army encouraged major changes in the social composition of the cadets at the Military Academy,

[75] See Whittam, *The Politics of the Italian Army*, pp. 26, 49, 146–147.

where the nobles had become a decided minority by the 1850s. While the Piedmontese military establishment and its traditions provided the model for the Italian army that emerged the following decade, the passage of a third of the officers from Savoy to France in 1860 and the entrance of large numbers of Lombards, central Italians, and southerners into newly formed mixed brigades after unification further reduced the aristocratic make-up of the officers corps. By the late 1880s, the corps was a overwhelmingly middle-class body, with only 3 percent to 4 percent of the officers coming from noble families.[76]

Nonetheless, the continued prominence of the old Piedmontese elite at the top of the military hierarchy and its close ties to the House of Savoy made it possible for the new Italian army to still perform traditional social functions. In this respect, neither professionalization nor the increasing social heterogeneity of the officer corps appears to have diminished the prestige of military service for young men from titled families in the decades after national unification. Indeed, the actual number of aristocratic officers from the region remained relatively constant between 1861 and World War I. A survey of various years of the *Annuario Militare del Regno d'Italia* reveals that Piedmontese noble families contributed from 200 to 248 officers on active service at any given moment throughout the period. Such continuity is especially striking, since the total number of aristocratic officers from all regions of the peninsula dropped substantially in the second half of the nineteenth century.[77]

Social considerations still seem to have dictated the distribution of titled officers within the armed forces. As table 4.5 indicates, Piedmontese nobles tended to concentrate in the traditionally prestigious cavalry and elite infantry regiments, where roughly three-quarters of them served. Another fifty nobles, on average, appear to have given precedence to duty and professionalism by serving in the ostensibly more bourgeois artillery. By and large, Piedmontese nobility avoided the Carabinieri and Engineers Corps.

A variety of sources attest to the fact that the military remained the preferred choice of most nobles who pursued careers in the second half of the nineteenth century. According to the electoral rolls, for instance, the army was the designated profession of more aristocratic voters in Turin than all other professions combined in the mid-1870s.[78] Nor had

[76] See *ibid.*, pp. 61–68; Del Negro, *Esercito, stato, società*, pp. 63–64; Ceva, "Forze armate," p. 285.

[77] According to Lucio Ceva, the number of noble officers went from 855 in 1863 to 430 in 1887. See his "Forze armate," pp. 284–285.

[78] ACT, Lista elettorale amministrativa, 1875.

Table 4.5 *Piedmontese aristocratic officers*

Branch	1875	1885	1895	1905	1914
Cavalry	88	87	114	102	101
Infantry	65	82	68	68	51
Artillery	33	47	56	65	52
Carabin.	6	11	7	3	3
Engineers	8	4	3	4	0
Total	200	231	248	242	207

Note: The data on distribution of Piedmontese aristocrats within the survey is drawn from lists in the Annuario Militare for the years 1875, 1885, 1895, 1905, 1914.

this pattern changed four decades later. On the eve of World War I, noble families resident in the regional capital had 214 men serving in the army officers corps as compared to only 19 in the legal profession, 18 in the judiciary, and 8 in engineering or architecture. The same families had virtually no presence in the church or professoriate.[79] A very similar picture emerges from the membership lists of the Società del Whist. From its founding in the 1840s until World War I, a substantial majority of the titled members of Turin's most exclusive and aristocratic men's social club held commissions and had served on active duty in the officers corp. Included in their ranks were some forty-four generals and admirals.[80]

The enduring prestige and status which the Piedmontese nobility continued to attach to military service also made the officer corps a primary route of access for new men to aristocratic circles in the second half of the nineteenth century. Although the king no longer routinely bestowed hereditary titles on officers who had entered the high command, distinguished service in the army remained one of the surest paths to ennoblement after 1861. Of the 106 new nobles created between unification and World War I whose professions can be identified, 38, or more than a third, came from the officer corps. In the last decade and a half before the war alone, fifteen officers received hereditary titles.[81]

More importantly, the military profession remained a crucial ingredient in a larger process of aristocratic socialization of young men from newly ennobled families who lacked a tradition of service in the army.

[79] See *La Guida commerciale ed amministrativa di Torino, 1913* (Turin, 1913), pp. 624–676, 749–766, 905–923, 977–1043.

[80] See Società Cavour, *Un secolo di vita*, pp. 111–218 for biographical sketches of the members.

[81] See Bertini Frassoni, *Provvedimenti nobiliari*, pp. 3–35.

Much as in the past, the acquisition of a patent of nobility in nineteenth-century Italy rarely produced immediate social rewards for its recipient; a title was an investment that could be realized only by the sons and grandsons of the original successful merchant, banker, or statesman. In Piedmont, this process typically involved the younger generations pursuing commissions and embracing careers in the military. Over the course of the century, a number of newly ennobled families began to develop their own modest military traditions. The Barel di Sant'Albano, for instance, a prominent banking family whose title came shortly before the French Revolution, sent six sons to the Royal Military Academy between 1816 and 1870, and produced four generations of army officers prior to World War I. Another family of bankers and merchants, the Rignons, had four men serving in either the artillery or cavalry between the 1820s and 1914. Other newly ennobled banking families like the Gonellas (1845), the Casanas (1852), and the Ceriana-Mayneri (1881) as well as families from the professions and administration like the Nasi (1836), the Fassini-Camossi (1860), and the Voli (1899) followed a similar pattern of involvement in the military. On the eve of the Great War, these families still had ten of their men serving in the fashionable units of the cavalry and infantry, alongside the sons of old titled families.[82]

In an era of increasing professionalization and meritocratic reform within the Italian army, Piedmontese aristocrats owed their strong attachment to military service to a combination of social, cultural, and economic circumstances. The importance of rural culture and social inheritance have long been recognized as crucial factors in the making of career officers in both Europe and the United States. Rural life encouraged an out-of-doors existence and a concern with sports, weapons, and the virtues of physical prowess that were well suited to the requirements of the traditional military establishment.[83]

In his memoirs, the cavalry officer, Marchese Mario Incisa della Rocchetta testified to the crucial formative role played by family tradition and country life. As he recalled it, "when I was quite little, I had firmly decided that I would be a soldier just as had been my father, his father, and his father's father: in the Cavalry, of course . . . "[84] The rituals of everyday life in the countryside recapitulated and revitalized this tradi-

---

[82] For information on the careers of the members of some forty families ennobled in the nineteenth century, I used Manno, *Il patriziato subalpino*, vols. I–XXVII. On the numbers serving in 1914, see *Annuario militare, 1914*, pp. 136–197.

[83] See Morris Janowitz, *The Professional Soldier: A Social and Political Portrait* (New York, 1960).

[84] Incisa della Rocchetta, "Impressioni e ricordi," p. 51.

tion. At an early age, for example, Incisa della Rocchetta and his
brothers learned the intricacies of horsemanship, 'first on a donkey, then
on a 'pony', then on a 'country horse' and finally on a *real* horse."
Before they were in their teens, the boys were already accompanying
their father on two to three-hour rides several times a week to oversee
the various seasonal agricultural activities. Special events such as the
passage of a cavalry regiment through Rocchetta or the two royal visits
by Vittorio Emanuele III to the family estate made a tremendous
impression on the young Incisa della Rocchetta and confirmed his commitment to military service.[85]

Once young men from old titled families made the decision to enter
into officers' training, their special social connections often ensured
them benevolent attention from their superiors as the case of Count
Eugenio De Genova di Pettinengo illustrates. When Count Eugenio
decided in 1889 to abandon the "comfortable, but lazy and deleterious
life of the society and porticos of Turin" and followed the "most noble
example of his father" by enrolling in the Military School of Modena,
he came into contact with a number of career officers who had served
under his father, General Ignazio De Genova di Pettinengo, one-time
Commandant of the Military Academy of Turin and then general director of the Ministry of War. The value of family connections emerges
clearly from the letters of one of the general's former subordinates who
wrote to assure him that "in taking an interest in your son I am obeying
longstanding sentiments of devotion and respect for you so that for me
it is almost like looking after another of my own sons."[86] It is difficult
to evaluate the impact of these mechanisms of informal influence on the
subsequent military careers of men from noble families. They were
probably of little help to the incompetent wastrel, no matter how
exalted his family name and social contacts. Still, the careers of the
twenty-nine youths from titled backgrounds who entered the Military
Academy of Turin between 1861 and 1870 suggest that aristocratic
status remained a decided asset in the Italian army. Although this group
made up less than 4 percent of the cadets who passed through the
Academy that decade, fourteen generals and seven colonels eventually
emerged from its ranks.[87]

In Piedmontese aristocratic circles, a career in the army not only
meant a gentlemanly pursuit; it also provided much needed employment for sons who might otherwise divide and fragment the family

---

[85] *Ibid.*, pp. 12–20, 29–33.
[86] *AST*, Prima Sezione, Archivio De Genova di Pettinengo, b. 8, f. 2, letter to General
Ignazio De Genova di Pettinengo, no date 1890.
[87] Rogier, *La R. Accademia Militare*, vol. II, pp. 279–411.

patrimony. Especially, in the era of more egalitarian inheritance laws, the military profession offered titled families an honorable way of preserving intact much, if not all, of their patrimony as it passed from one generation to the next. As officers, the younger sons earned a steady income that allowed them to receive their share of the inheritance in annual installments over decades rather than in one lump sum. This was precisely the strategy that Baron Pietro Antonio Guidobono Cavalchini urged in the 1850s on his four younger sons, three of whom did pursue military careers, while the fourth entered the diplomatic corps.[88]

Nearly four decades later, the economic value of a military career was not lost even on a wealthy nobleman like Count Ernesto Balbo Bertone di Sambuy. Although he would die a multi-millionaire in 1909, Count Ernesto insisted as early as the 1880s that his four sons had "to work out of necessity if they want to be in a position to support their families . . ." Appropriately, all four wound up in the armed forces, three as cavalry officers and one in the navy.[89]

Varying combinations of social prestige, family traditions, and economic necessity explain the enduring attraction of both the aristocratic first-born and their brothers to service in the army officers corps. While the majority of noble officers, whose families resided in Turin in 1913, were cadets, nearly half (48 percent) were oldest sons who often stood to inherit the lion's share of their fathers' estates.[90] Of course, military service did not necessarily have the same meaning for all concerned. The principal heirs of wealthy old families like Marchese Maurizio Luserna di Rorà, Marchese Emanuele San Martino di San Germano, or Count Emanuele Cacherano di Bricherasio seemed to treat the cavalry as a congenial pursuit and an obligatory rite of passage before they married or stepped into their fathers' shoes. Others, like Marchese Carlo Compans di Brichanteau, used the military as a stepping stone to a career in politics.

These men may have fitted the aristocratic stereotype of the dilettante officer, but they were not necessarily typical. In fact, many of the first born, especially those from old military families, retained their commissions long after they had come into their inheritances. Count Ferdinando Avogadro di Collobiano, for instance, inherited a large fortune

---

[88] For the inheritance strategy advanced by Baron Guidobono Cavalchini, see his last will and testament in AST, Testamenti pubblicati, vol. 42, p. 69. On the careers pursued by his sons, see Manno, *Il patriziato subalpino*, vol. xiii, pp. 666ff.

[89] URST, b. 788, f. 17, testament of Count Ernesto Balbo Bertone di Sambuy, February 11, 1889. On the military careers of his sons, see Manno, *Il patriziato subalpino*, II.

[90] See *Guida di Torino, 1913*, pp. 638–674.

from his father in the 1860s, but remained an officer for an additional two decades in the cavalry where he retired at the rank of major general.[91] Roughly two-fifths of a sample of aristocratic officers, whose names reappear on the active rolls of the Cavalry or Artillery in the *Annuario militare* over a period of two to four decades between 1875 and 1914, were first sons. On the eve of World War I, the ranks of oldest sons in the armed forces still included a large number of career officers: fifteen generals, three admirals, nine colonels, and ten majors.[92] Such numbers attest to the enduring efficacy of family customs and elite education in reproducing the distinctive aristocratic military ethos of the Piedmontese nobility.

Not surprisingly, the officer corps enjoyed a prominent place in the social life of Turin before World War I. As Marchese Incisa della Rocchetta recalled, in that era the genuine "gentlemen, that is to say . . . the only social category that 'counted' then [were] officers and people that lived off of rents."[93] The prestige enjoyed by the officer corps in the Piedmontese capital both reflected and depended, in turn, upon the survival of a strongly aristocratic high society with its own distinctive values, institutions and patterns of sociability.

ARISTOCRATIC SOCIABILITY: THE SOCIETÀ DEL WHIST

The blend of tradition and innovation that helped to perpetuate the army officer corps as a marker of social position for the sons of Piedmontese titled families was also strikingly evident in a new gentlemen's club, the Società del Whist, which increasingly gave structure to aristocratic social rituals in the second half of the nineteenth century. Such an institution developed, in part, in response to the transformation of court life in the Kingdom of Sardinia, especially after 1848.

In the first decades of the Restoration, the nobility had been able to rely once again upon the House of Savoy and its highly traditional court to provide both a focal point and an exclusive setting for many of their social activities. Indeed, the rigid etiquette observed at the courts of Vittorio Emanuele I, Carlo Felice, and Carlo Alberto ensured that titled status remained a virtual prerequisite for admission to royal festivities.

---

[91] Count Ferdinando Avogadro di Collobiano, the principal heir of an estate valued at over L. 2 million in 1868, continued to pursue his military career into the late 1880s. See *Annuario militare, 1885*, vol. II, p. 25. On the dimensions of the fortune he had inherited from his father, Count Filiberto, see URST, b. 13, f. 36, 1868.

[92] See *Guida di Torino, 1913*, pp. 638–674; on the length of service of noble officers, see sources indicated in Table 4.5.

[93] Incisa della Rocchetta, "Impressioni e ricordi," pp. 161–163.

Years later, Count Charles Arrivabene recalled how the Sardinian Court was so strict in such matters that, he claimed, "no one would have been admitted to the Court balls, had he not been able to show at least two centuries of nobility." While Arrivabene probably exaggerated the importance of lineage, the House of Savoy and its court were unquestionably the centerpiece of a traditional high society in Turin in the first half of the nineteenth century, a society that continued to be overwhelmingly aristocratic in character and membership.[94]

The Piedmontese–Sardinian Court, however, no longer played this role for the nobility in the wake of the Revolutions of 1848, the proclamation of the *Statuto*, and the accession of Vittorio Emanuele II to the throne. From the outset, the introduction of parliamentary elections and equality before the law required the new limited monarchy, which gradually took shape in the following decade, to open its court to a much broader and more socially heterogeneous political class. For his part, Vittorio Emanuele II showed little interest in maintaining the traditional etiquette of court, most of which he abolished in 1848. The new king's preference for a life of hunting and horseback riding at his castles at Stupinigi and Moncalieri led him largely to abandon the royal palace in Turin. Well before his court transferred south to Florence and then Rome, it had ceased to serve as the center of an aristocratic high society.[95]

The social vacuum created by the disappearance of traditional court life was at least partially filled in the decades after 1848 by a new gentlemen's club which had first appeared in Turin only in 1841. That club, the Società del Whist, traced its origins to an informal gathering of wealthy young men at the Caffè Fiorio, a fashionable coffee house in the heart of Turin. In March 1841, the future architect of Italian unification, Count Camillo Cavour, launched the idea of a club similar to the ones he had frequented in London during travels abroad, a club that would provide a much needed gathering place away from the "querulous and noisy promiscuity" of the varied clientele at the Caffè Fiorio where he and his friends often gathered.[96] Although Cavour began with a narrow conception of the club as an entity "dedicated to the game of whist and that of chess," the Società del Whist that finally emerged had a broader scope, namely "the gathering together, in an appropriate setting, of persons of education and refinement who can keep each

---

[94] Arrivabene, *Italy under Victor Emanuel*, vol. 1, p. 20. For additional descriptions of Sardinian court life in this period, see Gerbore, *Dame e cavalieri del Re*, pp. 16–25, 29–32, 34–44; Falletti, *Saggi*, pp. 176–177.

[95] See Gerbore, *Dame e cavalieri del Re*, pp. 65–71.

[96] See Società Cavour, *Un secolo di vita*, pp. 19–20.

other company there with conversation, with permissible games, and with the reading of books and magazines." In line with these aims, the physical layout of the new club, which occupied the "noble floor" of a palace designed by the great baroque architect Juvara, included suitably furnished rooms as well as a dining area for the daily "social dinner."[97]

Ironically, this new but highly selective gentlemen's club became in the second half of the nineteenth century the most exclusively aristocratic institution in the region and thus one of the strongest bulwarks of the old traditions associated with the Piedmontese nobility. From its inception, the Whist was popularly referred to as the "circolo dei nobili" and rumors circulated in Turin that it represented "an aristocracy within the aristocracy," admission to which required "proofs of four quarters of titled status."[98] A rapid glance at the names that appear in the club's published membership lists confirms the substance of these rumors. Of the 1,100 men who belonged to the Whist between 1841 and 1914, 995 or 90 percent came from titled families. Aristocratic predominance became even more striking when we consider that a third of the 105 untitled members were admitted in the first decade of the club's existence. More than any other single factor, it was noble birth that defined the members of the Whist.[99]

Titled status may have been a virtual prerequisite, but it did not automatically guarantee admission to the Whist. In fact a more detailed analysis of 459 men from noble families whose estates went through probate between 1862 and 1912 suggests that traditional values and older hierarchies with their subtle gradations of status remained important determinants of acceptance. Only a minority of these men, some 164 or little more than a third, were ever club members. This select group was distinguished from the rest of the hereditary nobility in a few key respects.

Ancient lineage appears to have counted for more than wealth or personal achievements. Club men were much more likely to come from old established families with generations of tradition and large networks of relatives than from recently ennobled families. There was a very marked correlation between antiquity of family title and membership in the Whist as the following table shows. These figures suggest that the club's admissions policies reaffirmed an older value system, one that ascribed the highest status to those families with the greatest stability and continuity over time. Accordingly, men who lacked the genealogical

---

[97] *Ibid.*, pp. 32–38.

[98] Quoted in the essay on men's clubs by Giuseppe Gloria in *Torino*, pp. 277–289.

[99] These statistics are based on the detailed biographical information contained in Società Cavour, *Un secolo di vita*, pp. 111–218.

Table 4.6 *Lineage and Whist membership*

Antiquity of title	Percentage in Whist (%)
Pre-1723	48
Post-1723	25
Restoration	18
Post-1861	10

For genealogical information, I have relied on Manno, Il *patriziato subalpino*, vols. I–XXVI.

Table 4.7 *Wealth and Whist membership*

Wealth groups	% of group in Whist
Below L. 100,000	31
L. 100,001–250,000	28
L. 250,001–500,000	30
L. 500,001–1,000,000	39
Above L. 1,000,000	70

attributes to go along with their titles found the path to acceptance considerably more difficult.

On the other hand, wealth *per se* did not seem to be a crucial determinant of membership in the Whist. Only in the case of the very richest individuals, did it seem to make a dramatic difference (see Table 4.7). The limited importance of wealth, especially when unaccompanied by a sufficiently lengthy pedigree, becomes strikingly evident when we compare the percentage of members among the men from old and new noble families with roughly the same levels of wealth. Predictably, those men who enjoyed both great wealth and ancient family titles were most likely to be members of the Whist. But as Table 4.8 shows, the prestige associated with pedigree was such that relatively impoverished men from old aristocratic families found access to the club easier than considerably wealthier nobles who had acquired their titles in the nineteenth century. Even when personal income and property holdings had become quite negligible, as in the cases of men like Marchese Tommaso Ferrero della Marmora and Marchese Lodovico Della Chiesa di Cinzano, ancient descent might prove sufficient to ensure inclusion.[100]

---

[100] At the time of their deaths, both men left estates in which debts exceeded the total capital value of their assets.

Table 4.8 *Wealth, lineage and Whist membership (percent)*

Total value	Pre-1723 titles (%)	19th C. Titles (%)
Below L. 100,000	40	4
L. 100,000–250,000	40	20
L. 250,001–500,000	35	16
L. 500,001–1,000,000	50	25
Above L. 1,000,000	83	22

With such a pronounced emphasis on lineage, it is hardly surprising that the close ties of blood, marriage, and genealogy that characterized Piedmont's aristocratic elite also played a major role in the processes of selection of members. From the outset, the nucleus of men who founded the Whist had all been related to each other as cousins or in-laws. The consanguinity of the founders remained a basic feature of the Whist's membership in the ensuing decades. More than two-thirds of the club men in the probate survey were linked by marriage to other old families of the Piedmontese nobility. In general, relatives of members far outnumbered those without prior connections among men taken into the Whist. Of the 1,475 individuals who belonged to the Whist between 1841 and 1940, roughly 800 came from a comparatively small group of 164 families with three or more members each. An even tighter circle of some 15 families accounted for over 10 percent of all members in the club prior to World War II.[101]

The Società del Whist not only reflected and reenforced the ties of blood and marriage, but also developed ties based on the members' involvement in certain traditional areas of public service. Relatively few of the club men in the probate survey (11 percent) conformed to the aristocratic stereotype of the detached gentleman of leisure. Most displayed a strong sense of duty to the House of Savoy in accordance with the longstanding military traditions of the Piedmontese nobility. The army officers corps far outdistanced all others combined as the preferred profession of the members prior to World War I. In fact, a solid majority (94 individuals or 57 percent) of the club men in the probate survey served in the army.

[101] See Società Cavour, *Un secolo di vita*, pp. 273–282 for an alphabetical listing of all members. On the families ties among the Whist's founders, see *ibid.*, p. 29. Roughly a quarter of the Whist members in my survey were bachelors. Of those who were married, 68 percent had spouses from pre-nineteenth century noble families, while 17 percent married women from aristocratic families outside of Piedmont. Only fifteen titled members had spouses from non-noble backgrounds.

The aristocratic ethos of the Whist also found expression in the club's particular institutional way of life. As the Whist's rituals, customs, and traditions developed over time, they did little to encourage what Nelson Aldrich Jr. has referred to as "hot commerce in goods, services, and selves." On the contrary, they were designed to make the club a privileged refuge and a "quiet zone of belonging" for members, distinguished by its exclusivity and its distance from the pressures and strains of the vulgar world outside.[102]

In accordance with these aims, the Whist embraced a code of comportment that emphasized, in the words of Count Ignazio Thaon di Revel, "a genuine cordiality, great tolerance, respect for other opinions, and a mutual esteem." Members were expected to behave in the dining room with "that dignified demeanor that is normally maintained . . . in the most distinguished private families." To encourage this behavior, there was an unwritten prohibition against any discussion of politics or religion. Within the confines of the club, all members were supposed to be on an equal footing, with no special privileges or prerogatives to anyone regardless of his public prominence. Indeed, it was considered extremely bad form for members to flaunt their standing in the outside world. General Enrico Morozzo della Rocca, one of the most decorated men in the country, could still claim: "when I enter the Club I am no longer a knight of the Annunziata (highest of the royal orders), but Cavalier della Rocca and nothing more."[103]

The events and activities sponsored by the Whist also reflected its role as an aristocratic refuge. More than half a century after the club's founding, the president, Count Massimo Biandrà di Reaglie, proudly affirmed in 1901 that the Whist was "an entirely private association adverse to external displays" that had never "taken part in any public demonstration."[104] Such views perfectly suited a club whose mostly old-line members felt no need to prove or publicize their high status. The avoidance of public display by the Whist carried over to seemingly innocuous symbolic actions. Until 1911, for instance, it was policy never to display the national flag from the central balcony of the club even on the most important national holidays.

The few external activities supported by the Whist tended to be of a sporting nature, usually involving enthusiasts of horse racing, cycling, hunting, and race cars. The club almost never sponsored official banquets that involved outsiders; the few that did take place commemo-

---

[102] Aldrich, *Old Money*, pp. 50–51.
[103] Società Cavour, *Un secolo di vita*, pp. 60–76. On the importance of courtesy within the club, see Gloria, *Torino*, pp. 277–289.
[104] Società Cavour, *Un secolo di vita*, p. 58.

rated some war or military hero. Those group events that occurred with some regularity inside the Whist tended to be of a smaller, more intimate character and were associated with other primarily aristocratic institutions. Thus, the club provided a setting for annual reunions of prestigious cavalry regiments and the alumni of the Royal Carlo Alberto College of Moncalieri.[105] In this fashion, the Whist's organized initiatives, much like its admissions policies and rituals, helped to perpetuate and transmit an older set of aristocratic values that exalted birth over achievement, status over profit.

The Società del Whist offers then a graphic illustration of how in the nineteenth century newly created institutions could serve to patch up and reconstruct elements of an old order well after those elements had been ostensibly abolished by statute. With the disappearance of the nobility's legally defined hereditary superiority and the traditional life of court, the Whist emerged as the most visible institutional embodiment of an enduring aristocratic establishment. As such, the club not only strengthened social contacts and relationships within the nobility; it also helped to perpetuate a set of common values and modes of comportment. In the process, the Whist provided its members with the final confirmation of an ascriptive social status and identity already firmly grounded in their sense of lineage, family upbringing, education, and state service.

At the same time, the pretensions of aristocratic families to continued elite status also required the development of fresh strategies of selective emulation, assimilation and/or exclusion to meet the unavoidable challenges that came from emerging new power groups in the nineteenth century. Above all, after the introduction of complete civil equality in 1848 and the impressive mobilization of capital in industry, trade, and banking the following decade, the hereditary nobility no longer stood alone as the sole ruling elite in Piedmont. Instead they became just one component of a much larger and heterogeneous class of wealthy notables who collectively dominated political and economic life in the second half of the nineteenth century. In this context, the survival of aristocratic families as a coherent and distinct group depended not only on their internal integration, but also on the forms and limits of interaction that developed between them and wealthy non-titled landowners, successful businessmen, and professionals.

[105] *Ibid.*, pp. 57–70.

CHAPTER 5

THE LIMITS OF FUSION: ARISTOCRATIC–BOURGEOIS RELATIONS IN NINETEENTH-CENTURY PIEDMONT

As old juridical and institutional barriers disappeared in the course of the nineteenth century, the degree to which the aristocracy survived as an identifiably separate group at the upper reaches of Piedmontese society depended on more than recasting and reproducing traditional values, customs, and practices. It also entailed a restructuring of relations with other wealthy and influential non-noble elements who emerged to challenge the primacy of the old titled families within a new and greatly expanded ruling class. In this arena, aristocratic survival involved a mixture of flexibility and rigidity. From the stand point of the law, nobles had become only one among the various strata of the bourgeois world by the second half of the century. Moreover, changing political and economic realities in Piedmont and on the Italian peninsula necessitated an unprecedented level of cooperation and collaboration between nobles and non-nobles in virtually all areas of public life, especially after 1848. Rubbing elbows on elective municipal councils or on the boards of voluntary associations, however, did not automatically lead to more intimate connections in private life. On the contrary, the persistence of relatively closed social networks at least in Piedmont served to reinforce a caste consciousness and isolation that delayed genuine integration of old and new elites.

Contemporary observers tended to embrace the view that noble and bourgeois groups merged easily and relatively quickly in nineteenth-century Italy to form a new class of notables in which property supplanted birth and privilege as the measure of social distinction. Less than twenty years after unification and the definitive abolition of all legal status distinctions on the peninsula, one old conservative aristocrat informed the social investigator, Leandro Carpi, in 1878, that "castes no longer exist; there are those who are richer and those who are less rich, those who are poorer and those who are less poor . . . But there are no more castes."[1] Two decades later, Luigi Villari noted how the Italian word *aristocrazia* had come to mean something quite different from its English counterpart, aristocracy: "The [former] does not signify the titled classes alone, or those who are of old family. It is best translated by 'good society.' The nobility are, of course, included in it, but so are a certain number of higher Government officials, most of the wealthy business men . . . and a few professional men."[2] These contemporary perceptions have found a clear echo in the recent interpretations of social historians who argue that Italian noble groups either declined rapidly or else lost their old distinctiveness by blending into a more heterogeneous class of landed proprietors.[3]

The case of the Piedmontese aristocracy challenges this vision of rapid assimilation. In Piedmont contact between old and new elites was restricted largely to the public sphere and rarely occasioned more intimate relations at least prior to World War I. In fact, distinctively aristocratic and bourgeois patterns of investments, marriage partners, professions, residences, and life styles all point to the persistence of parallel but socially separate elites in the region.

MINGLING IN THE PUBLIC REALM

The turbulent years of the late 1840s appear to have marked a watershed in relations between the titled nobility and other segments of Piedmont's educated and propertied classes. With the introduction of the *Statuto* and additional egalitarian legal reforms in the early 1850s, the anti-aristocratic rhetoric that had so captured the attention of contemporary observers in 1848–1949 largely disappeared from public discourse. Indeed, the very distinction between noble and bourgeois, which had been such a fundamental issue during the Restoration, no longer received much attention at all in the second half of the century either in the political debates or in the popular press.

Changes in rhetoric accurately mirrored certain shifting realities of state organization and public life. Much like the old privileged classes elsewhere on the Italian peninsula, those Piedmontese aristocrats who did not wish to withdraw completely from the public realm had little choice but to recognize and associate with their fellow citizens on terms

[1] See Carpi, *L'Italia vivente*, p. 52.

[2] Villari, *Italian Life*, p. 17. Foreign commentators like Roberto Michels tended to agree with Villari, stressing the comparative weakness of social distinctions in Italy. See R. Michels, *Il proletariato e la borghesia nel movimento socialista italiano* (Turin, 1908), pp. 298–310.

[3] See Introduction, pp. 3–5.

of relative equality in the decades after 1848. To begin with, the growing size and complexity of the Savoyard state entailed a level of expertise and professionalism that unavoidably required officials from an aristocratic background to work with men recruited from the middle classes. This progressive mingling of patrician and plebeian was nowhere more strikingly evident than in the army officers corps. As we have seen in Chapter 4, this last bastion of the nobility had become a predominantly bourgeois institution, at least in its social composition, by the last decades of the nineteenth century.[4]

The special status that the military enjoyed within the Piedmontese aristocracy meant that a commission in the cavalry or artillery made it easier for middle-class men to overcome caste barriers and engage in more intimate forms of sociability with members of the old nobility. In Turin they were incorporated into the ceremonies and social rituals of the city's high society and ducal court life, provided of course that they had the suitable income and manners. Dashing young officers were a necessary presence at the costume balls, charitable benefits, and solemn state occasions that marked Turin's winter season. Cavalry officers of non-noble origins enjoyed additional social opportunities in the spring and fall through their participation in the favorite sports of the old titled elite. While Marchese Mario Incisa della Rocchetta insisted that fencing was "the only sport played by 'gentlemen' and officers," equestrian sports and hunting parties probably afforded the most important occasions for extensive interaction.[5]

Middle-class officers could meet and have regular contact with their aristocratic colleagues not only in military schools, barracks, and playing fields, but also in more leisurely and informal settings. Incisa della Rocchetta recalled that prior to World War I there were a number of tables at the fashionable Caffè Fiorio in Turin that "were in tacit but uncontested possession of the 'clan' of cavalry officers, a few men from artillery admitted 'ad personam' and their carefully selected friends."[6]

Shared experiences in the officers corp could provide the basis for lasting friendships and social contacts between bourgeois and aristocrats as the experience of Giovanni Agnelli indicates. The future giant of the Italian automobile industry began his public life as an officer in the cavalry in the late 1880s, where he established solid ties with young nobles like Count Giulio Figarolo Tarino di Gropello, with whom he first discussed his entrepreneurial aspirations. The social connections

---

[4] See Chapter 4.
[5] Incisa della Rocchetta, "Impressioni e ricordi," pp. 161–163.
[6] *Ibid.*, pp. 165–166.

Agnelli made in the military paid off in the summer of 1899 when he joined with Count Emanuele Cacherano di Bricherasio, another cavalry officer and automobile enthusiast, and other men from the aristocratic and financial communities of Turin, to found Fiat.[7]

Nor was Agnelli's experience unique. In fact, the officer corps became the single most important path of access for non-nobles to the aristocratic Società del Whist and even to marriage into a titled family. The army furnished three times as many of the bourgeois members of the Whist as the other two fashionable professions, law and diplomacy, combined in the years between 1841 and 1915.[8] The relationships developed in the barracks and the Whist could lead in turn to visits to ancestral palaces and country homes that afforded introductions to other members of aristocratic families. Although hardly a commonplace, such encounters occasionally resulted in the most intimate form of social fusion with bourgeois officers actually becoming in-laws to some of Piedmont's oldest and most prominent lineages in the decades leading up to World War I.[9]

The officer corps also remained the primary institutional path for new men to official noble status in the second half of the nineteenth century. Although the king no longer ennobled on a regular basis bourgeois officers who had entered the high command of the army, the military service still represented an extremely valuable asset for aspirants to an hereditary title. Of the 106 new nobles created between 1861 and 1915 whose professions can be identified, 38 or more than a third came from the ranks of the officers corps. The army appears to have lost little of its importance in this respect with the passage of time. On the contrary, in the last decade and a half before World War I, the king ennobled fifteen military men.[10]

The army officers corps, however, represented only the tip of the iceberg of new shared experiences linking the titled nobility to the propertied, educated middle classes. The dismantling of the old absolutist regime and its hierarchical, corporative bodies opened the way to an

---

[7] See Biscaretti di Ruffia, *Il cinquantesimo anniversario*, pp. 37–41.

[8] Of the 106 bourgeois members of the Whist before 1915, 44 were army officers. See Società Cavour, *Un secolo di vita*, pp. 111–218.

[9] A partial list of the families with a bourgeois son-in-law in the officers corps included the Biscaretti di Ruffia, Cacherano di Bricherasio, Castellani Varzi de'Merlani, Del Carretto di Moncrivello, Gozani di San Giorgio, Lovera di Maria, Martini di Cigala, Mella Arborio, and Morozzo della Rocca di Brianze, Ripa Buscetti di Meana, Rovasenda di Rovasenda, and Tornielli-Bellini. See Manno, *Il patriziato subalpino*, vols. I–XXVI.

[10] See Cardoza, "Ennoblement," pp. 600–601 and "An officer and a gentleman," p. 196.

extraordinary flowering of voluntary associational activity that progressively structured public life in the urban centers of Italy during the second half of the nineteenth century. These years witnessed in Turin the founding of an array of new philanthropic and charitable societies, cultural institutions, sports and recreational clubs, and economic interest-group associations. By 1900, the *Guida di Torino* listed more than fifty societies working on behalf of hospitals, the poor, sick, and dying; over twenty recreational clubs that promoted everything from chess and bee keeping to tennis, cycling, and football; and at least another dozen institutions concerned with maintaining the city's museums and monuments or promoting the fine arts.[11]

Individuals from all segments of the local propertied classes sat side by side on the boards and jointly participated in the activities of these organizations. The Turinese women's section of the Italian Red Cross, for instance, brought together *grand dames* from some of Piedmont's oldest aristocratic families like the D'Oncieux de la Batie and Luserna di Rorà with the matrons of leading financial and manufacturing families such as the De Fernex, Denina, and Geisser. Likewise, the twin passions of Arturo Ceriana, a member of one of the city's top banking families, for classical music and horse racing led him to sit on the boards of both the Società di Concerti and the Società per le Corse di Cavalli where he came into regular contact with not only Giuseppe Engelfred, heir to a larger manufacturing and real estate fortune, but also the prominent, old-line aristocrats Count Emanuele Cacherano di Bricherasio, Marchese Giovanni Guasco di Bisio, and Marchese Fernando Scarampi di Villanova. In this fashion, these voluntary associations encouraged the development of new social configurations based less on ascriptive status than on shared interests and enthusiasms.[12]

Steadily widening access for the children of merchants, industrialists, and bankers to the educational opportunities afforded by elite Catholic schools represented a potentially more powerful instrument of aristocratic–bourgeois cohesion; here students from all segments of the propertied classes received a set of early, common educational and social experiences. From their founding in the middle decades of the nineteenth century, these institutions depended upon the patronage not only of the old titled elites, but also of leading bourgeois families. As a result, wealth as much as birth came to guide the admissions policies of the schools whose doors were open to boys from all segments of the

---

[11] See *La guida commerciale ed amministrativa di Torino, 1900* (Turin, 1901), pp. 489–545, 559–678.

[12] For lists of board members, see *ibid*.

propertied or "civilized" classes. In the case of both the Jesuit Istituto Sociale and the Collegio S. Giuseppe, aristocratic youths never accounted for more than a small percentage of the total enrollments. Even the most socially exclusive of the academies, the Royal Carlo Alberto College, was drawing the majority of its students in the last quarter of the century from bourgeois landed, professional, and business families. This often meant that, from as early as the age of ten, young nobles lived in close and virtually constant contact with affluent middle-class boys, sharing classrooms, living spaces, and the rituals of life in boarding school.[13]

Physical presence in the same institutional spaces, however, did not automatically translate into genuine social mixing. As the work of Gary Wray McDonogh on the "good families" of Barcelona has shown, the presence of middle-class students in elite schools can just as easily confirm as erase social distinctions and boundaries. Giovanni Agnelli's recollections of his time in the least aristocratic of the local private schools, the Collegio San Giuseppe, strongly suggests that the former was the case in Turin. Despite his respectable background as the son of a wealthy landowner, Agnelli found as a student there in the 1880s that "the majority of the boys, being nobles, were not permitted to greet someone who was not one."[14] Social distance was thus expressed not only in the differences between institutions, but also in the hierarchies within each institution that limited meaningful contact between students. Even stronger reservations could be advanced regarding the social impact of the voluntary associations which afforded considerably less constant and intimate contacts between nobles and other segments of the propertied classes.

Where the possibilities of real social mingling did exist, as was the case in the army officer corps and the Società del Whist, it tended to take place on terms that reenforced the role of the old titled families as arbiters of elite conduct, education, and modes of consumption. Acceptance within these institutional settings tended to require non-nobles to accept and imitate aristocratic values and life-styles. Aristocratic models of comportment, for instance, continued to inform the etiquette manuals that were designed to guide middle-class officers in their dealings outside of the garrisons.[15] The same officers were also expected to follow an unwritten code of honor that found its most

---

[13] See Chapter 4 for information on the social composition of the student bodies of the three leading elite schools in Piedmont.

[14] See Agnelli, *Vestivamo alla marinara*, p. 79. For the elite schools in Barcelona, see McDonogh, *Good Families of Barcelona*, pp. 122–126.

[15] See Mazzonis, "Usi della buona società," pp. 229–253.

dramatic expression in the enduring knightly custom of the duel. In his memoirs, Marchese Mario Incisa della Rocchetta recalled how in his youth in the opening decades of the twentieth century duels still typically took place between gentlemen, "namely between recognized and esteemed members of the only category that 'counted' then: officers and people who lived from rents." Aristocratic traditions rather than considerations of military professionalism continued to dictate appropriate behavior in settling "questions of honor." Officers who engaged in duels faced immediate arrest, but those who refused to fight, Incisa claimed, "were compelled to resign from their position and even from their profession."[16]

A similar pattern of adaptation and emulation characterized the social mixing that took place within the Società del Whist. Most of the tiny minority of bourgeois members seemed to have gained acceptance to the club by embracing the dominant values and pastimes of the aristocratic majority. Much as in the case of his noble colleagues, wealth alone was decidedly not the key to an untitled gentleman's admission into the Whist. Of the eighty-one wealthiest bourgeois men in the probate survey, those with estates valued at over L. 1 million, only two were ever members of the Whist. Both of them were sons of members who were distinguished less by their enormous wealth than by great landed status in one case and by marriage into a prestigious Milanese aristocratic family in the other.[17]

A bourgeois gentleman's involvement in certain "honorable" occupations appears to have counted for more than wealth in the eyes of club men. As we have already seen, the special prestige and status enjoyed by the officers corps within the Piedmontese nobility made the military profession the single most important avenue of access to the Whist for the untitled before 1914. Those bourgeois members without a military background were most often "men of the world" (uomini del mondo) who divided their time between philanthropic activities and leisured events such as hunts and races.[18]

---

[16] Incisa della Rocchetta, "Impressioni e ricordi," pp. 161–163. Mazzonis, "Usi della buona società," pp. 249–253 provides a fuller discussion of the meaning of questions of honor and duels in the Italian military.

[17] The two wealthy bourgeois members in the survey were Cesare Vitale and Giuseppe Engelfred. At the time of his death in 1906, Vitale left a landed estate of 615 hectares in the province of Cuneo. Engelfred, one of the six wealthiest individuals in my survey, was married to N. D. Beatrice Falcò dei Principi Pio di Savoia. See URST, 1906, b. 700, f. 39 and 1912, b. 824, f. 22.

[18] See Società Cavour, Un secolo di vita, pp. 111–218; 45 of the 105 untitled members had a military background, 12 were lawyers and 8 belonged to the diplomatic corps, while 20 were designated as "uomini del mondo."

As the cases of the officers corps and the Società del Whist attest, what little social mingling that did take place was on terms that favored the aristocratic element. For their part, the old titled families did not display much of a corresponding willingness to embrace or emulate the behavior and pastimes associated with the emerging new elites of industry and commerce. The old nobility's reluctance to adapt contributed significantly to maintaining social distance between the two elites, and thus to limiting the process of aristocratic–bourgeois fusion in Piedmont prior to World War I.

THE LIMITS OF ECONOMIC INTERPENETRATION

Georg Simmel observed in 1908 how "the full measure of the elegance and exclusiveness" of the nobility's situation lay not so much in their exclusive privileges as in what was "forbidden" to them. Simmel chose as his primary example "the prohibition on trading that runs through the whole history of the nobility."[19] Accordingly, one way of measuring the merging of old and new elites involves looking at the degree to which men from aristocratic families were prepared to abandon their traditional caste prejudices and become involved in the business world. In the case of England, for instance, F. M. L. Thompson has argued that the agricultural crisis of the late nineteenth century triggered a fundamental shift in the outlook of the aristocracy and gentry toward wealth generated by non-landed sources. As agricultural incomes fell, wealthy landowners began to depend increasingly upon the profits of urban real estate and their investments in joint-stock companies. This shift coincided with a massive influx of peers on to the boards of directors of these companies. In Thompson's view, such developments encouraged a growing identity of outlook and interest between landowners and businessmen, paving the way for aristocratic alliances with wealthy new families.[20]

Case studies of various prominent Tuscan, Roman, and Genoese aristocratic families have led students of Italian history to argue that a similar process of economic interpenetration was taking place in the peninsula in the second half of the nineteenth century. One of the wealthiest titled families on the peninsula, the Corsini, liquidated most of their old prestige investments in the decades after unification and instead became heavily involved in railroad development and high finance. Significantly, this major change in investment strategy coincided with the

[19] Simmel, "The Nobility," pp. 201–203.
[20] See Thompson, *English Landed Society*, pp. 299–307.

Corsini forging marital alliances with two of Italy's leading banking families, the Bastogi and Fenzi.[21] The same years saw Baron Bettino Ricasoli follow a like path with substantial investments in agricultural processing and marketing operations as well as in railroad companies, investments that brought the Florentine aristocrat into close contact with the banker Pietro Bastogi. By the time of his death in the late 1870s, Ricasoli's portfolio of stocks and bonds had grown dramatically, accounting for about a third of his estate.[22] Great Roman aristocratic landowners such as Prince Paolo Borghese and Prince Don Prospero Colonna also came to rely increasingly on non-landed sources of income and to expand their activities in the business world. Financial investments and urban rents surpassed rural estates in importance for Prince Borghese in the last decades of the century; by the 1890s they were providing the bulk of his family's revenues. On the eve of World War I, Prince Colonna chaired the board of a large chemical company and sat on the board of another firm engaged in real estate development. These initiatives paled in comparison to the activities of the Genoese patrician, Marchese Giacomo Durazzo Pallavicini, who presided over the boards of five joint-stock companies: two in mining, one each in the metallurgical, automotive, and real estate sectors.[23]

On the surface, the early history of the automobile industry suggests that a similar process of aristocratic infiltration into the business world took place in Piedmont at the turn of the century. From the outset, men from a few prominent titled families were heavily involved in this new sector of production. In fact, the key figure, along with Giovanni Agnelli, in the launching of Turin's automotive industry was the scion of one of Piedmont's older aristocratic lineages, Count Emanuele Cacherano di Bricherasio. It was Count Emanuele who first advanced in February 1899 the idea of building a modern new industrial complex. In the ensuing months, he took the initiative in establishing relations with banking interests and in rounding up a group of wealthy investors. Appropriately, the elegant Bricherasio palace provided the setting for the official founding of the Fabbrica Italiana Automobile di Torino or Fiat in July of the same year. Count Emanuele not only served as the first vice-president of the company's board of directors, but also

[21] See Moroni, "Le ricchezze dei Corsini," 79–106; Coppini, "Aristocrazia e finanza in Toscana," pp. 297–332.

[22] See Biagioli, "Vicende e fortuna di Ricasoli imprenditore," pp. 77–102.

[23] For changes in the distribution of the Borghese family's annual revenues, see Pescosolido, Terra e nobiltà, pp. 304–305. For information on the positions held by both Colonna and Durazzo Pallavicini, see Credito Italiano, Società Italiane per Azioni: Notizie Statistiche, 1916 (Rome, 1917).

supplied the land that was initially chosen as the site for the new factory.[24] Nor was Cacherano di Bricherasio alone. Count Roberto Biscaretti di Ruffia was also a founding partner and member of the board, while the ranks of early stockholders in Fiat and other local automobile companies included more than a dozen titled nobles.[25]

Aristocratic enthusiasm for the automobile, however, did not necessarily signify undiluted acceptance of capitalist, profit-oriented attitudes on the part of the nobles involved. For the most part, men like Cacherano di Bricherasio and Biscaretti di Ruffia were essentially dilettantes whose commitment to the automobile sector expressed less a burgeoning entrepreneurial spirit than a fascination with sports in general and the racing car, in particular, as a new source of adventure and leisurely diversion. Count Emanuele, who seems to have viewed the automobile as an extension of his equestrian interests, quickly emerged as an advocate of high-performance sports cars, while Biscaretti's interest grew out of his own direct participation in an automobile race between Turin and Alessandria in 1898. Not surprisingly, this sporting attitude did not translate into an enduring commitment to corporate life. By 1908, the names of old-line nobles had disappeared from the board of directors of Fiat.[26]

More importantly, the involvement of blue bloods in the automobile industry, such as it was, appears to have been the exception rather than the rule. Indeed, the composition of boards of directors, the minutes of stockholders' meetings and other corporate organizational proceedings all confirm that the worlds of finance and industry continued to be largely alien territories to Piedmont's aristocratic families in the second half of the nineteenth century. Much as in the case of the old patrician families of Milan, the security of their landed incomes and the paucity of non-agricultural sources of revenue on their estates reinforced traditional caste prejudices to keep them away.

Few aristocrats from the region followed Prince Corsini's path into the realm of high finance. The names of a mere fifteen Piedmontese nobles appear in the survey recently carried out by Alessandro Polsi of

---

[24] See Biscaretti di Ruffia, "Origini, nascita," pp. 37–39 and Castronovo, *Giovanni Agnelli*, pp. 10–11. Zoning problems led the board to drop its plans to buy Bricherasio's property and instead to purchase a plot of land elsewhere in the city, owned by the newly ennobled Peracca family. See *I primi quindici anni della Fiat*, vol. i, pp. 67–89.

[25] See Castronovo, *Storia del Piemonte*, p. 187n. For the activities of Biscaretti di Ruffia, see Biscaretti di Ruffia, *I cinquantesimo anniversario*, pp. 39–40.

[26] On the attitudes of Cacherano di Bricherasio and Biscaretti di Ruffia, see *I cinquantesimo anniversario*, pp. 37–40 and *I primi quindici anni della Fiat*, vol. i, p. 80 and vol. ii, pp. 450–451.

all major investors (over L. 10,000) in Italian joint-stock banks founded in the quarter century from 1853 to 1878, and most of them did not have particularly extensive investments. Moreover, the three men with a substantial involvement in more than one bank – Baron Ernesto Casana, Marchese Paolo Solaroli di Briona, and Baron Ignazio Weil-Weiss – were, in fact, from newly ennobled banking families.[27] The only financial institution in which aristocrats played a prominent role was the Cassa di Risparmio. Between the 1850s and World War I, titled families like the Alfieri di Sostegno, Thaon di Revel, and Valperga di Masino furnished all but one of the presidents and twenty-two of the Cassa's directors. Their presence, however, was more a reflection of the bank's philanthropic traditions than of any entrepreneurial enthusiasm on the part of the nobility.[28]

Aristocratic gentlemen were no more likely to be found on the boards or among the major stockholders of Turin's joint-stock companies in the last two decades of the century. In 1884, for instance, the names of only sixteen old-line nobles appeared in the public records concerning business activity in the city of Turin. These few titled corporate directors and stockholders tended to shun the more dynamic and modern sectors of local industry and to concentrate instead in two older and well-established areas: insurance and public utilities. Thus, more than a dozen prominent nobles sat on the general council of the Royal Company for Insurance against Fire, while the board of the local water company was chaired by Marchese Vittorio Del Carretto and included among its directors Count Cesare Valperga di Masino, Marchese Luigi Cisa di Gresy, and Count Alessandro Pernati di Momo. Conversely, the names of only two nobles appear as major stockholders in railroad companies in 1884; none show up in the documents relating to textiles, metallurgy, chemicals, or the machine industry. The same pattern of marginal aristocratic involvement in business enterprises continued into the 1890s. In 1894, just thirteen old-line nobles appear to have been actively involved in the city's companies, and they were concentrated almost exclusively in one insurance company and two public utilities firms.[29]

---

[27] Alessandro Polsi kindly furnished me with a list of Piedmontese nobles based on his ongoing research on major stockholders in Italian joint-stock banks. His list included some nineteen individuals, but four of them were residents in Turin from other regions. Weil-Weiss was a big investor in five banks, Solaroli in three, and Casana in two. On the reluctance of the Milanese patriciate to become involved in industrial activities, see Zanetti, *La demografia del patriziato milanese*, pp. 42–44.

[28] See *La Cassa di Risparmio*, pp. xxxvii–xxxxv, for a list of officers and directors.

[29] AST, Sez. Riunite, Atti di Società, 1884, vols. I–VI and 1894, vols. I–VI bis. On the prominent role of aristocrats in the Royal Company for Mutual Insurance, see the brochure in AST, Sez. Riunite, Archivio Thaon di Revel, b. 112.

At first glance, the extraordinary industrial take-off that began to transform Turin in the following decade and a half does seem to have sparked a dramatically expanding involvement of Piedmontese nobles in the corporate world. By 1905, the number of titled gentlemen sitting on company boards or in assemblies of stockholders had tripled. Furthermore, they could now be found in what were becoming some of the most dynamic industrial sectors. Count Edoardo Barel di Sant'Albano, for example, was the fourth largest stockholder in the Itala automobile company as well as a founding partner and major stockholder in the Società Anonima Carrozzeria Automobile Alessio and a director of the S.A. Industrie Metallurgiche Torino, while Count Paolo Costa della Trinità, patriarch of one of the oldest and wealthiest feudal families in the province of Cuneo, chaired the board of the Navigazione Alta Italia, sat on the board of the Società Veneziana di Navigazione a Vapore, and was the sixth largest stockholder in the Cantiere Navale di Muggiano.[30]

Yet a closer examination of corporate boards and lists of large stockholders or officials of trade associations during the Giolittian era reveals a persistent reluctance on the part of the established aristocratic families to participate in the business world. The great majority of titled corporate directors and stockholders, and virtually all of those from the old-line families like Count Ernesto Balbo Bertone di Sambuy and Marchese Maurizio Luserna di Rorà, still limited their activities to the traditional sectors of insurance, public utilities, mining, and food processing. A few other nobles became early investors in more glamorous, but marginal enterprises involving the performing arts. Count Guido Arnaldi di Balme and Alessandro Canera di Salasco, for example, were founding partners and the two largest stockholders in the Società Generale Italiano il "Cinematografo" in 1905. But on the whole, it was recently ennobled banking and business families like the Rebaudengo, Boarelli, and Ceriana-Mayneri who furnished the nobles actively involved in the newer and more dynamic sectors of heavy industry.[31] Old-line nobles were no more likely to be found serving as officers or sitting on the boards of Turin's leading commercial and industrial interest-group associations. In 1900, not a single noble was acting in an

---

[30] *Ibid.*, Sez. Riunite, Atti di Società, 1905, vols. I–IV for names of aristocratic directors and major stockholders. See Credito Italiano, *Società Italiane per azioni. Notizie statistiche, 1914* (Rome, 1915) for Costa della Trinità's role in the shipping sector.

[31] AST, Sez. Riunite, Atti di Società, 1905, vols. I–XI, and 1914, vols. I–VI. For additional information on the role of Piedmontese nobles in 1914, see Credito Italiano, *Società per Azioni, 1914*, which lists thirty-six Piedmontese nobles as being on corporate boards.

official capacity within the Chamber of Commerce, the Società Promotore dell'Industria Nazionale, the Lega Industriale e Commerciale Torinese, the Confederazione fra Industriali e Commercianti, or the Associazione dell'Industria Meccanica.[32]

The aristocratic investment patterns that emerge from the probate records and local tax rolls provide additional proof of the relative social distance from the business world that Piedmont's old-line nobles steadfastly maintained in the late nineteenth and early twentieth centuries. As the tables in Chapter 3 illustrate, investments by rich aristocrats in personal assets, and stocks and bonds in particular, were considerably smaller than those of other affluent non-noble groups, both as a factor in their own estates and as a contribution to the total wealth of Turin's wealthy upper classes in the decades from 1862 to 1912. More than a third (35.7 percent) of the top aristocratic wealth holders in probate left less than L. 1,000 in stocks and bonds; only nine nobles possessed over L. 500,000 in such assets at the time of their death.[33]

The rolls of the municipal tax on *ricchezza mobile* or personal income, which provide another window on the business community in Turin in the first years of the new century, tell a similar story. They show that in 1903, for instance, a total of 370 individuals or businesses had declared personal incomes that exceeded L. 1500. Heading this list were the leading cotton manufacturers, Mazzonis (L. 205,000) and Wild and Abbegg (L. 181,670), followed by the liquor distiller, Martini and Rossi (L. 162,000), and the military supplier Giovanni Gilardini (L. 112,044).[34] The same list included the names of only twenty-two nobles, half of whom were women. All but six of these titled individuals had declared taxable incomes below L. 10,000. Of the top six, three owed their personal income to marital ties to wealthy bourgeois families. Two of the other three, Count Felice Rignon and Baron Ignazio Weil-Weiss, came from banking families ennobled in the middle of the nineteenth century, while the third, Adolfo Baudi di Selve, had a lucrative legal practice. For their part, the wealthy old titled families were mostly absent from the personal income tax rolls.[35]

The experiences of more adventurous nobles like Count Giuseppe d'Harcourt and Count Carlo Beraudo di Pralormo in the rough and tumble world of industry did little to encourage a shift in aristocratic attitudes. In the mid-1870s, Count d'Harcourt, who already possessed a sizeable fortune based primarily on real estate and money lending,

---

[32] See *Guida di Torino, 1900*, pp. 707–780.
[33] See Chapter 4 as well as Cardoza, "La ricchezza e i ricchi," pp. 299–340.
[34] ACT, "Imposta sulla Ricchezza Mobile, 1903."   [35] *Ibid.*

became involved with the industrialist Giuseppe Allemano, owner of a machine factory in Turin.[36] An initial loan to Allemano of L. 250,000 by the wealthy noble in 1875 led to more intimate collaboration three years later when the two formed a partnership jointly to operate the factory and market its products. According to the terms of their agreement, d'Harcourt furnished an additional L. 200,000 in capital and handled the finances of the company, while Allemano supplied the plant and equipment, and managed the processes of production. In exchange for his already substantial investment, Count Giuseppe was supposed to get all the net profits of the company; Allemano was to receive only a salary of L. 6,000 per year. Within months it became clear that d'Harcourt had made a very unwise commitment. He had to provide more of his own capital to pay off Allemano's debts assumed by the partnership, while according to his lawyer "not a dime (un soldo) of profit entered into the [company] coffers."[37] Although d'Harcourt moved quickly to dissolve the partnership in March 1879, he had already invested nearly three-quarters of a million lire with virtually no return, a figure that climbed to over a million by the end of that year. Allemano's reluctance to honor his obligations resulted in a court case that dragged on for years and provided the aristocrat with only partial compensation. As late as the mid-1880s, d'Harcourt had still not recovered over L. 400,000 that he had put into the industrial venture.[38]

Two decades later, Count Carlo Beraudo di Pralormo suffered proportionately greater losses because of his overly enthusiastic forays into the stock market. The largest single landowner in the commune of Pralormo in the 1860s, Count Carlo began to liquidate his estate, farm by farm, to his tenants between 1881 and 1909. While he retained his family's ancestral castle overlooking the village, his rural properties were reduced to one-fifth of what they had been in 1860. Enthralled by the new investment opportunities in industry, Beraudo di Pralormo used the capital from these sales to amass an impressive and diversified portfolio that included shares in a number of textile, railroad, shipping, and sugar refining companies which accounted for nearly half of all his assets in early 1907. Unfortunately for his heirs, Count Carlo underestimated the risks of the stock market and suffered heavy losses as a result of the financial crisis of 1907. The value of his portfolio, which was worth

---

[36] In 1867, d'Harcourt had a gross income of L. 107,604, with the largest portion coming from apartment buildings in the city of Turin. See AST, Sez. Riunite, Archivio D'Harcourt, b. 74, f. 13, "Consegne dei reditti, 1867.

[37] Ibid., Sez. Riunite, Archivio D'Harcourt, b. 74, f. 29, "Causa sommaria del appello commerciale, 1879."

[38] Ibid., Sez. Riunite, Archivio D'Harcourt, b. 95, f. 8, b. 96 f. 13.

L. 416,899 at the time of purchase, collapsed; his heirs estimated its value at under L. 250,000 after his death in 1909.[39]

Significantly, the nobility's marginal involvement in the worlds of industry and commerce was matched in the last decades of the nineteenth century by a growing reluctance on the part of the rich bourgeoisie to invest in land, the Piedmontese aristocracy's traditional source of wealth and status. As the survey of probate records shows, bourgeois investments in rural properties, which were already comparatively modest in the first years after Italian unification, provided a steadily shrinking share of the total value of estates possessed by rich non-nobles in the ensuing decades. In the period after 1900, a full quarter of the wealthiest bourgeois in probate left no landed assets at all. Conversely, the place of stocks and bonds in their fortunes grew steadily in importance, so that by the last decade before the war such assets accounted for three-quarters of the value of the personalty owned by rich non-nobles.[40]

These contrasting patterns of investment and productive activity indicate that, in one of the pillars of Italy's industrial triangle, no great convergence of economic interests or outlook had come to link the old nobility with the newer business elites in the decades before World War I. Indeed, the material interests of the two may well have become even more divergent in the late nineteenth century. Despite the host of new challenges and opportunities that emerged in the years after 1880, the composition of the nobility's fortunes and their role in the region's economic life remained considerably more traditional than those of other segments of the wealthy propertied classes. Much as in the past, the bulk of aristocratic wealth in Piedmont stayed solidly rooted in the countryside and in inherited landownership, while most titled gentlemen continued to eschew any significant personal involvement in business activities. Conversely, the same years also witnessed the transformation of Turin's bourgeoisie from a class of largely propertied rentiers to one composed increasingly of entrepreneurs and merchants actively involved in industry, commerce, and finance.[41] The resulting

---

[39] Information on land sales and stock holdings are contained in the *Archivio privato Beraudo di Pralormo* which is in the possession of the family. I am grateful to Count Filippo Beraudo di Pralormo for the opportunity to consult his family's papers.

[40] In the period 1862–1873, rural property accounted for 26 percent of the total value of grand bourgeois wealth in probate. That figure fell to 18 percent the following decade, and to 13 percent in the period 1901–1912. Stocks and bonds, which provided 15 percent of bourgeois wealth in the decade after unification, contributed 38 percent of the total value in the period after 1900. Cardoza, "La ricchezza e i ricchi," pp. 297–340.

[41] See *ibid.*, pp. 319–328 for data on the composition of aristocratic fortunes and the occupational distribution of wealthy non-nobles who passed through probate.

absence of much real contact on corporate boards or in stockholders' assemblies delayed the development of new affinities and thereby helped to perpetuate the social distance between the old titled aristocracy and the upper bourgeoisie.

LINEAGE, WEALTH, AND INTERMARRIAGE

Anthropologists, social historians, and social theorists have long emphasized the importance of studying marriage patterns to understand changes in status hierarchies. As Weber expressed it, when marriages take place between groups, they are "the typical characteristics of mutual esteem among status equals; their absence signifies status differences."[42] Accordingly, one of the most reliable indicators of the social fusion of old and new elites is intermarriage: the degree to which established aristocratic families were prepared to accept the sons and daughters of wealthy industrialists, bankers, and merchants as suitable partners for their own children.[43]

In the case of the Piedmontese, contemporary observers insisted that even after the elimination of all legal privileges and distinctions after 1848, aristocratic prejudices against marrying outside the ranks of the old titled families remained very powerful. Count Charles Arrivabene, for example, saw little change in their mentality in the early 1860s:

> The proud aristocracy of the Piedmontese capital, far from mixing with the commonality, as in other Italian towns, does not associate or marry with any lower class. A Turinese . . . nobleman would think himself humiliated were his daughter to marry a gentleman without title. With few exceptions, the nobility of Turin are very bigoted . . . [44]

Echoing these sentiments the following decade, Leandro Carpi praised those Piedmontese nobles who "honor the new aristocracy of talent that is emerging from all social classes," but concluded that "unfortunately . . . the number of these is still restricted and not enough to allow individual merit to outshine caste."[45]

On the whole, the available quantitative evidence provided by the probate records and published genealogies for the period 1862–1912 confirms the impressions of contemporary observers about the strongly endogamous tendencies of the Piedmontese nobility. In a period when

---

[42] Weber, *From Max Weber*, p. 300.
[43] For a fuller discussion of the issue of marriage patterns and intermarriage, see Stone and Fawtier Stone, *An Open Elite?*, pp. 156–157.
[44] Arrivabene, *Italy under Victor Emanuel*, vol. I, p. 17.
[45] Carpi, *L'Italia vivente*, p. 151.

Table 5.1 *Aristocratic marriages*
(all married nobles)

Spouse's Social Status	Number	Percentage
Piedmontese nobility	382	68
Non-Piedmontese nobility	63	11
Bourgeoisie	117	21
Totals	562	100

Table 5.2 *Aristocratic lineage and endogamy*
(all married nobles: 1862–1885, 1901–1912)

Lineage of spouse	Pre-1722 (%)	Post-1722 (%)	Restoration (%)	New nobility (%)
Nobility				
Pre-1722	62 (197)	26 (41)	16 (13)	0 (0)
Post-1722	10 (31)	35 (54)	19 (15)	5 (1)
Restoration	2 (7)	8 (12)	15 (12)	10 (2)
New	1 (3)	1 (1)	1 (1)	10 (2)
Non-piedmontese	13 (41)	11 (17)	6 (5)	5 (1)
Bourgeois	12 (37)	20 (31)	43 (34)	70 (14)
Totals	100	101	100	100

it became more usual for young aristocrats elsewhere on the peninsula to marry outside of their class, the pattern of the Piedmontese remained quite traditional.[46] As the data indicate (Table 5.1), the substantial majority of all married nobles who passed through probate after 1862 honored the traditions of caste by finding their spouses within the ranks of titled families; barely a fifth wed non-nobles. Even this latter figure exaggerates the extent of intermarriage between old-line nobility and bourgeoisie, since it includes a large number of newly ennobled individuals who were themselves not fully accepted in more established aristocratic circles.

A more delineated analysis reveals significant variations in marital patterns and propensities within the nobility, above all between the *ancien régime* families and those who had acquired their titles in the nineteenth century (Table 5.2). The data that emerge from this table indicate first of all a strong correlation between aristocratic lineage and endogamy. On the one hand, those nobles whose families had acquired their titles

---

[46] See for example, Zanetti, "The Patriziato of Milan," pp. 745–760.

Table 5.3 *Nineteenth-century nobility: distribution of mixed marriages (by wealth group)*

Estate value	Restoration nobility (%)	Post-1861 nobility (%)
Less than 100,000	21	29
100,001–250,000	32	22
250,001–500,000	35	14
500,001–750,000	12	14
750,001–1 mill	0	0
More than 1 million	0	21
Totals	100	100

only in the nineteenth century accounted for a disproportionately large share of the mixed marriages in the survey. In fact, as a group, they were more likely to intermarry with non-nobles than with other aristocrats. Only in the case of the very richest individuals, who were also second-generation nobles, was there much variation in the selection of marital partners (Table 5.3). Such a propensity was, however, less a sign of aristocratic–bourgeois fusion than an indicator of the obstacles encountered by the newly ennobled in gaining social acceptance by established noble families. For the most part, alliances between old and new titled families were rare, suggesting that individuals, who lacked the requisite genealogical attributes to go along with their titles, found access to the inner circles of the aristocracy illusive.

The behavior of old-line families, on the other hand, revealed a considerably more traditional attitude toward intermarriage with non-nobles. As the data in Table 5.2 show, less than an eighth of the married individuals in the probate survey, who could trace their family's titles back before 1722, wed outsiders. In fact, richly pedigreed nobles were more likely to marry into titled families from other countries or other regions of Italy before they let a "commoner" into their midst. The Avogadro di Cerrione, for example, were linked by marriage to such prominent Milanese and Genoese patrician families as the Trotti Bentivoglio, Visconti d'Aragona, Durazzo, and Grimaldi.[47] This did not mean, of course, that there were not scions of distinguished old titled families who conformed to late-nineteenth-century stereotypes by marrying wealthy, but unpedigreed heiresses. Marchese Lodovico Della Chiesa di Cinzano could trace his family's titles back to the fourteenth

---

[47] See the family tree compiled by Lodovico Avogadro di Cerrione in the typescript "MS Avogadro" which the family has kindly allowed me to consult.

century, but ancient lineage did not prevent him from marrying the daughter of Baron Ignazio Weil-Weiss di Lainate, a rich and newly ennobled Jewish banker in 1870.[48] Still, in Piedmont, men like Marchese Lodovico were decidedly the exception. As a rule, the older its pedigree, the more likely a family was to eschew alliances with non-titled elements and instead to establish marital links with another aristocratic family of comparable antiquity.

The classic coalescence of new wealth and old status that characterized so much of late-nineteenth-century high society in Milan, Rome, and most European capitals appears to have been largely absent in Turin. If the people who passed through probate after 1862 are any indication, intermarriage between wealthy bourgeois and aristocrats continued to be a true rarity in the Piedmontese capital. Of the 125 richest non-nobles in my survey (with fortunes over L. 750,000), only 6 – 3 men and 3 women – forged marital alliances with noble families and none of these were with the old titled elite of wealth. Four of the noble families involved in these marriages had only gained their titled status in the nineteenth century or else came from outside Piedmont.[49] Nor did the situation change dramatically in the following generation. The children from these wealthy bourgeois families were not much more likely to marry into the nobility than their parents. My survey uncovered just fourteen cases of mixed marriages involving heirs of rich non-nobles. Such results strongly suggest that, in the absence of lineage, wealth alone still did not provide the social acceptance and high status that "good" marriages with old stock confirmed.

Economic considerations, however, appear to have played a prominent role in the calculations of that tiny minority of men and women from *ancien régime* aristocratic families who did break with tradition and wed outside their class (Table 5.4). Titled gentlemen from the wealthiest of these families virtually never married outside their caste; only three old-line nobles with estates over L. 750,000 had non-noble spouses. In sharp contrast to the pattern displayed by more recent nineteenth-century aristocrats, nearly two-thirds of the marriages linking old titled and bourgeois families involved relatively poor nobles who left estates under L. 100,000; a quarter of them had less than L. 20,000 in total assets at the time of their death.

[48] See Manno, *Il patriziato subalpino*, vol. VII.

[49] The seven individuals involved in mixed marriages were: Giuseppe Engelfred (Beatrice Falcò dei Principi Pio di Savoia, from Milan), Severino Grattoni (Delfina Baudi di Selve), Giovanni Racca (nob. Giuseppina Ceppi), Baroness Palmira Andreis (nee Molino), Countess Giuseppina Gallina (nee Vicino), and Countess Augusta Rosa Ricardi di Netro (nee Gattino).

Table 5.4 *Old nobility: mixed marriages*
(by wealth group)

Estate value	Pre-1722 nobility (%)	Post-1722 nobility (%)
Less than L. 100,000	60	61
100,001–250,000	27	23
250,001–500,000	5	10
500,001–750,000	3	3
750,001–1 mill.	3	3
More than 1 million	2	0
Totals	100	100

The marital patterns that emerge then from the probate and genealogical records indicate that the elimination of legal status distinctions and increased public interaction in the mid-nineteenth century did not lead to more intimate familial ties between most segments of the nobility and other sectors of Piedmont's propertied classes. Titled families continued to exchange marital partners with each other; mixed marriages remained more the exception than the rule in the second half of the century. When such marriages did take place, they tended to be confined to titled families of lesser status and prestige, due either to their relative poverty or to their lack of a sufficiently lengthy pedigree.

The meaning of this persistent endogamy is of course ambiguous. In part, it may have reflected the new self-confidence and social autonomy of the wealthy business elite that had little or no interest in being accepted. More likely, it attested to the stubborn refusal on the part of the Piedmontese nobility to treat even the wealthiest merchants and industrialists as social equals. But regardless of who rejected whom, the rarity of mixed marriages meant that aristocratic and bourgeois kinship networks continued to develop along quite distinct and mutually exclusive lines. As a result, the economic and social alliances and exchanges so vital to the consolidation of a dynamic and cohesive upper class remained relatively undeveloped in the late nineteenth century.

CULTIVATING DIFFERENCE: PATTERNS OF RESIDENCE AND DISPLAY

The social distance that continued to characterize relations between old and new elites in Piedmont found expression not only in the persistence of endogamous practices, but also in more symbolic ways involving distinctive life-styles, leisure-time activities, and patterns of sociability. Tastes and preferences displayed in these areas reflected important differences in values and attitudes within the propertied classes. Moreover, they acted as visible signs of distinction and social position that defined informal borders between old stock and new wealth.[50] Especially for a small group of rich titled magnates, high levels of expenditures on servants and carriages, traditional patterns of residence and the maintenance of dual residences, and a preference for country life helped to distinguish them from other equally wealthy elements of the propertied classes. At a purely social level, gentlemen's clubs, private parties and receptions, as well as vacation locales provided additional settings to display and reinforce the legally invisible barriers that separated old aristocratic families from the new fortunes being made in commerce and industry.

First of all, the upper tiers of the nobility who possessed the requisite resources still showed a stronger proclivity toward certain traditional forms of conspicuous display than other elements of the propertied classes in the decades leading up to World War I. Judging by the luxury taxes they paid, for example, the scions of titled houses were much more likely than rich industrialists to maintain a large staff of servants and a number of elegant carriages, which of course prominently displayed their family crests. In 1900, sixty-two of the seventy-six biggest contributors to the municipal tax on servants (those paying over L. 40) came from the ranks of the nobility. Their presence was even more dominant at the very highest levels. With Count Cesare Valperga di Masino heading the list, the eminent old-line aristocrats Count Ernesto Balbo Bertone di Sambuy, Marchese Emanuele Thaon di Revel di St. Andrea, Marchese Emanuele Coardi di Bagnasco, and Marchese Giuseppe Pallavicino-Mossi, together with the newer nobles Count Carlo Conelli de'Prosperi and Baron Ignazio Weil-Weiss di Lainate, accounted for all but one of top eight contributors (those paying L. 70 or more). Moreover, the only non-noble to compete with these titled gentlemen in this arena of display, Giuseppe Engelfred, embraced an aristocratic ethos in most other respects, through his marital ties with a Milanese titled family and through his status as a substantial landowner, member of the Società del Whist, and leading philanthropist. Generally, the few bourgeois families with large staffs of servants tended to be a part of the old business elite of Piedmont that had long emulated the nobility's patterns of conspicuous leisure.[51]

[50] See Lamont, *Money, Morals, and Manners*, pp. 174–187 and Charle, "Noblesse et élites," pp. 427–432.

[51] See ACT, Ruolo: tasse domestici, 1900. The original tax rolls for that year list alphabetically the names of 8,746 contributors who paid a total of L. 63,015. According to

Private carriages provided a more highly visible means of aristocratic display. In his memoirs, Count Giovanni Figarolo di Gropello recalled that rides in his family's carriages in the early years of the century were still surrounded with great pomp and ceremony. Count Giovanni was struck in particular by the constant presence of a coachman, dressed "in livery and truely very stylish." Whenever members of the family entered the carriage, he "did a 'present-arms' with his whip raised and held vertically in front of him."[52] Not surprisingly, many of the same blue bloods with large domestic staffs also featured prominently on the carriage tax rolls, where they accounted for three-quarters of the major contributors at the turn of the century.[53]

As the account books of Marchese Giuseppe Pallavicino-Mossi attest, luxury tax contributions represented only a small portion of the expenditures involved in maintaining an aristocratic family in the grand style. In the 1890s, when the annual salary of the most established managers in the cotton industry ranged from L. 4000 to L. 10,000, Pallavicino-Mossi spent on average over L. 4,000 per year on the physical upkeep of his family's palace in Turin, nearly L. 8,000 to stock its kitchen and wine cellars, about L. 5,700 on livery and servants, and another L. 2,300 on horses and carriages. All this came in addition to the expenses for the family's villa in Rivoli and the ancestral country house in the province of Vercelli.[54]

Such conspicuous expenditure and display was more than just a reflection of the substantial wealth of these families, whose patrimonies had in fact already been surpassed by new business fortunes; it was also an expression of their distinctively aristocratic values. As a result, the industrial "take-off" experienced by Turin in the opening years of the new century did not fundamentally alter these patterns. After a decade in which nearly two-thirds of the millionaires to pass through probate came from outside the ranks of the nobility, titled families still dominated Turin's luxury tax rolls in the last years before the war. In 1912, for instance, they accounted for two-thirds of the individuals paying more than L. 30 in servant taxes and nine of the top eleven contributors

the regulations enacted in 1898, the tax on each male domestic was L. 10, L. 5 for each female domestic. Doormen and servants hired specifically to care for the sick were excluded from the tax.

[52] "Diario dell'Ammiraglio di Divisione, Count Giovanni di Gropello," p. 5.

[53] ACT, "Ruolo: Tassa vetture private 1899." One-horse carriages paid a levy of L. 40, two-horse L. 50. Carriages emblazoned with a family coat-of-arms paid double.

[54] These estimates are based on data from AST, Sez. Riunite, Archivio Pallavicino-Mossi, b. 19, "Ragguaglio delle Entrate e delle Spese" for the years 1890, 1891, and 1892. On the salaries earned by managers in the cotton industry, see Romano, L'industria cotoniera lombarda, pp. 438–439.

(over L. 70). In a year in which Count Luigi Valperga di Masino and Count Eugenio De Genova di Pettinengo paid L. 80 and L. 90 respectively, the two leading figures in Turin's automobile industry, Giovanni Agnelli and Dante Ferraris, were each assessed a mere L. 20 for their considerably more modest domestic staffs.[55]

Wealthy nobles also did not hesitate to embrace the new form of luxury consumption represented by the automobile, which quickly supplanted the carriage as the preferred mode of transportation for the Turinese upper classes in the last years before the war. The Figarolo di Gropello family, for example, replaced their horses and carriages in 1911 with an elegant Fiat limousine that had a "convertible roof in the back" and sat five people, separated with fixed glass from the chauffeur "with whom one communicated by means of a small portable telephone."[56] A few prominent industrialists and bankers like Giovanni Battista Biglia and Luigi Marsaglia did show a new willingness to outspend their aristocratic counterparts in the consumption of luxury automobiles, but even in this arena twenty-seven of the thirty-six biggest contributors (over L. 100 annually) to the private vehicle tax were titled nobles in 1913.[57] Thus, the greater wealth enjoyed by successful businessmen did not seem to increase their inclination to compete with the titled nobility. At least in terms of these forms of luxury and display, the old and new elites remained socially distinct.

Changing elite residential patterns in the last decades before World War I created an additional obstacle to aristocratic–bourgeois fusion by physically accentuating the social distance between the nobility and the newly rich business class. These changes marked a decisive break from the previous era when most segments of the propertied classes had lived in close proximity to each other within the vertically stratified residential buildings of the old and relatively compact historical center of Turin. Virtually all the city's aristocratic palaces had been designed to generate at least some income from commercial leases on the ground floor and rental units on the higher floors, providing the owners in this fashion with prestige and profits. Well into the nineteenth century, Piedmont's most exclusive titled families as well as its leading bankers, manufacturers, and merchants were still concentrated in a zone surrounding the royal palace that could easy be traversed on foot in a half

---

[55] ACT, "Ruolo Tassa Domestici 1912." That year 10,224 individuals paid a total of L. 74,375. Out of this number 187 were assessed over L. 30 – 60 non-nobles and 127 nobles.

[56] "Diario Figarolo di Gropello," p. 21.

[57] *Ibid.*, "Ruolo tassa vetture private 1913." That year 320 people contributed L. 24,811. Of that total 36 paid assessments over L. 100, 27 nobles and 9 bourgeois.

hour. The family of Count Giuseppe d'Harcourt, for example, occupied the "noble floor" of the building they owned in via della Provvidenza, but leased out spacious apartments on the floors immediately above theirs to the families of the bankers Giuseppe Bolmida and Giuseppe Arduino.[58] The residential intermingling of old and new elites, however, became increasingly less common in the decades before World War I.

The rapid expansion of the city in the late nineteenth century ushered in an era of significant change both in the form and location of the residences of Turin's prosperous bourgeoisie. Indeed, the last years of the century witnessed an exodus of wealthy business families from apartments in the historical center of the city toward newly developed neighborhoods on the periphery like the Crocetta, where many of them constructed their own imposing mansions. By 1914, this exodus was well under way as a sample study of the residences of thirty wealthy businessmen and industrial leaders in the last decade before the war reveals. All but four of these men lived outside of the old historical center, most having made the move to the newly fashionable Crocetta district. In this area of broad avenues and spacious mansions could be found on the eve of war the addresses of the better part of Turin's business elite. The key figures in the Lega Industriale di Torino and the Confederazione Italiana dell'Industria, Luigi Craponne-Bonnefon and Gino Olivetti, the banker and insurance executive Eugenio Pollone, the automotive executive Dante Ferraris, the distiller Enrico Cora, and the textile magnates Rodolfo De Planta, Napoleone Leumann, and Emilio Wild all had homes in the Crocetta.[59]

The most prominent elements of the aristocracy did not participate in this exodus and were thus largely absent from these elegant new neighborhoods before World War I. The great majority of old–line titled families continued to live in what amounted to Turin's aristocratic quarter, an area encompassing a small number of streets like Via della Rocca, Via Bogino, and Via Cavour as well as the elegant piazzas San Carlo, Maria Teresa, and Bodino, all in close proximity to the old royal palace. In the last decade before the war, for example, 70 percent of the membership of the Società del Whist and virtually all the heads of the

---

[58] AST, Sez. Riunite, Archivio d'Harcourt, b. 67, f. 7, lists of tenants at via della Provvidenza, 31.

[59] This sample included the largest non–noble contributors to the luxury tax rolls in 1907 and 1912 as well as the list of the leadership of the top industrial associations in the city in 1913, published in *La guida, 1913*, pp. 1174–1175. For similar developments in Germany, see Augustine, "Arriving in the upper class."

old families had their primary residence in this zone of the city. The same families also still occupied twenty-five of Turin's forty-four oldest and most important aristocratic palaces prior to 1914.[60]

Aristocratic and business elites were separated not only by the location of their residences, but also by the number and function of the residences they possessed. On the one hand, virtually all the top old-line titled families continued to maintain at least one second home outside the city, usually an ancestral castle or villa in the Piedmontese countryside. As a rule, these country houses were attached to landed estates that provided the site of the family residence. In addition to a rent palace that occupied the better part of a city block in Turin, the Valperga di Masino also still possessed their ancient castle, located appropriately in the commune of Masino in the Turinese countryside. Even more imposing were the residences of Count Ferdinando Avogadro di Collobiano. At the time of his death in 1904, he owned three ancestral castles in the Vercellese countryside as well as a palace in Turin's elegant Piazza San Carlo.[61] These aristocratic country houses represented more than luxurious retreats for their owners; they were also an important embodiment of lineage and tradition crucial to a titled family's identity and status, as well as vital bases of operations for the effective management of their landed estates.

The wealthy bourgeois elite, on the other hand, were much less likely to possess castles, manors, or landed estates. In fact, fully a third of the richest non-nobles in probate had no second home outside of the city. Those who did have another home usually chose one in close proximity to their primary residence in Turin in order to conciliate luxurious display with business responsibilities. Typically, they owned villas located in the foothills immediately flanking the city along the eastern side of the Po River. Since they were in easy reach of their owners' place of work, these villas could serve as full-time residences or else as weekend retreats.[62] In either case, they carried with them none of the rituals and obligations traditionally associated with the country houses of the titled nobility.

The increasing physical separation and divergent functions of Turin's

---

[60] See Società del Whist, *Elenco dei soci per l'anno 1907* (Turin, 1907). Boggio, *Lo sviluppo edilizio di Torino*, pp. 19–30, provides a list of the palaces and the families that owned them in 1907.

[61] See *URST*, m. 648, f. 42, 1904, Count Cesare Valperga di Masino; m. 655, f. 38, 1905, Count Ferdinando Avogadro di Collobiano.

[62] Nearly a third (32 percent) of the non-nobles with estates over L. 750,000 possessed property in the countryside valued at less than L. 1000. See Cardoza, "La ricchezza e i ricchi," pp. 328–329.

aristocratic and bourgeois residential neighborhoods unavoidably had the effect of widening the social gap between old and new elites by reducing the opportunities for informal, face-to-face sociability. Mutual isolation encouraged in turn the persistence and even the strengthening of separate patterns of social networking and friendship that found expression in the clubs, balls, and private engagements that defined "high society" in Turin.

THE LIMITS OF FUSION: GENTLEMEN'S CLUBS AND HIGH SOCIETY

Much like the changes in residential patterns, the evolution of the Turin's two leading gentlemen's clubs, the Società del Whist and the Accademia Filarmonica, in the late nineteenth century served to obstruct rather than facilitate the fusion of aristocratic and bourgeois elites. Despite the intentions of its founders, who wanted the club to reduce the gap between the nobility and other segments of the propertied classes, the Società del Whist never displayed more than a very cautious and tentative opening to the untitled. Between 1841 and 1870, sixty-five non-nobles gained admission; they represented about 12 percent of all entrants to the club. The high point of assimilation came in the decade after the creation of the Kingdom of Italy, when the bourgeoisie contributed nearly one-fifth of the new members.[63]

Significantly, the aristocratic club became even less inclined to accept "new men" as social equals in the decades after 1870. Between 1871 and 1914, the bourgeois minority within the club fell, both in numbers and percentage terms, as the Table 5.5 shows. The narrowness and caste consciousness that underlay this pattern of recruitment stood in sharp contrast to the Whist's closest counterpart in Milan, the Società dell'Unione, which drew nearly two-fifths of its membership from outside the titled nobility in the early 1890s.[64] The non-nobles who did enter the Whist after 1890 came largely from one of two categories; they were either relatives of members or military officers.

Noticeably absent from the club roster were business magnates actively engaged in industry and commerce. Of the 383 men listed as directors or top officers of joint-stock companies in Turin in the early years of World War I, just 8 were members of the Whist, and all of them were from titled families. Likewise, none of the leadership of the Lega Industriale di Torino, the Federazione Industriale Piemontese, the

---

[63] See Società Camillo Cavour, *Un secolo di vita del Whist*, pp. 111–163 for a chronological listing of members in the order of their admission to the club.

[64] See Meriggi, "Lo 'spirito di associazione'," p. 416.

Table 5.5 *Bourgeois members of Whist*

Period	Entrants	Percentage
1861–1870	23	17
1871–1880	11	9
1881–1890	8	7
1891–1900	7	6
1901–1910	6	5

Confederazione Italiana dell'Industria or the Associazione Generale fra Industriali e Commercianti in Torino belonged to the aristocratic club. The few members who did come from prominent business families like Severino Denina and Vittorio Sella had long since distanced themselves from the economic responsibilities and social milieu of their predecessors and had adopted most of the traditional markers of an aristocratic style of life.[65]

As the data in Table 5.5 attest, the Società del Whist, far from acting as an agent of social fusion, had become by the turn of the century an increasingly impregnable and caste-like enclave of titled society that actually made for less contact between the classes than had been the case a half century earlier. Contemporaries were aware of the changes. Already in 1877, a group of respectable but untitled young gentlemen formed a new association, the Giovine-Club, largely because they were convinced, according to Giovanni Gloria, that in the case of the Whist "access to postulants was extremely difficult." Four years later, Gloria, himself a member of the Whist, lamented the lack of "cohesion" and "fusion" in local high society, a situation that he attributed primarily to the "orgogliuzzi di casta."[66]

It is not altogether clear that the other major gentlemen's club, Accademia Filarmonica, managed to provide the interaction and intermingling denied by the Whist. Titled nobles always represented a distinct minority within the former musical society, accounting for 18 percent of all members between 1814 and World War I. Moreover, many of these nobles lacked the ancient lineage so highly esteemed by

---

[65] The data on the paucity of businessmen in the Whist is derived from a comparison of the names on the complete roster of the members in Società Camillo Cavour, *Un secolo di vita* with the lists of corporate boards in Credito Italiano, *Società per azioni, 1916* and list of officers in the "Associazioni per la tutela degl'interessi industriali e commerciali" in *La guida, 1913*, pp. 1174–1175.

[66] See the essay on the men's clubs by Gloria in *Torino*, pp. 275–277.

the Whist; nearly half of them had acquired their titles in the nineteenth century.[67]

The Filarmonica developed along decidedly different lines from the aristocratic club, evolving into the premier social retreat of Turin's business elite. In sharp contrast to the Whist, wealth and success in the business world counted for more than birth in gaining a membership in the former musical society. Forty-one of the eighty-one bourgeois millionaires who passed through probate had been members, a figure considerably higher than the two found in the Whist. Similarly, nine of the eleven biggest non-noble luxury taxpayers in 1899–1900 belonged to the club.[68] In the last decades of the nineteenth century, the great cotton manufacturing families – Mazzonis, Poma, Rolle, Tabasso, Leumann – and major distillers such as Enrico Cora and Teofilo Rossi all became members. At the onset of World War I, members presided over the boards of twenty-six corporations in the city and sat on the boards of another seventy-nine. The ranks of the Filarmonica also included such notables as Luigi Craponne-Bonnefon, the president of the Lega Industriale and the Confindustria, Felice Piacenza, head of the Lega Industriale Biellese, and the influential automobile executive, Dante Ferraris.[69]

It appeared for a brief period that the Accademia Filarmonica might also become an agent for upper-class fusion, a role rejected by the highly exclusive Whist. The 1880s, in particular, saw a sudden influx of aristocrats into the former musical society. Of the 163 members from titled families in the Filarmonica between 1840 and 1915, 70 joined that decade, and more than half of these men were also members of the Whist. The year 1882 alone saw 27 nobles assume dual-membership status.[70]

These developments, however, failed to produce any significant lowering of social barriers. Titled gentlemen might attend the dances and concerts offered by the Filarmonica or enjoy the sporting activities of its chalet on the Po, but this did not translate into more intimate familial or business relations with non-nobles. Moreover, whatever interaction and

---

[67] See *Cronistoria dell'Accademia*, pp. 129–145. Of the 1,078 men who belonged to the Filarmonica between 1814 and 1915, 191 came from titled families. Of these, 89 were newly ennobled. See Manno, *Il patriziato subalpino*, vol. I, for list of new nobles in the nineteenth century.

[68] See ACT "Ruolo tasse vetture private, 1899" and "Ruolo tasse domestici, 1900."

[69] On the presence of industrial leaders in the Filarmonica, see *Cronistoria dell'Accademia*, pp. 129–145; Castronovo, "Formazione e sviluppo," pp. 773–849; *La guida, 1913*, pp. 1174–1175; Credito Italiano, *Società per azioni, 1916*.

[70] See *Cronistoria dell'Accademia*, pp. 139–145; Società Cavour, *Un secolo di vita*, pp. 174–218.

networking did take place in the 1880s did not establish any enduring precedent. On the contrary, after 1890, the number of nobles who entered the club dropped sharply. In the following two and a half decades, only twenty-three titled men joined. As a result, the Filarmonica became steadily less successful at bringing together and blending men from Turin's new and old elites before World War I.[71]

The patterns of social isolation and exclusion displayed by the gentlemen's clubs carried over to the less institutionalized forms of upper-class sociability in the late nineteenth and early twentieth centuries. Long after the transfer of the royal court away from Turin in the 1860s, the resident members of the House of Savoy continued to serve as the centerpieces and chief arbiters of local high society. The presence of the Duke and Duchess of Aosta, the Duke and Duchess of Genoa, or the heir to the throne, the Count of Turin, at a society event added significantly to its luster and virtually guaranteed its success, while the most sought after invitations were those to the grand balls and receptions hosted by members of the royal family. The enormous prestige enjoyed by the House of Savoy in the city provided the nobility with advantages that no other old elite on the peninsula enjoyed in the late nineteenth century. Royal family members with their inevitable aristocratic entourage gave Turinese high society a distinctively traditional cast that tended to relegitimize and reinforce both the rituals and status of the hereditary titled establishment.[72]

The social calendar in Turin displayed a certain regularity each year with a fairly predictable series of semi-public and private events and entertainments. Much as in other urban centers of Italy, the year began with *Carnevale* in late January and early February which marked the busiest period of the season. As an enthusiastic chronicler for the local society weekly, *Il Venerdì della Contessa*, reported in February 1891 "these nights, one dances with indescribable abandon everywhere; in families, theaters, clubs."[73] That year, for instance, the paper provided accounts of some twenty private house parties as well as larger gatherings at the Circolo degli Artisti and Accademia Filarmonica in a two week span that culminated with a grand ball sponsored by the Duke and Duchess of Genoa at Palazzo Chiablese.[74] February also marked the beginning of the sporting calendar as well with a series of weekly hunting parties that continued into May, typically presided over by the

---

[71] *Ibid.*

[72] On the special status enjoyed by the House of Savoy in Turin and Piedmont in general, see Levra, "Torino tra primazia risorgimentale," pp. 81–172.

[73] *Il Venerdì della Contessa*, n. 6, February 6, 1891.

[74] *Ibid.*, n. 5–7, 1891.

Duke of Aosta in the countryside surrounding the city. During the months of March, April, and May, social life tended to revolve around concerts and other musical events. In June, the race track became the favorite locale for upper-class display and socializing. In accordance with the longstanding traditions of Piedmont's aristocratic elite, the social life of the regional capital came to a halt in July with the summer exodus of Turin's upper classes to their country homes or to fashionable retreats in the mountains or by the seaside. As the *Il Venerdi della Contessa* noted in mid-August 1904, "our city exhibits a strange dreariness . . . deserted squares, cheerless streets and avenues . . . everyone gone."[75] Nor was Turin's social calendar much more lively in the autumn months when about all the society paper had to report on were hunting parties. Throughout the year, theater premières and even services at the city's more fashionable churches provided additional opportunities to see and to be seen. *Il Venerdi della Contessa* regularly reported the names and attire of the socially prominent women who attended opening nights in the Regio, Carignano, Alfieri, Balbo, and Vittorio Emanuele Theaters or who had been seen at mass in the Churches of San Filippo, SS. Martiri, Sant'Agostino, Angioli Custodi, and Madonna degli Angeli.[76]

Of course, the regularity of Turinese high society was occasionally disrupted by special events such as weddings and funerals. The receptions and ceremonies surrounding the wedding of Marchese Giuseppe Pallavicino-Mossi and Countess Irene Avogadro di Collobiano, for instance, marked the high point of the winter season of 1895–1896 and, as such, attracted large crowds of onlookers as well as receiving extensive coverage in the local press. The prenuptial reception given by the bride's family in their palace in Piazza San Carlo a week before the wedding had a guest list that included, *La Stampa* reported, "the names of almost all the Turinese aristocracy" and members of the royal family. The Church of Santa Teresa, where the wedding itself took place in mid-February, had "never embraced," according to *Il Venerdi della Contessa*, "so much of the Turinese aristocratic world."[77] The death of Count Ernesto Balbo Bertone di Sambuy in February 1909 was a sadder

[75] *Ibid.*, August 17, 1904.

[76] In its issue of March 26, 1904, for example, *Il Venerdi della Contessa* listed the names of thirty-six society ladies who had attended mass at the Church of San Filippo that week. The list included some of the most prominent families of the old nobility as well as newer families like Mazzonis, Ceriana, and Poma. For similar lists, see *ibid.*, March 12, 1904.

[77] See *La Stampa*, February 9, 1896 and *Il Venerdi della Contessa*, February 14, 1896. The wedding was also covered by *Italia Reale*, *La Tribuna Biellese*, *La Patria* of Turin as well as *L'Italie: Journal Politique Quotidien* of Rome. For clippings, see AST, Sez. Riunite, Archivio Pallavicino-Mossi, b. 16.

but no less major event which attracted the cream of high society as well as large crowds of mourners. Participating in the huge funeral procession, which wound its way along the main avenues of the city, were the Duke of Aosta, the mayor, military commanders, church officials, representatives from the Senate, Chamber of Deputies, judiciary, and "numerous patrician families."[78]

While those aspects of high society associated with semi-public or public institutions continued to be dominated by the great titled families, they did offer at least the physical possibility of social contact between Turin's old and new elites. Both aristocratic women and non-titled matrons could be found, for instance, at theater premières and concerts or in the fashionable churches on sunday. Opening night at the Carignano Theater in January 1912, for example, was attended not only by old-line aristocrats such as Countess Irene Avogadro di Collobiano, but also by the wife of the prominent business magnate Giuseppe Durio and one of the leading lights of the local Jewish elite, Baroness Faustina Levi de Veali.[79] The guest lists of the "charitable" balls given by the Accademia Filarmonica, the Circolo degli Artisti, and members of the royal family reflected a similar heterogeneity. Thus, the dance given on behalf of the Congregazione di Carità during Carnevale in 1904 brought together, according to the society press, "the aristocracy of blood, that of talent, and the aristocracy of money." Likewise, the boxes at the race track included not only old-line nobles, but also members of prominent bourgeois families like Ceriana, Denina, Voli and Sella.[80]

The circles of the nobility and the haute bourgeoisie, however, rarely intersected in the more intimate receptions, house parties, summertime diversions, and rural sporting events that filled much of the leisure time of Piedmont's upper classes in this period. Social isolation was especially evident during Carnevale. As the *Il Venerdì della Contessa* expressed it, "every social class has its own parties."[81] Judging by the accounts that appeared in the society weekly, private parties and receptions continued to be largely segregated along social and religious lines before World War I. On the whole, the families of the old-line nobility preferred to remain in splendid isolation and maintained a low profile. The soirées that took place in aristocratic town houses were extremely exclusive

---

[78] See *La Stampa*, February 27, 1909 for a detailed account of the funeral.

[79] See *Il Venerdì della Contessa*, January 9–10, 1912.

[80] These conclusions are based upon a careful reading of the lists of names of those people in attendance at these receptions and sporting events that appear in *Il Venerdì della Contessa* during the years 1891 and 1904. For the account of the charitable ball for the Congregazione di Carità, see *ibid.*, February 10, 1904.

[81] *Ibid.*, n. 6, February 6, 1891.

affairs that rarely included any bourgeois guests. When the Countess Riccardi di Lantosca, for example, gave a private party during Carnevale in 1891, the paper provided the names of some twenty-five aristocratic men and women in attendance, including the heir to the throne, the Count of Turin, but mentioned not a single non-noble. Little had apparently changed more than a decade later when *Il Venerdi della Contessa* reported in February 1904 on an "extraordinarily elegant reception at Palazzo di Rorà" hosted by Marchesa Luserna di Rorà that was attended exclusively by women from old titled families like the Del Carretto di Moncrivello, Thaon di Revel, and Perrone di San Martino.[82] At the same time, aristocratic families continued to hold themselves as aloof as possible from the other cliques and coteries. Accordingly, the names of prominent nobles rarely appeared on the guest lists of receptions, parties, and concerts that industrial or banking families hosted in their homes or in the city's major hotels. These groups, in turn, rarely took part in the private gatherings given by prominent members of Turin's Jewish community.[83]

Traditional rural sports, associated with the equestrian and military customs of the nobility, served as additional mechanisms of social differentiation. Hunting, in particular, received extensive coverage in the society press which characterized it as the most "aristocratic sporting event."[84] Hunts still took place with surprising regularity in the first decade of the new century on royal domains and parks near Turin, or else on the estates of titled nobles. The Duke and Duchess of Aosta were invariably in attendance, along with a coterie of old-line nobles and cavalry officers. After the rides, the family hosting the hunt usually invited participants to a lunch at their country house or ancestral castle. Few if any bourgeois riders took part. In 1904, for instance, the only non-nobles mentioned by *Il Venerdi della Contessa* in its accounts of the hunts were from a few prominent, old families like the Nasi, Engelfred, Ceriana, and Bonvicino, most of whom also had members in the Società del Whist.[85]

Even less social mingling between old and new elites took place during the summer months. Titled families tended to follow their traditional custom of passing the summer as well as the better part of the fall at their ancestral estates in the provinces. Here they renewed ties with

[82] *Ibid.*, February 13, 1891 and February 10, 1904.
[83] See, for example, *ibid.*, January 16, 1904 for the party given by Debenedetti. Conclusions regarding the social composition of the parties given by non-nobles are based on the lists of guests in the society weekly.
[84] *Ibid.*, October 26, 1904.
[85] That year *Il Venerdi della Contessa* had reports on a dozen hunting parties.

local notables, oversaw the harvests, enjoyed their favorite outdoor sports, and exchanged visits with other old families from neighboring estates. The Compans di Brichanteau, for example, left their town house in July each year and went to their castle overlooking the village of Mercenasco in the province of Turin, where they remained until November. Once there, younger members of the family helped to harvest the grapes and took trips to the castles of cousins like the Valperga di Masino and the Seyssel d'Aix, while the parents, for their part, hosted a steady stream of relatives and intimate friends such as the Scarampi di Villanova, Oreglia d'Isola, and Maffei di Boglia.[86] Similarly, as late as 1904, all the members of the Figarolo di Gropello clan, with their respective wives, husbands, and off-spring were still gathering together each summer at Beltondino, site of the family's principal country house and most extensive properties in the province of Alessandria.[87]

Bourgeois families, for their part, were more inclined to vacation at fashionable resorts in the mountains or else in the new grand hotels that sprang up along the Italian Riviera in the late nineteenth century. During the summer months, *Il Venerdi della Contessa* kept a running account of the locales where Turinese notables had been sighted. The familiar names of Piedmont's old aristocratic elite remained largely absent from these accounts. In August of 1904, for example, while old titled families retreated to their ancestral estates, the society weekly reported that only prominent bourgeois families like the Denina, Voli, Bonvicino, Nigra as well as Cesare and Teofilo Rossi of the liquor dynasty were vacationing at the Hotel Royal in Courmayeur. In such resorts, the city's upper-middle class was more likely to meet and socialize with wealthy American, British, and French tourists than with Piedmontese nobles.[88]

Taken together, these various indicators of social interaction between Piedmont's old and new elites reveal a situation that differed noticeably from other regions of Italy where a new hybrid ruling class emerged in the nineteenth century through the fusion of the hereditary aristocracy with influential segments of the haute bourgeoisie. The interaction that did take place among the various segments of the propertied classes in Piedmont was largely restricted to the public sphere and did not lead to more intimate relations prior to World War I. On the contrary,

---

[86] The AST, Sez. Riunite, Archivio Compans di Brichanteau contains a number of letters written by family members in Mercenasio between 1865 and 1918.

[87] See "Diario Figarolo di Gropello," February 4, 1986, p. 9.

[88] *Ibid.*, August 6, 1904. In that issue, the society weekly reported that, in addition to the local families in residence, there was a "numerous colony of Americans, British, and Frenchmen."

contrasting attitudes toward industry and commerce, separate patterns of investment, marriage partners, residences, and lifestyles all point to the persistence of parallel but socially distinct elites. In fact, there are indications, such as the evolving recruitment policies of the gentlemen's clubs, that caste consciousness and barriers became more rather than less pronounced in the late nineteenth and early twentieth centuries. The few bourgeois families who gained some measure of acceptance did so only by adopting the values and culture of the old-line nobility.

The evolution of aristocratic–bourgeois relations in Piedmont proved to be something of a mixed blessing for old-line families. On the one hand, as the apparent hardening of social barriers in the late nineteenth century indicates, the survival of the titled nobility as a prominent, influential, and wealthy element in Piedmontese society did not depend upon any significant social or economic accommodation with the industrial or commercial middle classes. Subalpine nobles were able to maintain so much of their traditional caste consciousness and exclusivity without sacrificing influence largely because of two circumstances. First, they proved to be very skillful at accepting new institutions and then using them to bolster their own wealth and old way of life. Second, they benefited from being members of a regional society that still exhibited a strong sense of social hierarchy and deference, a society where the monarchy, church, and military continued to enjoy widespread prestige and respect.

On the other hand, social isolation and exclusivity also had their costs, since they limited the ability of old-line families to coopt or convert newer elements of the propertied classes to an aristocratic way of life. While some local industrialists continued to pursue hereditary titles and to ape the nobility in other respects in the last decades before World War I, most of Turin's new entrepreneurial families appear to have found the terms of social acceptance by the nobility to be too difficult and/or too humiliating. Instead, they increasingly accepted and perhaps even preferred to participate in a "good society" of their own making with institutions, neighborhoods, and social rituals separate and distinct from those of the nobility. As a result, the aristocracy became increasingly cut off from new centers of wealth, leadership, and power. The reluctance or inability of old-line families to diversify and modernize their presence in society and to continue absorbing talented and wealthy new men as in the past not only contributed to the impoverishment of their own ranks, but it also condemned them to a not-so-splendid isolation in the twentieth century.

CHAPTER 6

RETREAT AND ADAPTATION IN THE TWENTIETH CENTURY

As the preceding chapters have argued, the Piedmontese aristocracy proved to be more successful than their titled counterparts elsewhere on the Italian peninsula at maintaining a combination of landed wealth, social exclusivity, cultural traditions, and political influence in the second half of the nineteenth century. The same cannot be said for the following century. The extraordinary growth of industry in Piedmont, the rapid advance of mass politics, recurrent problems in the agricultural sector, demographic weakness, two wars, and ultimately the fall of the monarchy combined to transform irrevocably the identity, status and, material circumstances of the nobility in Piedmont by the middle of the twentieth century.

Old-line aristocratic families responded to these challenges in a variety of ways. Some conformed to popular stereotypes by squandering the remains of the ancestral patrimony on gambling, mistresses, and the high life or by retreating to their decaying country houses and palaces where they led a proud, but increasingly impoverished existence before simply dying off. For others, preeminence was followed not so much by decadence and disappearance as by adaption and survival. In fact, a number of titled families became active participants in a process of adjustment to the difficult circumstances that confronted them particularly after 1914. As a result, they remained an affluent and prominent component of Piedmontese high society in the decades that followed. But even successful adaptation unavoidably transformed most of these nobles into plutocrats and industrial-financial managers who lost much of their distinctive identity and cohesion as they merged into a broader and more diverse upper class.

World War I and its aftermath were clearly the decisive developments in this process of decline and transformation. From the perspective of the late twentieth century, however, the first signs of a change in aristocratic values and patterns of behavior appeared before 1914. Titled families already began to experience new economic challenges in the

196

last decades of the nineteenth century as a direct consequence of a prolonged world-wide depression in agriculture. The resultant drop in
prices, incomes, and rents did not necessarily spell disaster for the
nobility as a whole, but it did have the effect of reducing their wealth,
widening the gap between rich and poor nobles, and forcing old families
to begin to alter their way of life and to reconsider some of their traditional values and social customs.

THE AGRICULTURAL CRISIS AND THE PIEDMONTESE ARISTOCRACY

Both contemporary observers and subsequent scholarly opinion have
tended to view the great agricultural depression of the late nineteenth
century as a watershed in the history of Europe's landed elites. From the
corn regions of Britain to the Russian steppes, the structure of agricultural society was severely shaken in these years and the power and
prestige of landowners permanently undermined. With the importation
of cheap grains from overseas in the 1870s and the resultant prolonged
decline in farm prices, many landowners saw their agricultural incomes
fall dramatically. In order to maintain a semblance of their former style
of life and occasionally to avoid bankruptcy, they often had to choose
between drastic retrenchment and the pursuit of new sources of income
in the world of finance and industry. In either instance, their responses
diminished the social prestige traditionally associated with the land and
led to fundamental changes in rural social habits.[1] In the case of Italy,
the depression in the countryside has been linked both to the impoverishment of the old nobility and to their flight from the land as a result of
increased indebtedness, the liquidation of rural property, and a new propensity to invest in state bonds and corporate stocks.[2]

As I have argued in Chapter 3, Piedmont's landed aristocracy also felt
the effects of the crisis.[3] Its impact was especially pronounced in the rice
growing areas of Vercelli and Novara where some of the largest aristocratic estates were located. The price of wheat fell 31 percent between
1880 and 1895; the price of rice dropped 20 percent already in the first
half of the 1880s. In the short run, the big absentee landowners were protected from the worst effects of depression by their relatively long-term
(nine to twelve years) leases with the tenants who were still obligated to

---

[1] See Thompson, *English Landed Society*, pp. 308–324; Spring (ed.), *European Landed
Elites*; Lieven, *The Aristocracy in Europe*, pp. 74–100.
[2] See Banti, "I proprietari terrieri nell'Italia centro-settentrionale," pp. 14–15;
Coppini, "Aristocrazia e finanza in Toscana," pp. 297–332; Petrusewicz, *Latifondo*.
[3] See Chapter 3, pp. 109–110.

pay rents established in the economic climate of the previous decade. As a result, the commercial leaseholders and other tenant farmers initially bore the brunt of the situation brought on by falling prices, reduced production, tight credit, and increased expenses. But as leases expired or tenants dropped out, rental rates began to fall (Pugliese estimates by about 35 percent between 1881 and 1890) and the income of the large estate owners suffered accordingly.[4]

The estate records of the Pallavicino-Mossi, Gazelli di Rossana, and d'Harcourt families provide a good indication of the agricultural depression's delayed impact on aristocratic landed incomes. Gross farm revenues from the Pallavicino-Mossi properties in the provinces of Vercelli and Turin, which had averaged around L. 170,000 per year in the second half of the 1870s, fell only slightly (8 percent) in the first four years of the following decade. The situation changed drastically in the five years after 1884 when annual farm income dropped another 38 percent to L. 97,000, a trough in which the properties would remain for the rest of the century. The more modest land holdings of the Gazelli di Rossana family, some 350 hectares in the provinces of Cuneo and Asti, followed a similar pattern of decline. Their farm revenues remained relatively unchanged through the first half of the 1880s, but then began to drop steadily. Their average annual income in the years 1889 to 1894 was roughly half (52 percent) what it had been a decade earlier. Count Giulio d'Harcourt fared little better in the management of his father's estate in the province of Turin where average net revenues dropped 35 percent in the second half of the 1880s.[5]

Not all segments of the nobility shared equally the economic hardships and losses associated with the agricultural depression. Grouped by time period, aristocratic probate returns reveal an increasing polarization of wealth in the wake of the crisis in the countryside. One apparent consequence of the agricultural slump was that the ranks of "poor" nobles (less than L. 100,000) expanded steadily in the late nineteenth and early twentieth centuries, especially at the very lowest levels. While there had been no really impoverished nobles (those who possessed less than L. 1,000 in total assets) in probate prior to 1886, in the twelve years after 1900 they accounted for about 4 percent of all the titled individuals in the survey. More importantly, the same period also witnessed a decline in the

---

[4] See Pugliese, *Due secoli di vita agricola*, pp. 178–208; Castronovo, *Il Piemonte*, pp. 93–108 provides a general treatment of the agricultural depression in the region.

[5] See AST, Sez. Riunite, Archivio Pallavicino-Mossi, b. 19, entrate e uscite, 1879–1900; Archivio d'Harcourt, b. 75, f. 18, reddito: Tenuta d'Azeglio, 1880–1902; Archivio Gazelli di Rossana (Biblioteca Provinciale di Torino) b. 50–20, entrate e uscite 1880–1902.

Table 6.1 *Distribution of wealth within nobility by period (percent)*

Category	1862–1873 (%)	1874–1885 (%)	1901–1912 (%)
Less than 100,000	37	41	46
100,001–250,000	27	29	26
250,001–500,000	19	16	13
500,001–750,000	7	7	4
750,001–1,000,000	3	2	2
1,000,001–2,000,000	4	4	7
More than 2,000,000	3	2	2

numerical importance of the intermediate or middling nobles (between L. 100,000 and L. 500,000). By the opening decade of this century, they accounted for less than two-fifths of the aristocratic fortunes in probate.

The length and severity of the agricultural depression created problems for those nobles who depended exclusively on the rental income from their estates and some ancient families actually went under as a result. The case of Count Carlo Broglia di Casalborgone shows how financial catastrophe might await those landowners who were already in difficulty before the slump in farm revenues. The first son of the former Minister of War and signer of the *Statuto*, Lieutenant General Count Mario Broglia di Casalborgone, Count Carlo inherited the ancestral family seat and over 250 hectares of attached farm land in Casalborgone in the late 1850s. Even before the downturn of the 1880s, rents from the estate were not sufficient to support a large household that included six children, two younger brothers, and a staff of six in the luxuriously aristocratic style favored by Broglia and his wife. By 1880, interest payments on a debt of L. 221,400 were already absorbing a large chunk of their annual income. The collapse of farm prices in the ensuing decade made a difficult financial situation impossible. By 1891, the family's total indebtedness had reached over L. 367,000 with interest payments exceeding annual revenues, despite the decision to give up the elegant residence in Turin and retreat to the family castle. After the death of Count Carlo in 1893, the entire Casalborgone estate including the castle had to be sold to pay off debts, and the family disintegrated. The only surviving male heir, Count Mario, died in 1896 at the age of thirty-three as a miner in Brazil; his unmarried sisters ended their days in the Regio Convitto delle Vedove e Nubili di Civile Condizione, an institution in Turin that cared for destitute women from good families.[6]

[6] AST, Sez. Riunite, Archivio Broglia di Casalborgone, b. 31 and 34, carte varie di

In a similar if less dramatic vein, Marchese Tommaso Ferrero della Marmora, the scion of one of Piedmont's most distinguished titled families and the principal heir to a large landed fortune in the middle decades of the century, died in 1900 virtually propertyless and in debt. The land registry carried out in 1850s listed Marchese Tommaso as the second largest landowner in the commune of Pralormo with nearly 500 hectares of property. At the time of his death in 1900, the capital value of all Marchese Tommaso's land holdings amounted to a mere L. 1,800; his total estate was valued at L. 87,021.58, while there were over L. 100,000 in claims against it.[7]

Wealthy aristocrats, however, appear to have weathered the economic crises of the late nineteenth century with considerably less difficulty than their more modestly endowed colleagues. There is little indication that the great landed magnates suffered catastrophic losses as a consequence of the agricultural depression. Even in the worst years of the early 1890s, Marchese Giuseppe Pallavicino-Mossi's annual income, for instance, still exceeded L. 100,000.[8] Although the average value of their estates fell slightly (5.5 percent), the rich titled elite (over L. 750,000) actually accounted for a larger share of the nobles in probate after 1900 than they had in the period before 1886. Likewise, the average level of indebtedness among the large titled landowners in probate did not show any significant change in the wake of the crisis.[9] Finally, the depression did not provoke any immediate or massive flight of the nobility from the countryside comparable to what took place in certain provinces of Emilia-Romagna where the average size of aristocratic landholdings fell sharply.[10] For the large titled landowners in par-

---

carattere patrimoniale (1881–1904). On the fate of Count Carlo's children, see b. 9 and 11.

[7] See *Catasto Rabbini*, f. 95 and AST, Sez. Riunite, Insinuazioni, 1854, Inventario del Marchese C. E. Ferrero della Marmora for the landed property of the family at mid-century; for the impoverished circumstances of Marchese Tommaso at the time of his death, see *URST*, vol. 557, 1901, f. 24.

[8] AST, Sez. Riunite, Archivio Pallavicino-Mossi, b. 19, Entrate e spese negli anni 1893, 1894, and 1895.

[9] See note 3. The average level of indebtedness among the 319 aristocrats in probate between 1874 and 1885 was L. 54,538 or 21 percent of the gross value of the estate. Ten estates were in the red. In the period from 1901 to 1912, the average indebtedness among the 247 aristocrats was L. 35,805 or 22 percent; twelve estates were in the red.

[10] In the province of Ravenna, for instance, the average size of their properties dropped from 474 hectares in 1835 to 224 in 1898–1900. Titled nobles saw their land holdings contracted even more dramatically in the province of Piacenza, where they went from an average of 171 hectares before the crisis to a mere 71 at the beginning of the twentieth century. See Banti, "I proprietari nell'Italia centro-settentrionale," p. 14.

ticular, rural properties remained far and away the most important assets in their portfolios prior to World War I. Despite the trials and tribulations of the 1880s and 1890s, two-thirds of the large landed estates and nine of the eleven wealthiest landowners to pass through probate between 1901 and 1912 still came from the ranks of the aristocratic elite.[11]

Nor did the agricultural slump lead to any sudden or drastic decline in the standard of living enjoyed by the great landed families, if a large staff of servants and elegant carriages are any indication. As Chapter 5 has shown, the luxury tax records attest to how they continued to maintain a lavish style of life that clearly distinguished them from the vast majority of bourgeois families.[12]

Yet beneath this facade of stability and continuity, the agricultural depression had affected the competitive position of the great noble families and encouraged subtle changes in their attitudes toward the estates. Most wealthy aristocrats survived the crisis with their fortunes largely intact, but they still had experienced a relative impoverishment. While they had been largely marking time, new fortunes were being made in commerce and industry that noticeably altered the social composition of the region's wealthiest class by the first decade of the twentieth century. Between 1901 and 1912, little more than a third of the millionaires in probate still came from the old aristocratic families. Furthermore, the new wealth was on a scale without parallel. The fortune left by Alessandro Martini of the "Martini and Rossi" vermouth dynasty in 1905, for example, was nearly twice that left by the richest aristocratic family in the nineteenth century, the Falletti di Barolo.[13]

The slump and the challenge to their status from new wealth may not have driven the old families to abandon the countryside, but it did lead them to regard their estates less as a trust to be passed to future generations and more as an economic asset to be judged in the cold light of investment returns. And in this light, large rural properties seemed to have lost some of their attraction. Most of the great landed magnates ceased to acquire new land in the 1880s, a trend that continued after the depression had ended. Indeed, I have not found a single noble family whose landed estates actually increased because of land purchases after

---

[11] Data drawn from materials cited in note 3.

[12] ACT, Ruolo tasse vetture private, 1899; Ruolo tasse domestici 1900. For a more detailed discussion of aristocratic spending, see Chapter 5.

[13] Between 1901 and 1912, there were seventeen aristocratic fortunes over 1 million lire and six over 2 million; during the same period there were thirty bourgeois millionaires and twelve multi-millionaires. The estate left by Martini was valued at L. 11,854,133, that of the Marchesa Falletti di Barolo at L. 6,390,781.

the 1880s. The economic motives are not hard to deduce. As the lawyer for Marchese Giuseppe Pallavicino-Mossi noted, in 1893, the family's estates were barely yielding 2 percent per year of their capital value, while Marchese Giuseppe was paying 5 percent interest on his loans from the Cassa di Risparmio and on his sisters' portions of their father's estate. These circumstances led the young title holder to break with family traditions and pressure one of his sisters into accepting land instead of the standard cash settlement for her portion of their father's inheritance.[14]

Aristocratic landowners with estates in the plains were also encouraged to take a less romantic view of their rural properties by the erosion of traditional patterns of peasant deference and subservience, a tendency which the agricultural depression accentuated in the last decades of the century. Although the change did not, for the most part, assume the form of agricultural unions and strikes as in other regions of the Po Valley, it was evident to the landed magnates and their agents. According to the priest in the parish supported by the Pallavicino-Mossi family near their estate of Torrione in the province of Vercelli, religious observance had declined sharply "in the villages infected by socialism such as ours." For his part, Marchese Giuseppe Pallavicino-Mossi became less inclined to follow his father's paternalistic treatment of the local population. Thus, in the 1890s he informed local authorities that he no longer would furnish as in the past the "premises for the school in Torrione."[15] The break with aristocratic tradition was even more evident the following decade when prominent nobles like Marchese Vincenzo Ricci and Carlo Arborio di Gattinara played leading roles in the militant new agrarian associations that emerged in the rice growing areas after 1900 to "stem the . . . absurd demands of the workers."[16]

Elsewhere old titled families saw signs of declining deference in the minor disputes with the villages that tended to estrange them from their rural dependents. The experience of the Figarolo di Gropello, one of the most prominent aristocratic families of Alessandria, is illustrative. In 1901, Vittorio Figarolo di Gropello inherited a large estate in the locality of Zinasco. During the nineteenth century, his grandfather had been the chief patron of the locality, investing in the construction of irrigation canals and even building the local church at his own expense. Nonethe-

---

[14] See AST, Sez. Riunite, Archivio Compans di Brichanteau, category 4, b. 9, f. 6, letter from avv. Cattaneo to Marchesa Leontina Pallavicino, no date 1893 as well as b. 28, f. 14, Pallavicino pro-memoria, Rome, 1905.

[15] *Ibid.*, b. 12, correspondence regarding the estates of Saletta and Torrione. On the issue of strikes and rural unions, see Castronovo, *Piemonte*, p. 104.

[16] See Confederazione Nazionale Agraria, *Atti del II Congress*, pp. 32–36.

Table 6.2 *Changing structure of aristocratic wealth (>L. 750,000)*

Category	1862–1873 %	1901–1912 %
Real property	84	69
Rural property	66	50
Urban property	18	19
Personal property	12	20
Stocks	0.5	8
Bonds	3	7
Ban deposits	3	1
Farm equipment	0.5	1
Credits	5	3
Intervivos gifts	2	9
Other	2	1
Totals	100	100
Liabilities	21	9

less, Vittorio sold the estate in the first decade of the new century because, his nephew later recalled, he was "disgusted by the constant disputes with the peasants and petty local authorities, ungrateful for all the good done in the village by the house of Gropello."[17]

The probate records reflect a subtle shift in the attitudes of the Piedmontese aristocracy toward landownership in the wake of the *crisi agraria*. The percentages in Table 6.2 confirm that no sweeping restructuring of aristocratic wealth or large-scale exodus from the countryside took place in late-nineteenth-century Piedmont. Indeed, the fortunes that belonged to the titled rich in Turin continued to be fairly traditional in structure into the last decade before the war. Real property remained considerably more important than mobile assets. Land holdings, in particular, were still the largest single component of the estates belonging to noble families who accounted for three-fifths of the total value of all elite rural property in probate between 1901 and 1912.

These older forms of wealth, however, no longer enjoyed the same popularity and importance in aristocratic circles by the first decade of the twentieth century. The contribution of rural property to the fortunes of the wealthy nobility fell by about fifteen percentage points, while the share of rich aristocrats with over L. 1 million in landed assets dropped from 48 percent in the first decade after unification to 29 percent in the last decade before the Great War. The departure from tradition also was evident in the reduced importance of the old legacies, pensions, and annuities that had previously burdened most aristocratic

[17] "Diario dell'Ammiraglio di Divisione, Conte Giovanni di Gropello," p. 33.

estates. As a result, liabilities absorbed a considerably smaller portion of the noble fortunes in probate after 1901, but at a price — the abandonment of centuries-old charitable and paternalistic customs.

The diminished economic attractiveness and social appeal of landed estates encouraged a gradual shift in the habits and values of the younger generation of Piedmontese aristocrats who emerged from the crisis. Skepticism about the value of landed status and the country life came precisely when attractive investment opportunities and new life-styles seemed to be presenting themselves on the urban frontier.

CHANGING PATTERNS OF ARISTOCRATIC INVESTMENT AND SOCIAL BEHAVIOR

Chapter 5 has argued that Piedmontese nobles tended on the whole not to follow the movement of their patrician counterparts in Florence, Rome, and Genoa in the direction of increased economic interpenetration with new business elites. In fact, as Table 6.2 shows, real property continued to be considerably more important than mobile assets in the fortunes of aristocratic families in Turin before World War I, with land holdings still the largest single component of their estates. Nonetheless, this apparent traditionalism should not obscure the gradual changes that had begun to take place in the investment strategies of wealthy titled families before 1914. Indeed, the success of the titled rich in weathering the hard times of the 1880s and 1890s can be traced in part to their responding to the opportunities offered by urban real estate and new forms of financial capitalism.

A few old-line families were well situated to exploit the urban real estate market. Well before the agricultural downturn of the 1880s, great landed aristocrats were also some of the leading landlords in the city of Turin as well as among the principal property owners in the surrounding commune in the 1850s.[18] Investment in urban rent palaces offered some wealthy aristocrats distinct advantages, with the drop in rents and income from land. The rental income from the huge palace owned by Count Gustavo Ferrero d'Ormea in Piazza Carlina, for instance, more than made up for the reduced revenues from his farm properties, accounting for nearly half of the family's annual revenues by 1892.[19] Marchese Giuseppe Pallavicino-Mossi's palace in via Santa Teresa, which he had inherited from his father in 1879, produced an

---

[18] See Chapter 3, pp. 110–111.

[19] AST, Prima Sez., Archivio Ferrero d'Ormea, b. 95, list of revenues for the year 1892. While rural rents totaled L. 32,472 that year, the rent palace yielded L. 41,566.

annual rental income that exceeded 4 percent of its capital value in the late 1880s and the early 1890s, more than twice the return on his landed estates in Vercelli. Such economic considerations led Marchese Giuseppe to purchase two additional commercial buildings adjoining his palace in 1892, which he turned around and sold to the *Banca Commerciale* in 1898. He then invested the profits from that sale in three more buildings, including a large and lucrative rental palace on the newly developed Corso Vittorio Emanuele. By the last years of the pre-war era, income from these urban properties accounted for approximately two-fifths of his family's annual revenues.[20] Other prominent aristocrats such as Count Paolo Costa della Trinità, Marchese Carlo Compans di Brichanteau, and Count Saverio Capris di Cigliè followed a similar strategy that made them some of the principal property owners in the city in last years before World War I.[21]

For men like Pallavicino-Mossi, real estate in the city came to mean something quite different from what it had for the previous generation of wealthy old-line aristocrats. Although they and their families continued to reside in elegant palaces, considerations of status and prestige played a secondary role in their urban investment strategies. Their buildings now represented an important source of rental income as well as an increasingly valuable investment. Accordingly, they became more inclined to exploit them as purely economic assets, buying and selling them as market conditions dictated.

Still, this aristocratic interest in urban real estate development was rather modest in scale, especially when compared to the investments of wealthy non-nobles. It certainly did not entail any massive transfer of assets. Overall, both the average value of urban real estate and its importance within the portfolios of the wealthier noble families in my survey were only slightly higher (about 6 percent) in the first decade of the new century than they had been in the period before 1885. Few nobles figured prominently among the big urban proprietors in probate. A mere four rich aristocrats in the decade after 1900 had more than L. 500,000 invested in buildings in Turin, only one had more than L. 750,000, and none over L. 1 million. During the same period, the urban property bequeathed by rich non-nobles registered an impressive 56 percent increase, while the average value of their urban assets rose by nearly a third (30 percent).[22]

[20] AST, Sez. Riunite, Archivio Pallavicino-Mossi, b. 11, "Entrate e Uscite," 1912. For information on purchases and sales of buildings in the 1890s, see b. 13.

[21] See Chapter 3 for sources on urban properties. For lists of owners of buildings in Turin, see *La Guida commerciale ed amministrativa di Torino, 1913*.

[22] Between 1874 and 1885, twenty-three wealthy aristocrats left a total of L. 6,897,313

The more successful titled families also began to take advantage of new opportunities in business and commerce as the statistics in Table 6.2 reveal. Not only did the share of personal assets in their fortunes increase, but the composition of those assets showed important modifications. The place of stocks and bonds in the estates of wealthy aristocrats in probate quadrupled in importance, while more old-fashioned forms of mobile wealth such as credits and bank deposits declined. In this respect, they differed sharply from the nobility in less industrialized areas such as Piacenza, who still had 85 percent of their wealth in rural property at the beginning of the century.[23]

Count Gustavo Ferrero d'Ormea and Count Ernesto Balbo Bertone di Sambuy embodied the moderate investment strategy of gradual diversification pursued by some of the more prosperous aristocratic families. Both men were heirs to large fortunes that included substantial rural properties, but virtually no liquid assets. Neither man displayed any interest in abandoning his country estates or family seat as a result of the agricultural crisis. On the contrary, they held on to most of their rural properties throughout the difficult years and well beyond, selling off only outlying farms and unconnected patches of land to pay off their younger siblings' portions in the estate and to reduce their debts.

But at the same time both men curtailed any further purchases of land and began to invest their surplus income in an array of paper assets. Count Gustavo 'started cautiously, buying a limited number of shares mostly in the Banca Nazionale and the Ferrovie Vittorio Emanuele that had a total capital value of L. 155,451 by 1890. Over the course of that decade, he greatly expanded his shareholdings in other railroad companies so that his stock portfolio was worth L. 410,430 in 1898. The economic expansion and relative prosperity of the Giolittian era encouraged Ferrero d'Ormea to increase the range and value of his stockholdings. Less than two years before the war, Count Gustavo not only held stock in nine railroad companies, but also had substantial investments in the hydro-electric, mining, and machine firms. Together these stocks had a capital value of well over L. 800,000 in 1912, making

---

in urban properties with an average value of L. 299,883. In the years 1901 to 1912, twenty-four of them bequeathed L. 7,601,500 for an average of L. 316,729. The wealthiest aristocratic urban proprietor in the later period, Count Alberto Brondelli di Brondello left L. 798,650 in fixed assets in Turin in 1902; his total fortune was valued at L. 1,365,541. See *URST*, 1903, b. 239, f. 24. Between 1901 and 1912, the fifty-five wealthiest non-nobles in probate left L. 29,985,018 in urban properties, up form L. 19,183,325 in the period 1874–1885.
[23] See Banti, *Terra e denaro*, p. 29.

Table 6.3 *Aristocratic elite: lineage (>L. 750,000)*

Category	1862–1873 (%)	1874–1885 (%)	1901–1912 (%)
Pre-1722	92	70	67
Post-1722	4	13	8
Restoration	4	9	8
Post-1861	0	9	17

them the single most important component of the Ferrero d'Ormea patrimony.[24]

Count Ernesto Balbo Bertone di Sambuy followed a similar, if somewhat more conservative, program of diversified investments. While Count Ernesto sold a few small properties in the province of Alessandria in order to extinguish inherited debts, he left untouched the old family estate, San Salvà, as well as two other estates he had inherited from his mother and grandmother; these rural possessions remained the primary assets and main sources of revenues at least until his death in 1909. At the same time, Count Ernesto, whose public image was that of "the ultimate personification of aristocratic and feudal traditions," slowly began to diversify his assets, building up a securities portfolio that included stockholdings in railroad, machinery, automotive, and chemical fertilizer firms. By the time of his death, his stocks and bonds were worth L. 342,000 or roughly one-seventh of his total patrimony.[25]

These slight alterations in the structure of aristocratic fortunes coincided with and perhaps reflected gradual changes in the social origins and customs of the people who comprised the wealthiest segment of the nobility in Turin. Before World War I, there were initial signs that ancient lineage, endogamy, and primogeniture – classic elements of the noble ethos – had begun to lose some of their importance as the defining features of the aristocratic wealthy. As Table 6.3 indicates, the old families continued to provide the bulk of large fortunes within the nobility before World War I, but increasingly they had to make room at the top for new nobles like the bankers Count Felice Rignon, Baron Ernesto Casana, and Marchese Paolo Solaroli di Briona, and the cotton manufacturer Baron Paolo Mazzonis, all men who possessed titles but

---

[24] See Archivio Ferrero d'Ormea, b. 98, Successioni: Tancredi Ferrero d'Ormea, 1877 and b. 96, Gustavo, crediti e valori, anni diversi.

[25] Archivio Balbo Bertone di Sambuy, Cart. XVIII-C, b. b, f. 4, patto di famiglia, 1 November 1909 includes a list of all Count Ernesto's stocks and bonds. For his public image, see the lengthy obituary in *La Stampa*, February 25, 1909.

Table 6.4 *Aristocratic elite: spouse's lineage (>L. 750,000)*

Category	1862–1873 (%)	1901–1912 (%)
Pre-1722	79	57
Post-1722	4	0
Restoration	0	0
Post-1861	0	5
Bourgeois	4	10
Non-Piedmontese nobility	13	29

Table 6.5 *Aristocratic elite: family position (>L. 750,000)*

Category	All periods (%)	1862–1873 (%)	1874–1885 (%)	1901–1912 (%)
First Son	66	70	74	54
Cadet	10	7	9	13
Collateral	4	4	9	0
Daughter	20	19	9	33

remained actively involved in the worlds of urban real estate, finance, and industry.

The more varied pedigree of the titled rich carried over only partially to their choice of marriage partners. Wealthy aristocrats in the last decades before the war were less likely to limit their choice of spouses to the same small circle of old Piedmontese families, although endogamy remained strong (see Table 6.4).

The drop in the percentage of spouses from local titled families and a corresponding rise in marital alliances with noble families from outside the region can be traced in part to the effects of Italian unification which reduced provincial isolation and brought the heavily service-oriented Piedmontese aristocracy into frequent contact with prominent regional elites elsewhere on the peninsula. In this respect, they offer evidence for the gradual emergence of a genuinely national high society in the decades after 1861. At the same time, the data in Table 6.4 suggest that most wealthy aristocrats were still reluctant to abandon caste taboos and marry women from untitled families.

The commanding position of first sons within the wealthy titled elite also began to erode in the last decades before the war as the data in Table 6.5 shows. The retreat from the practice of primogeniture apparent in these statistics suggests that certain changes in the structure and values of aristocratic families were taking place. The shrinking number of first sons in the ranks of the wealthy reflected in part a distinct lack of demographic vitality. In fact, the specter of biological decline confronted a number of prominent old families who failed to reproduce themselves and accordingly died out in the decades after 1862 (see Table 6.6). The threat of extinction seems to have been especially acute at the very top of the aristocratic pyramid of wealth where ten of the eighteen richest old families in probate produced no sons and disappeared in the second half of the nineteenth century. Their ranks included some of the most prestigious names in Piedmont: Benso di Cavour, Alfieri di Sostegno, Taparelli d'Azeglio, Dal Pozzo della Cisterna, and Falletti di Barolo.

Whatever the reasons may be – an excessively small pool of suitable marriage partners, late marriages, the failure to marry at all, or some form of birth control – the resultant demographic decline had a devastating impact on a number of large aristocratic patrimonies. In virtually every case, failure to find a male heir led to the fragmentation and sale of much of the estates, often to the benefit of the institutions of the Catholic Church. When the Marchesa Giulia Falletti di Barolo died childless in 1864, for instance, her entire estate with its vast landholdings passed to the Opera Pia Barolo. Administrators of the Catholic charitable organization wasted no time liquidating a large part of the landed patrimony; between 1864 and 1871 they sold over 2,500 hectares.[26]

A similar course was followed by the last male members of three of Piedmont's most famous aristocratic families: Marchese Emanuele Taparelli d'Azeglio, Marchese Aynardo Benso di Cavour and Marchese Carlo Alfieri di Sostegno. All three men owed their great wealth and landholdings primarily to the fact that they had been only sons and therefore had inherited most if not all of their respective family estates. At the same time, it was precisely this singular status and their failure to provide male heirs that condemned their families to extinction and their landed patrimonies to dispersion. Ironically, in the case of Marchese Emanuele Taparelli d'Azeglio, aristocratic caste traditions may have been a contributing factor. After a youthful romance was effectively sabotaged by his parents who deemed the young woman socially inappropriate, d'Azeglio never married. When he died in 1890, his sizeable rural properties passed to the newly founded Opera Pia Taparelli in Saluzzo which had as its primary mission the care of the sick and home-

---

[26] Archivio Falletti di Barolo, b. 51, f. 1. Sales netted L. 2,519,388. For a brief discussion of some of the factors that contributed to the crisis of family continuity in the nineteenth century, see Stone and Fawtier Stone, *An Open Elite?*, p. 282.

Table 6.6 *Aristocratic elite: demographics (>L. 750,000)*

Category	1862–1873 (%)	1874–1885 (%)	1901–1912 (%)
Celibate	7	17	4
Married	93	83	96
Total	100	100	100
No children	16	26	29
W/children	84	74	71
Total	100	100	100
No sons	36	37	39
One son	24	37	22
More than one son	40	26	39
Total	100	100	100

less from the communes of Lagnasco, Genola and Maresco, "ancient fiefs of the Taparelli family."[27]

Much like d'Azeglio, the last Marchese di Cavour was a life-long bachelor who as an only son had inherited the great bulk of his father's estates as well as those of his famous uncle. His death in 1875, however, resulted in the rapid division of the family's landed patrimony. According to the terms of his will, Marchese Aynardo distributed his rural properties among seven legatees, with the largest and most valuable portion (the 1,215 hectare estate of Leri in the Vercellese plains) going to the Ospizio di Carità in Turin.[28] Marchese di Cavour's brother-in-law, Marchese Carlo Alfieri di Sostegno, made a considerably more valiant effort to carry on his family name, but two marriages, to Ernestina Doria di Cirìè and Giuseppina Benso di Cavour, yielded only two daughters. As a result, Marchese Carlo in his last will and testament distributed his large family patrimony between his daughters and the Istituto di Scienze Sociali Cesare Alfieri in Florence.[29]

---

[27] Borbonese, *Gli ultimi Azeglio*, p. 53; Maldini Chiarito, "Trasmissione di valori e educazione familiare," pp. 54–55.

[28] URST, 1876, vol. 68, f. 2. Marchese Aynardo left the remainder of his rural properties to his cousins, Ortensia De-Sellon and Count Eugenio di Roussy di Sales, his two nieces, Luisa and Adelina Alfieri di Sostegno, his private secretary, and the city of Turin. Significantly, the only thing he left to his sister, Giuseppina Alfieri di Sostegno was part of the family silverware and linen and then only on the condition that she not "interfere in the division . . . of said personal effects."

[29] AST, Prima Sez., Archivio Alfieri di Sostegno, b. 19, f. 8, testamenti del Marchese Carlo Alfieri di Sostegno.

In other cases where there was a number of sons, the skills increasingly required to maintain and manage family patrimonies led wealthy nobles to abandon the principle of primogeniture to ensure that their ablest offspring would be in charge. This appears to have been the logic behind the decision of Marchese Giuseppe Dalla Valle di Pomaro to leave the bulk of his large estate to his second son, Marchese Alessandro, despite the fact that he was still single at the time of his father's death.[30]

The rising number of cadets and women with large fortunes may have also resulted from a growing reluctance on their part to subordinate their individual economic interests and rights to the dynastic interests of the family as embodied in the first son. Marchesa Albertina Compans di Brichanteau and her husband Marchese Carlo, for instance, waged a bitter court battle with her mother and only brother, Marchese Giuseppe Pallavicino-Mossi, over the value and division of the huge fortune left by their father in 1879. Marchese Lodovico Pallavicino-Mossi, who passed on an estate valued at around L. 4.5 million, failed to make clear in his will whether he wanted the *disponibile* or freely disposable half to go exclusively to his son or to be divided equally among his children. The widow and son claimed the *disponibile*, citing views expressed by Marchese Lodovico before his death. Marchesa Albertina and her husband, for their part, challenged that claim and demanded a third of the estate.[31]

Still, changes in the structure and social composition of aristocratic wealth did not add up to any radical transformation of Turin's titled elite in the period from unification to World War I. On the contrary, the upper levels of the Piedmontese nobility steadfastly maintained a certain balance between continuity and innovation that permitted cautious adaptation, but avoided any real abandonment of tradition. Aristocrats continued to follow a way of life that entailed social exclusivity, traditional pastimes, and the maintenance of dual residences with large staffs of servants. New interest in stocks and bonds and the growing presence of women, cadets, and the newly ennobled in their ranks

---

[30] For the last will and testament of the father, see Marchese Alessandro's probate file in *URST*, b. 694, f. 5, 1905.

[31] See the records in AST, Sezione Riunite, Archivio Compans di Brichanteau, Category 6, b. 6 and b. 28, f. 14, Pallavicino Pro-Memoria, Rome 1903, for various accounts of the ensuing court battles. According to the terms of the final settlement, Albertina and her husband gave up their claim to a third of the total value of the estate. In exchange, Marchese Giuseppe Pallavicino-Mossi and his mother accepted the larger estimate of the total value of the estate which had been advanced by the Compans di Brichanteau. As a result, Albertina's total share of her father's estate (including the dowry) came to L. 720,000. She then received another L. 120,000 after the death of her mother. See *ibid.*, f. 17.

should not obscure the fact that on the eve of the Great War most affluent nobles were still the first sons of old pedigreed families whose wealth lay predominantly in the land. In this respect, the composition of their fortunes remained considerably more traditional than those of the wealthy bourgeoisie.

Despite the laments of some landed magnates and their agents, the strong presence of the old-line families on the land also enabled them to continue playing an important leadership role in the countryside. As I have argued in Chapters 2 and 3, this role helped preserve vertical ties and local loyalties among certain strata of their rural dependents, combat the growth of more modern forms of class solidarity, and bolster traditional notions of "natural" leadership. In this fashion, they may well have contributed to the stability and social peace that so distinguished the Piedmontese countryside from other areas of the Po Valley in the late nineteenth century. They rarely had to contend with the militant agricultural unions and bitter strikes that beset their counterparts in Emilia and Lombardy. Between 1880 and 1901, the strike propensity of farm workers in Piedmont remained low, especially when compared to these neighboring regions. Socialist labor organizers encountered considerably greater difficulties founding peasant leagues in the Piedmontese plains, where provincial federations came late, were small in size, and proved to be short lived.[32] And even in those provinces such as Vercelli and Novara, where the leagues did manage to establish a base among rice workers, they met strong resistance in the fields and at the ballot box from a coalition of anti-socialist forces commanded by titled nobles.[33]

WORLD WAR I AND THE ECONOMIC CRISIS OF THE NOBILITY

In his last will and testament before his death in 1923, Marchese Carlo Alberto Scarampi del Cairo sadly informed his heirs that although he had never wasted "a dime (*un soldo*) . . . of our patrimony . . . it has been reduced by now to little value."[34] As his words suggest, the years after Italy's entrance into World War I were not easy ones for the local aristocratic elite. Indeed, the war proved to be a considerably more pivotal event than the agricultural depression of the 1880s and 1890s in

---

[32] For comparative data on strikes and rural labor militancy, see Charles Tilly, Louise Tilly, and Richard Tilly, *The Rebellious Century, 1830–1930* (Cambridge, MA, 1975), pp. 158–161; Giuliano Procacci, *La lotta di classe in Italia agli inizi del secolo XX* (Rome, 1970), pp. 78–81, 302–305.

[33] See note 16 in this chapter.

[34] *URST*, b. 1389, f. 19, Marchese Carlo Alberto Scarampi del Cairo, 4 February 1923.

the decline of Piedmont's nobility. As the previous section has shown, most aristocrats had managed to avoid any catastrophic financial collapse in the late nineteenth century. On the whole, they had charted a course of limited diversification that enabled them to preserve much of their wealth and the way of life that it made possible. The pace of economic and social change accelerated dramatically for the old families after Italy officially became a belligerent in May 1915. Even the most careful planning could not prepare the titled nobility for what now confronted them. World War I and its aftermath proved to be especially formidable challenges that few old-line families were able to surmount without substantial changes in attitude and behavior.

It is hardly surprising to find Piedmontese nobles actively involved in most aspects of the war, given their strong martial traditions and deep sense of loyalty to the House of Savoy. Even before Italy had officially entered the war, aristocratic notables like Count Emanuele Costa di Polonghera, Count Alessandro Rovasenda di Rovasenda, and Alfonso Ferrero di Ventimiglia played leading roles in the Comitato di Preparazione founded in early 1915 to promote and prepare for Italian intervention in the hostilities.[35] After the "radiant days of May," older titled gentlemen like Lt. General Alberto Morelli di Popolo, president of the Comitato della Mobilitazione Industriale per il Piemonte, bolstered the war effort on the domestic front, while younger nobles either volunteered or pursued their natural career choices on active duty in the armed forces. Between 1915 and 1918, some 300 aristocratic members of the Società del Whist alone were in uniform. Many honored the traditions of their lineages by serving with distinction; eighty-eight Piedmontese nobles were decorated for valor. Such bravery exacted a disproportionately heavy price. More than a dozen officers from local titled families were killed or crippled, another thirty were wounded in combat, and countless others were emotionally debilitated by the experience.[36]

World War I proved to be no less difficult for the Piedmontese nobles on the home front. Vera Zamagni and Adeline Daumard have argued that the war and its aftermath provoked a general loss of private wealth in Italy and France as a result of material destruction and "the forced diversion of private resources to the state."[37] The structure of

[35] See Castronovo, *Il Piemonte*, p. 283.

[36] For information on the role of local nobles in the war effort, see *Elenco dei nobili caduti, decorati* (Turin, 1918). On the number of members of the Whist in the war and their activities, see the Società Cavour, *Un secolo di vita*, pp. 94–96, 186–257.

[37] See Zamagni, "The Rich in a Late Industrialiser," p. 135, and Daumard, "Wealth and Affluence in France," pp. 111–112.

aristocratic fortunes in Piedmont, with their emphasis on real property and land holding, were particularly vulnerable to the worst effects of the war. Like absentee landowners elsewhere on the peninsula, they were hard hit by the effects of new economic conditions, military conscription, and state intervention during the war years. Government decrees, tax policies, and price trends all worked decisively to the disadvantage of those landowners who had leased out their lands prior to 1915. Because of the freeze on rents, they received none of the financial benefits of rapidly climbing farm prices, while they had to shoulder the burdens of increased property taxes and rising costs of living. Arrigo Serpieri has estimated that absentee landlords in the Po Valley saw their real income fall by as much as a third, leading to what he characterized as a massive "shift of wealth from the landowner to the leaseholder."[38]

The wartime revenues of the Pallavicino-Mossi estates in Vercelli provide a graphic example of the war's impact on landed income of the nobility in Piedmont. Between 1915 and 1920, the gross rental income from their farms remained frozen at L. 151,500 per year, while their net revenues fell from L. 98,186 in 1916–1917 to a low of L. 62,301 in 1919–1920. When inflation is taken into consideration, the actual net losses suffered by the family's agricultural properties were even more dramatic, since the real value of the post-war Italian lira was only about 37 percent of what it had been in 1914. In the case of the Pallavicino-Mossi family, these losses were counterbalanced by their dairy operations, whose annual revenues went from L. 44,317 in 1914 to L. 152,837 in 1919 and by their urban rents which rose about a third during the same period.[39] Few nobles, however, had so much land or lucrative non-agricultural sources of income to weather the war years as comfortably as Marchese Giuseppe Pallavicino-Mossi, who according to the Municipal Tax Commission headed a family that was "among the wealthiest in Piedmont."[40]

A survey of the roughly 4,250 estates that passed through probate during the years 1922–1923 confirms that both a general loss of wealth in Turin and an especially severe drop in the fortunes of the old titled families had taken place during the war and immediate post-war years. When inflation is taken into account, the data show that the number

---

[38] Serpieri, *La guerra e le classi rurali*, pp. 116–118.

[39] Information on the wartime finances of the family comes from AST, Sez. Riunite, Archivio Pallavicino-Mossi, b. 11, Entrate e Uscite, 1912–1930; b. 10, wartime revenues declared for the *Contributo straordinario di guerra*.

[40] AST, Sez. Riunite, Archivio Pallavicino-Mossi, b. 10. The comments of the Commissione were in response to Count Giuseppe Pallavicino-Mossi's appeal for a reduction in his tax assessment in 1918.

Table 6.7 *Large estates in probate*[a] *(annual average in 1914 lire)*

Category	1901–1912	1922–1923
L. 250,001–500,000	19	13
500,001–750,000	6	2
750,001–1,000,000	2	1
More than 1,000,000	5	0.5

[a] In order to convert post-war monetary values into 1914 lire, I have relied on the tables published in Istituto Centrale di Statistica, *Il valore della lira dal 1861 al 1965* (Rome, 1966), p. 66, which cites as the coefficients for converting into 1914 lire the years 1922 and 1923 as respectively 0.2414 and 0.2428.

and scale of the large estates in 1922 and 1923 were substantially smaller than they had been during the Giolittian era (Table 6.7). Great concentrations of wealth became exceedingly rare in the wake of the war. In fact, measured by the monetary values of the pre-war years, only one millionaire and no multi-millionaires passed through probate in the years 1922–1923.

At the same time, the wealth-holdings of the nobility, in general, fell dramatically from their pre-war levels (Table 6.8). The nominally "poor" (those titled individuals with less than L. 100,000 in assets) now constituted the vast majority of the nobles in probate, while the percentage of those who were truly impoverished (less than L. 1,000) was more than twice what it had been before 1912.

Not surprisingly, the old aristocratic families contributed a much smaller share of the large fortunes in probate after the war, even when the effects of inflation are not taken into account (Table 6.9). At least in terms of its wealth-holding, the Piedmontese upper class that emerged from the war was an overwhelmingly non-noble social formation in which the old families, with their titles and ancient lineages, occupied a rather marginal position.

The sharp decline in the nobility's share of the large fortunes coincided with important changes in the composition of their wealth. Above all, what had been a gradual and strategic withdrawal by aristocratic families from the countryside before 1914 became a full-scale exodus in the early 1920s. For many of them, the war and immediate post-war conditions in the countryside created extraordinary new pressures and incentives to sell their land holdings. On the one hand, a number of new factors made continued landownership extremely disadvantageous: increased death duties and steadily mounting tax burdens, a shortage of agricultural laborers as a result of high wages offered in industry and the cities, and an explosion of political radicalism and labor

Table 6.8. *Distribution of wealth within the nobility (1914 Lire)*

Category	1901–1912 (%)	1922–1923 (%)
Less than L. 100,000	46	70
100,001–250,000	26	17
250,001–500,000	13	9
500,001–750,000	4	4
750,001–1,000,000	2	0
More than 1,000,000	9	0

Table 6.9 *Changes in the distribution of large fortunes (post-war lire)*

Category	1901–1912		1922–1923	
Estate Size	Arist. (%)	Bourg. (%)	Arist. (%)	Bourg. (%)
L. 250,001–500,000	14.4	85.6	8.2	91.8
500,001–750,000	34.4	65.6	8.5	91.5
750,001–1,000,000	27.8	72.2	10.5	89.5
More than 1,000,000	30.6	69.4	17.1	82.9

militancy in the countryside that seemed to challenge the basic rights of private property. On the other hand, there were substantial financial advantages to selling landed assets in the immediate post-war period. The continual devaluation of the lira and a flood of eager buyers from the ranks of peasant tenants, who had done well during the war, drove up the price of farm lands to levels that had little relationship to their actual profitability. Under these circumstances, the selling off of rural properties represented a very attractive business proposition to landed families, since it provided immediate capital that could be invested elsewhere at a much higher rate of return.[41]

The results are evident in the probate returns for 1922–1923, which registered a significant drop in both the value and size of aristocratic rural properties. Of the fifty-two nobles in the survey, twenty-two left no land holdings at all, while another ten had landed assets with a capital value of less than L. 12,000 when corrected for inflation. Although farm land still constituted an important source of wealth for three of the seven richest aristocrats in the post-war survey, none qualified as a large landowner by pre-war standards.[42]

[41] See Istituto Nazionale di Economia Agraria, *Inchiesta sulla piccola proprietà*, pp. 53–54.
[42] Marchese Lorenzo Del Caretto di Torre Bormida and Marchesa Luisa Incisa di Cam-

The cases of two of the wealthier nobles, Baron Roberto Casana and Count Calisto Gay di Quarti, indicate how the paucity of aristocratic rural properties in probate was probably the result of land transfers made during and immediately after the war. In 1917, Casana, the principal heir of his father Baron Ernesto Casana, inherited an estate that included over 300 hectares of prime farm land mostly in the province of Novara. By the time of his own death in 1921, Baron Roberto had disposed of all of his land either by sale or transfer to his younger brothers. His sizeable estate consisted exclusively of urban rental palaces and stocks and bonds. In a similar fashion, Count Calisto Gay di Quarti held on to the family castle and park, but sold his last remaining rural properties in 1919 for a handsome sum that he then proceeded to invest in corporate stocks and government bonds.[43]

This aristocratic exodus from the land continued in the following two decades which saw a number of Piedmont's oldest landed families desert their ancestral properties in the countryside. The Costa della Trinità family offers a particularly striking case in point. In the pre-war era, Count Paolo Costa della Trinità had inherited a huge landed estate of over 1,300 hectares in the provinces of Cuneo and Turin. The estate he left to his son and daughter in 1930 included a mere 15 hectares of rural property; the chief asset of the family was an entire square block of rent palaces in the fashionable Borgo Nuovo quarter of Turin. Marchese Maurizio Luserna di Rorà, whose predecessors had been major landowners in the late nineteenth century, followed a similar course. Of the several hundred hectares his family had owned in the 1870s, only twenty-one remained in his possession at the time of his death in 1929. Much like his cousin, Count Paolo Costa della Trinità, Marchese Maurizio preferred to hold on to his family's urban properties, which together with his securities portfolio, made up the bulk of his substantial fortune.[44]

Marchese Carlo Compans di Brichanteau, perhaps the greatest aristocratic financial success story of his generation in Piedmont, best demon-

---

erana each left properties totaling 171 hectares with a capital value of approximately L. 250,000 (1914 lire); 192 fortunes in the pre-war probate survey included rural properties with a greater capital value.

[43] For the estates of Baron Ernesto Casana and his son Baron Roberto, see respectively URST, b. 1076, f. 2, 1917 and b. 1340, f. 47, 1922; that of Count Calisto Gay di Quarti is in b. 1358, f. 19, 1922.

[44] For the estates of Count Paolo Costa di Trinità and Marchese Maurizio Luserna di Rorà, see URST, b. 1503, f. 55 and b. 1474, f. 17. Information of the nineteenth-century landholdings of the two families can be found in AST, Sez. Riunite, Archivio Costa della Trinità, b. 5, Certificato di Denunzia, successioni Count Carlo Costa della Trinità, 1893; b. 11, Eredità Luserna di Rorà.

strated what it took for the scions of old titled families to amass and then preserve substantial wealth in the first decades of the twentieth century. While both his parents came from old-line families, neither was especially affluent. As a result, the inheritance Marchese Carlo received upon the death of his father in 1873 was a rather modest one, amounting to little more than L. 115,000.[45] After his marriage to Albertina Pallavicino-Mossi in 1876, the ambitious young aristocrat's financial prospects began to improve dramatically. Between her dowry and the portions of her parents' estates, Albertina brought L. 840,000 into her husband's household. With his excellent connections in the worlds of politics and business, Compans proved to be an astute investor of this new found wealth. In the 1880s and 1990s, he sold off much of his rural property and used the proceeds from the sales (and his wife's money) to purchase a number of rental buildings in Turin.[46] The following decades also saw him expand his family's investments in corporate stocks and treasury bonds. Despite the war and its aftermath, Marchese Carlo died a very wealthy man with a personal fortune estimated at L. 16,887,743 in the mid-1920s.

The estate he left to his heirs was distinguished not only by its size, but also by its structure which bore scant resemblance to the great aristocratic patrimonies of the previous century. An extremely diversified portfolio of stocks and bonds constituted the single largest component, accounting for nearly half (49 percent) of the total gross value of the estate. Urban rental palaces represented the second largest component (43 percent). Significantly, rural property, the traditional measure of noble wealth and status, played a negligible part in the Compans di Brichanteau fortune. While Marchese Carlo still owned his family's castle in Mercenasco as well as villas in Andrate and Massa (Tuscany), together they were valued at only L. 998,000 or less than 6 percent of the total.[47]

---

[45] AST, Sez. Riunite, Archivio Compans di Brichanteau, Cat. 8, u.a. 28, f. 10. The entire estate was valued at L. 210,950, with the most valuable assets being the Castle of Mercenasco and scattered properties in Ciriè, Rivarolo and in Tuscany that together amounted to little more than 100 hectares. Of little economic value, but as testaments to the ancient lineage of the family were the *annualità perpetue* owed the family by the communities of Ala (1724) and Lombriasco (1580). See *ibid.*, Cat. 4, u.a. 6, f. 24, denuncia di successione di Conte Alessandro Compans di Brichanteau.

[46] At the beginning of this century, Compans and his wife owned nine buildings in Turin, six in his name and three in hers. See *La Guida di Torino, 1900*. Albertina's dowry was worth L. 320,000; her share of her father's estate came to another L. 400,000, and she received L. 120,000 from her mother. AST, Sez. Riunite, Archivio Compans, c. 8, u.a. 28, f. 17, Report of Ragioniere Ferroglio, December 15, 1926.

[47] *Ibid.* Compans owned stock in some twenty different companies. Their estimated

Of course, not all aristocratic families liquidated completely their landed patrimonies. Those grandees like Marchese Giuseppe Pallavicino-Mossi and Count Augusto Avogadro di Collobiano, who had the bulk of their estates in the rich rice-growing areas of the Vercelli and Novara, remained big property owners. Yet even their rural properties and agricultural interests diminished significantly in the inter-war period. During the 1920s, Count Giuseppe, for instance, sold off his family's dairy operations and virtually cut his land holdings in half. As a result, agricultural revenues, which had provided 57 percent of his annual income in 1920, accounted for only 18 percent in the last years of the decade. By 1930, Count Giuseppe derived the major part (58 percent) of his sizeable annual income from his various financial operations.[48] Avogadro di Collobiano, who had inherited perhaps the largest single landed patrimony in Piedmont in the early twentieth century, appears to have followed a similar course. At the time of his death in the mid-1930s, Count Augusto was still a major landlord in the province of Vercelli, but his rural estates had dwindled to roughly two-fifths what they had been before World War I.[49] Titled families might still make annual pilgrimages to their country houses, but they had largely ceased to be the chief employers, patrons, and arbiters of a hierarchically organized rural society by the end of the inter-war period. Much like their country houses, they now stood in splendid isolation in the countryside without any concrete, ongoing connection to the population of the surrounding farms or villages.

ARISTOCRATIC SOCIAL RECONVERSION IN THE INTER-WAR PERIOD

Pierre Bourdieu has observed how reconversion strategies designed to safeguard or improve family or individual positions in social space become especially important "at a stage in the evolution of class societies in which one can conserve only by changing – to change so as to conserve."[50] For the old titled families of Piedmont, the decades after 1918 constituted just such a stage. The war did more than hurt these families

---

value was L. 8,260,557. His estate also included four buildings in Turin valued at L. 7,334,818. Adjusted for inflation, the total value of his estate (in 1914 lire) was L. 3,526,161.

[48] See Archivio Pallavicino-Mossi, b. 11, conti di casa 1920–30; b. 10, imposta sul patrimonio 1920; b. 6 f. 5, denuncia di successione 1945.

[49] For the estate of Count Ferdinando Avogadro di Collobiano, see URST, b. 655, f. 38, 1904. On the land holdings of his son, see Archivio Avogadro di Collobiano e della Motta, b. 157.

[50] Bourdieu, *Distinction*, p. 157.

in their pocketbooks; it also engendered a new society that seemed to bear little relationship to what they had known before 1914. The resulting disorientation, disillusionment, and cynicism severed many of the emotional bonds that linked a younger generation of aristocrats to the past, weakening in the process their attachment to norms and social practices that had previously defined the nobility as a separate and distinct elite within Piedmontese high society. Financial exigencies combined with a new indifference to tradition to induce a significant erosion of aristocratic taboos and prejudices in the 1920s and 1930s as a profile of the nobles who became members of the Società del Whist after 1918 clearly indicates.

Both in their educational background and in their career choices, this post-war generation of men from titled families differed in important respects from their predecessors who had entered the club in the two decades before 1915. To begin with, aristocratic men were much more likely to have received university degrees (Table 6.10). Prior to the war, only a small minority of the nobles in the Whist received their *laurea*. In the vast majority of cases (78 percent), those who did graduate from the university, took degrees in law usually as part of their preparation for careers in the diplomatic corps. Nearly twice as many members went to military school and then entered the officers corps. This traditional pattern changed noticeably in the decades after the war when the ranks of *dottori* virtually doubled, with university graduates outnumbering for the first time army officers among the new members of the Whist. Almost half of the titled men who entered the club between 1919 and 1940 had received a higher education. Moreover, a substantially larger number of these university trained aristocrats now took their degrees in fields such as engineering and economics that prepared them more for entry into the worlds of industry and commerce than state service.

Changing educational preferences coincided with the accelerated decline of old caste prejudices against involvement in business enterprise. The inter-war period saw a gradual expansion of "acceptable" occupations for young men from old-line families. After 1918, a growing number of nobles either chose or were forced to abandon the life of leisure and public service followed by their ancestors and to seek employment in Turin's business community. Of the 292 men from titled families who were admitted as members to the Società del Whist between 1919 and 1940, 38 held managerial positions in industry and banking, a work status that would have been unimaginable in the pre-war era.[51]

[51] See source cited in Table 6.10.

Table 6.10 *Aristocratic higher education (titled Whist members)*

Degree Field	1893–1914	1919–40
Law	56	78
Engineering	12	41
Economics	1	8
Agronomy	1	3
Chemistry	0	3
Mathematics	1	0
Medicine	1	0
University totals	72	133
% of cohort	28	46
Military	139	104
% of cohort	55	37

These statistics are drawn from Società Cavour, *Un secolo di vita*, pp. 186–257.

Aristocratic attitudes toward social contacts with business families changed accordingly, as both the admissions policies of the Whist and new marriage alliances attest. In contrast to the patterns that had prevailed in the two decades before 1914 when they accounted for less than 6 percent of the entrants into the Whist, non-nobles made up 13 percent of the new members admitted into the club in the inter-war years.[52] During the same period, it also became more socially acceptable, if not commonplace, for even the scions of Piedmont's wealthier old titled families to take the daughters of prominent industrial magnates as their brides. This merger of old stock and new wealth found its purest expression in the inter-war years in the marriage of Count Cesare Valperga di Masino to Vittoria Leumann in September 1929. The groom was the only son and principal heir to the substantial patrimony and titles of one of Piedmont's most ancient and prestigious aristocratic lineages. After serving with distinction in World War I, Count Cesare led the life of a gentleman of leisure, dividing his time between his palace in Turin and his ancestral castle in Masino. His new bride, on the other hand, came from a strikingly different social milieu. The Leumanns had only arrived in Italy in the 1830s and in three generations they went from being textile workers to heading one of the region's most important cotton manufacturing complexes. Nor was the Leumann–Valperga di Masino wedding a unique event; the same years also saw other prominent industrial families like the Mazzonis and Rossi di Montelera begin to intermarry with the old nobility.[53]

[52] *Ibid.*

[53] The marriage is noted in *Il libro d'oro della nobiltà italiana* (Rome, 1932), p. 1140. According to Manno, the Valperga di Masino were among the top four noble families

The triumph of Fascism did not fundamentally alter these patterns of economic and social reconversion. Much like their counterparts in Tuscany and Rome, aristocratic families in Piedmont emerged as beneficiaries of the collapse of parliamentary democracy and the consolidation of Mussolini's dictatorship in the 1920s, although they were neither early nor enthusiastic converts to the Blackshirts' movement.[54] After their virtual disappearance from political life in the immediate post-war period, titled aristocrats served in a whole host of governmental and party posts at the local level in the years from 1925 to 1943.[55]

The honors and offices that the Fascist regime bestowed upon titled nobles hardly represented, however, a restoration of aristocratic traditionalism in Piedmont. On the contrary, the old-line families sacrificed even more of their old social exclusivity by according the plebeian leaders of Fascism a degree of acclaim and acceptance that they had long denied the Duce's liberal predecessors.[56] More importantly, despite

in Piedmont who historically enjoyed precedence over all others on all solemn occasions and royal ceremonies. See Manno, *Il patriziato subalpino*, vol. xx, "Piossasco Asinari Derossi". For a biographical sketch of Count Cesare Valperga di Masino, see Società Cavour, *Secolo di vita*, p. 250. On the Leumann family, see Testa, "La strategie di una famiglia imprenditoriale," pp. 603–636. During the inter-war years, Count Alberto d'Harcourt married Ada Rossi di Montelera, while three of Cesare Mazzonis' children married into noble families: Schiari Riccardi, di Gresy, and Mocchia di Coggiola. See Manno, *Il patriziato subalpino*, vol. xv, and Levi, *L'idea del buon padre*, p. 8.

54 The available evidence indicates that aristocratic "fascists of the first hour" were a decided rarity in Turin and the surrounding region. Certainly no figure comparable to Marchese Dino Perrone Campagni, scion of an old Florentine noble family and *generalissimo* of the Tuscan squadrists, emerged from the ranks of the Piedmontese nobility. At least until 1925, most politically active nobles were at best *fiancheggiatori*, whose primary allegiances remained with the Liberal-Monarchist and Catholic camps. On the early days of the Fascio of Turin, see Bianchi di Vigny, *Storia del fascismo torinese*, pp. 143, 336, 339, 397. For additional information, see Missori, *Gerarchie e statuti del PNF*; Tuninetti, *Squadrismo*; Guasco, *Fascisti e cattolici*; Maggia, *Lotte sociale e lotte politiche*; Chiaramonte, *Economia e società in provincia di Novara*.

55 Some eighty-six aristocratic members of the Società del Whist served the Fascist regime in the following capacities: twenty-four podestà, four vice-podestà, ten federal secretaries of the PNF, four political secretaries of local fasci, eight members of disciplinary councils, fifteen in the economic corporations, and twenty-one in various other capacities. See Società Cavour, *Un secolo di vita*, pp. 186–257 and Missori, *Gerarchie e statuti*, pp. 158–292.

56 In 1928, the Società del Whist conferred the status of Honorary Member on Mussolini, who became the first and only non-noble and head of government to ever receive such a title. Breaking with another longstanding tradition of the club, that of political neutrality, the Whist held a special dinner four years later in October 1932 to honor the Duce, who became the first head of an Italian government to enter its rooms and address the membership since the days of Cavour. See Società Cavour, *Un secolo di vita*, pp. 88–89, for an account of the reception for Mussolini at the

their renewed political prominence, the aristocrats who entered public life during the inter-war period differed in important respects from their nineteenth-century predecessors. Measured by the traditional standards of their class, they were considerably less wealthy, leisured, service-oriented, and socially exclusive than their parents and grandparents. Unprecedented numbers of nobles no longer possessed the financial means to support their old genteel way of life. And even those titled families who remained financially well-off were much less likely to still constitute a landed aristocracy with their wealth and status in the countryside. By the late 1930s, the figure of the aristocratic landed gentleman of leisure had become much more the exception rather than the rule.

At the same time, the Great War and its aftermath left noble families demoralized and undermined their old sense of collective élan. Thus, with the retreat from the land came a decline in other traditions that had previously defined and distinguished the Piedmontese nobility. The generation of nobles who entered the Whist after 1918, for instance, no longer embraced the old military vocation with the same enthusiasm and unanimity as before the war. Instead, growing numbers of them took a decidedly bourgeois course, pursuing technical educations and careers in business that only a generation earlier had been viewed with utter contempt in respectable aristocratic circles. And as more young nobles began to enter the worlds of industry and finance, old caste barriers began to come down with the opening of the doors of the Whist to new men and the increasing frequency of intermarriage between noble and bourgeois families. By the end of the inter-war period, Piedmont's titled elite had gone a long way toward losing their distinctive identity and merging into a broader and more heterogeneous upper class.

World War II and its aftermath only carried to completion this process of social reconversion and fusion. In addition to its substantial material costs, the war drastically hastened the demise of the last two institutional bulwarks of aristocratic group identity and cohesion in Piedmont: the House of Savoy and the old, socially exclusive, Società del Whist. The abolition of the monarchy after a national referendum in 1946 and the resultant loss of legal status for hereditary titles deprived Piedmontese noble families of an institution that had provided the focus

Whist. The foremost regional luminary of Fascism, the newly ennobled (1925) Count Cesare De Vecchi di Cismon, was also accorded an unusually warm reception from the institutional bastion of the Piedmontese aristocracy. In 1929, the members of the Whist made him a *socio aggregato d'honore*, the first since 1865. Two years later the club admitted his son, Count Giorgio De Vecchi di Cismon, as a regular member. See *ibid.*, pp. 245, 260.

for their traditional ethos of duty and service as well as the figurehead that structured their social hierarchies.[57] Nowhere were the consequences of the fall of the monarchy more evident than in the armed forces, which more than any other body had defined the special identity of the Piedmontese nobility. In the absence of the House of Savoy, the Italian army officers corps ceased to be the fashionable, not to say obligatory, vocation it had once been in aristocratic circles.

World War II also dramatically hastened the collapse of the remaining barriers to elite social fusion. Such fusion found its most fitting symbolic expression in the post-war transformation of the Società del Whist. In December 1946, a special commission was formed by the membership to explore various solutions to the club's enormous financial problems and the physical damage of its old locale. Without the means to continue "the life of the club along the same lines as in the years preceding the war" and unwilling to accept "a reduced style of life," the members decided to open negotiations with "a similar club." These negotiations concluded in 1948 when the Whist merged with the leading bourgeois men's club, the Accademia Filarmonica, to form "a great club, a meeting place for all the best elements in the city."[58] Appropriately, the new hybrid club took up residence in the locale of the Filarmonica, a former aristocratic palace in Piazza San Carlo.

In the decades since World War II, Piedmont's titled noble families have not vanished altogether from the upper classes and high society in Turin as even the most casual glance at the leadership and membership of the Whist–Filarmonica clearly reveals.[59] Eight of the eleven presidents of the club between 1948 and 1977 were old-line nobles from such pedigreed families as the San Martino d'Agliè di San Germano, Provana di Collegno, and Giriodi Panissera di Monastero. As recently as 1977, 395 men or more than half the membership of what has remained one of Italy's most exclusive and socially prestigious gentlemen's clubs still claimed titles which they attached prominently to their names in the Whist–Filarmonica address book. While some nobles only acquired their titles after World War I, many others came from old-stock families. Indeed, a number of them continued to possess not only titles, but also the material trappings of aristocratic lineage. Prince Don Francesco Guasco di Bisio, for instance, resided in his ancestral palace on Via

---

[57] See Rumi, "La politica nobiliare," pp. 592–593.

[58] See a copy of the commission's report which is located in AST, Sez. Riunite, Archivio Compans di Brichanteau, u.a. 43, f, 1. 2. On the actual fusion, see Marazzi, *170 anniversario dell'Accademia Filarmonica*, p. 7.

[59] The data presented in this paragraph are drawn from the Società del Whist-Accademia Filarmonica, *Elenco dei soci per l'anno 1977* (Turin, 1977).

dei Guasco in Alessandria. Others like Count Luigi Valperga di Masino, Marchese Carlo Del Carretto di Moncrivello, Count Percivalle Roero di Monticello, and Marchese Alessandro Gay di Quarti e di Lesegno still remained the owners and occupants of castles that bear their names and had been in their families for centuries.

But these men represented a shrinking minority within a group of old families that now resided for the most part on the wide avenues of the newer "bourgeois" neighborhoods of Turin such the Crocetta and earned their livelihoods in the worlds of finance and industry. Significantly, some of the more successful nobles in the post-war era – Luca Cordero di Montezemolo, Gustavo Figarolo di Gropello, Filippo Beraudo di Pralormo, and Vittorio Caissotti di Chiusano – have served as high level executives and representatives of this Fiat industrial empire and the Agnelli family. As their achievements attest, the survival of the nobility has depended on the abandonment of an aristocratic culture of landed leisure and the acceptance of a new culture of work and industry.

BIBLIOGRAPHY

PROBATE RECORDS

Much of the quantitative data in this book rests on a survey of all surviving probate records from unification to the years shortly before World War I – approximately 30,000 files – which were stored in the Ufficio di Registro in the building of Intendenza di Finanza in Turin at the time that I consulted them. I located and examined about 90 percent of all the records for the years 1862 to 1885, and 1901 to 1912. In addition, I carried out a smaller post-war survey of some 4,250 files in probate in 1922 and the first half of 1923. Unfortunately, all records for the years 1886 to 1900 are missing, having either been lost or destroyed. Individual files or *fascicoli* were grouped in binders or *buste*. Each busta contained from 42 to 146 fascicoli. From these files I collected detailed patrimonial, genealogical, demographic, and professional information on all individuals from titled aristocratic families, some 837 individuals, as well as on a group of the 125 wealthiest non-nobles (with estates valued at over L. 750,000). That information was then entered into an SAS data set, using an IBM mainframe computer. With thirty-two variables, this data set permitted the systematic analysis of such factors as the form and scale of wealth, lineage, gender, primogeniture, and endogamy within the nobility over a span of a half century. At the same time, it also provided a more precise measure of the infiltration, interaction, intermarriage, and other forms of contact between nobles and new families from the worlds of industry, banking, and commerce.

The inaccessibility, disarray, and physical deterioration of the nineteenth-century probate records in Turin largely dictated a comprehensive survey. The documents for the period up to 1912 were crammed into a dark, damp, and filthy room in the basement below the Ufficio di Registro where they had been left largely untouched for decades. The condition of records for the period from 1913 to 1919, which were stored in a nearby room, were slightly better, but almost as inaccessible. The probate records for the period since the end of World War I were organized chronologically in larger and cleaner rooms in an adjoining warehouse. Although annual indexes do exist from 1862 onward, they were of little use for the period before 1919, since the actual volumes of documents themselves were no longer maintained in any systematic manner. A number of them could not be consulted or even identified due to water damage.

These conditions offered advantages as well as disadvantages. The lack of order and limited accessibility made it nearly impossible to do the in-depth samples of specific years that have permitted scholars to reconstruct the distribution of wealth among all classes in other cities on the peninsula. These conditions also dictated the decision to set the lower limit of the wealthy elites at the comparatively high level of L. 750,000. That cut-off point provided a sufficiently large pool of wealthy non-nobles, on whom I could gather detailed information and still be assured of completing the survey within the time allotted to me by the Ufficio di Registro and the Archivio di Stato di Torino. Although I lack detailed data on the structure and distribution of wealth within the group of non-nobles with estates valued at between L. 250,000 and L. 750,000, I did record the number of such estates annually in the periods covered in the survey. More seriously, the apparent destruction of all records for the years 1886 through 1900 precluded any analysis of the immediate, short-term consequences of the banking crisis and agricultural depression of the late 1880s and early 1890s.

For the study of aristocratic wealth, however, a survey of all surviving documents greatly reduces the problems of representativeness and the distortions created by exceptional cases, since it provides a much larger pool of estates than one finds by sampling only a limited number of years. Moreover, the neglected state of the records has meant that most of the files still contain not only the official tax forms, but also a host of supportive documents that include marriage contracts, wills, testaments, contracts, and leases. These documents offered more detailed information on the creation, preservation, and transfer of large fortunes over the course of their owners' lives.

LAND REGISTRIES AND OTHER PUBLIC RECORDS

Archivio Centrale dello Stato (Rome)

Ministero dell'Interno: Rapporti dei Prefetti, Alessandria, Cuneo, and Novara (1882–1888)

Archivio di Stato di Torino, Sezione Riunite

Catasto Francese (1812):
Province of Vercelli: Departments of Santhià, Vercelli, Stroppiana, Desana, Livorno, Crescentino, Cigliano, San Germano, Gattinara, Trino, Arborio.
Province of Turin: Communes of Carignano, Poirino, Fiano, Collegno.
Province of Cuneo: Communes of Cardè, Costigliole, La Manta, La Trinità, Carru, Margarita, Morozzo, Moretta, Polonghera, Faule, Bene, Rocca de' Baldi, Vottignasco, Torre di S. Giorgio, Centallo, S. Albano, Magliano, Caraglio, Venzuolo, Villanovetta.

Catasto Rabbini (1850s): Provinces of Novara and Turin.
Senato – Testamenti Pubblicati d'Uffico: 1817–1864
Atti Notarili: Insinuazioni (various years)

Archivio di Stato di Torino: Prima Sezione

Titoli di Nobiltà: 1825–1846
Archivio della Commissione Araldica Piemontese: 1889– 1942
Antonio Manno, "Il patriziato subalpino. Notizie di fatto storiche, genealogiche, feudali, ed araldiche," 26 vols. The first two volumes of this alphabetically organized work were published in Florence in 1895; the remaining twenty-four volumes are in typescript with the original in the Biblioteca Reale di Torino and carbon copies at the Biblioteca Nazionale di Torino and both sections of the Archivio di Stato di Torino.

Archivio Comunale di Torino

Ruolo della tassa sui domestici: 1900, 1907, 1912
Ruolo della tassa sulle vetture private: 1899, 1912, 1913
Ruolo della tassa sulla ricchezza mobile: 1903
Ruolo della tassa sulle aree fabbricabili: 1914
Lista elettorale amministrativa, 1875

FAMILY PAPERS

Archivio di Stato di Torino: Prima Sezione

Alfieri di Sostegno
Asinari di San Marzano
De Genova di Pettinengo
Ferrero d'Ormea
Ferrero Fiesco, Principi di Masserano
Ferrero Ponziglione di Borgo d'Ale
Provana di Sabbione

Archivio di Stato di Torino: Sezione Riunite

Avogadro della Motta e di Collobiano
Broglia di Casalborgone
Compans di Brichanteau
    Archivio di famiglia
    Archivio politico
Costa della Trinità e di Polonghera
D'Harcourt
Doria di Ciriè
Isnardi di Caraglio

Luserna di Rorà
Mazzonis
Pallavicino-Mossi
Sannazzaro
Thaon di Revel
Valperga di Masino
Villa di Villastellone

Biblioteca Provinciale di Torino

Cotti di Ceres
Gazelli di Rossana

Biblioteca Reale di Torino

Scarampi di Villanova

Opera Pia Barolo

Falletti di Barolo

Privately held family archives

Avogadro di Cerrione
Balbiano di Aramengo
Balbo Bertone di Sambuy
Beraudo di Pralormo
Figarolo di Gropello
Incisa della Rocchetta

BOOKS AND ARTICLES

Agnelli, Suzanna, *Vestivamo alla marinara*, Milan, 1975.
Aldrich Jr., Nelson W., *Old Money: The Mythology of America's Upper Class*, New York, 1988.
Alighiero Manacorda, Mario, "Istruzione ed emancipazione della donna nel Risorgimento. Riletture e considerazioni" in Simonetta Soldani (ed.), *L'educazione delle donne. Scuole e modelli di vita femminile nell'Italia dell'Ottocento*, Milan, 1989.
Anderson, Benedict, *Imagined Communities: Reflections on the origin and spread of nationalism*, London, 1991.
Annuario militare del Regno d'Italia (Rome, various years)
Antonelli, Raoul, *Il Ministero della Real Casa dal 1848 al 1946* in Segretariato Generale della Presidenza della Repubblica, Servizio biblioteca e documentazione, *Quaderni di Documentazione*, new series, n. 1, Rome, 1991.

Arnone, Carmelo, *Diritto nobiliare italiano: storia ed ordinamento*, Milan, 1935.

Arrivabene, Charles, *Italy under Victor Emanuel: A Personal Narrative*, 2 vols. London, 1862.

Assereto, G. (ed.), *I Duchi di Galliera, alta finanza, arte e filantropia tra Genova e l'Europa nell'Ottocento*, Genoa, 1991.

Astarita, Tommaso, *The Continuity of Feudal Power: The Caracciolo di Brienza in Spanish Naples*, Cambridge, 1992.

Astuti, Guido, "Gli ordinamenti giuridici degli stati sabaudi" *Storia del Piemonte*, vol. I, Turin, 1961.

Augustine, Dolores L., "Arriving in the Upper Class: The Wealthy Business Elite of Wilhelmine Germany" in Richard J. Evans and David Blackbourn (eds.), *The German Bourgeoisie: Essays on the Social History of the German Middle Class*, London, 1991.

Augustine-Perez, Dolores, "Very Wealthy Businessmen in Imperial Germany," *Journal of Social History*, 22 (1988).

Avogadro della Motta, Emiliano, *Saggio intorno al socialismo e alle dottrine e tendenze socialistiche*, 2 vols., Turin, 1854.

Balani, D., Carpanetto, D., and Turletti, F., "La popolazione dell'Università di Torino nel settecento," *Bollettino Storico-Bibliografico Subalpino*, 76:1 (1978).

Balbo, Cesare, *Pensieri ed esempi*, Florence, 1854.

Baldi Papini, Ubaldo, *La nobiltà e il diritto nobiliare. Saggio sociologico-giuridico*, Florence, 1939.

Banti, Alberto M., "Una fonte per lo studio delle elites ottocentesche: le dichiarazioni di successione dell'Ufficio del Registro," *Rassegna degli Archivi di Stato*, 43:1 (1983).

"Ricchezza e potere. Le dinamiche patrimoniali nella società lucchese del XIX secolo," *Quaderni Storici*, 56 (1984).

Terra e denaro. Una borghesia padana dell'Ottocento, Venice, 1989.

"I proprietari terrieri nell'Italia centro-settentrionale" in Piero Bevilacqua (ed.), *Storia dell'agricoltura italiana*, vol. II, *Uomini e classi*, Venice, 1990.

"Note sulle nobiltà nell'Italia nell'Ottocento," *Meridiana*, 16 (1994).

Storia della borghesia italiana: l'età liberale, Rome, 1996.

Barbagli, Marzio, *Educating for Unemployment: Politics, Labor Markets, and the School System – Italy, 1859–1973*, New York, 1982.

Sotto lo stesso tetto: mutamenti della famiglia in Italia dal XV al XX secolo, Bologna, 1984.

Barberis, Walter, "Continuità aristocratica e tradizione militare nel Piemonte sabaudo," *Società e Storia*, 13 (1981).

Le armi del Principe. La tradizione militare sabauda, Turin, 1988.

"La nobiltà militare sabauda fra corti ed accademie scientifiche: politica e cultura in Piemonte fra sette e ottocento" in *Les noblesses européennes au XIXe siècle*, Rome, 1988.

Barzini, Luigi, *From Caesar to the Mafia: Sketches of Italian Life*, New York, 1971.

Becker, Seymour, *Nobility and Privilege in Late Imperial Russia*, DeKalb, IL., 1985.

Beckett, John, *The Aristocracy of England, 1660–1914*, Oxford, 1986.

Berdahl, Robert M., *The Politics of the Prussian Nobility: The Development of a Conservative Ideology*, Princeton, 1988.

Berti, Domenico, *Cesare Alfieri*, Rome, 1877.

Bertini Frassoni, Count Raoul, *Provvedimenti nobiliari dei Re d'Italia*, Rome, 1968.

Biagioli, Giuliana, "Vicende e fortuna di Ricasoli imprenditore" in *Agricoltura e società nella Maremma Grossetana dell'Ottocento*, Florence, 1980.

Bianchi, Nicomede, *Storia della Monarchia piedmontese dal 1773 al 1861*, vol. I, Turin, 1877.

Bianchi di Vigny, Guerrando, *Storia del fascismo torinese, 1919–1922*, Turin, 1939.

Biscaretti di Ruffia, Carlo, *Il cinquantesimo anniversario della Fiat*, Turin, 1949.

"Origini, nascita e primi sviluppi della Fiat" in *I cinquant'anni della Fiat*, Milan, 1950.

Blum, Jerome, *The End of the Old Order*, Princeton, 1978.

Boggio, Camillo, *Lo sviluppo edilizio di Torino dall'assedio del 1706 alla Rivoluzione francese*, Turin, 1909.

Lo sviluppo edilizio di Torino dalla Rivoluzione Francese alla metà del secolo XIX, Turin, 1918.

Boldrini, M. and Alberti, A., "Il patriziato italiano nelle categorie dirigenti" in *Contributi del laboratorio di statistica dell'Università Cattolica del Sacro Cuore di Milano*, Milan, 1936.

Borbonese, Emilio, *Gli ultimi Azeglio*, Saluzzo, 1891.

Borelli, Giorgio, "Il problema della nobiltà (preliminari di una ricerca storica)," *Economia e Storia*, 17, 4, (1970).

Bourdieu, Pierre, *Distinction: A Social Critique of the Judgment of Taste*, Cambridge, MA, 1984.

Briano, Giorgio, *Il Marchese Cesare Alfieri di Sostegno*, Genoa, 1869.

Brofferio, Angelo, *Storia del Piemonte dal 1814 ai giorni nostri*, Turin, 1851.

Bulferetti, Luigi, "I piemontesi più ricchi negli ultimi cento anni dell'assolutismo sabaudo" in *Studi storici in onore di Gioacchino Volpe*, Florence, 1958.

Bullio, Pieraldo, "Problemi e geografia della risicoltura in Piemonte nei secoli XVII e XVIII," *Annali della Fondazione Luigi Einaudi*, vol. III, 1969.

Bush, M. L., *Noble Privilege*, New York, 1983.

Rich Noble, Poor Noble, New York, 1988.

Calendario Generale del Regno, Turin, various years.

Calendario Generale del Regno d'Italia, Rome, various years.

Cannadine, David, *The Decline and Fall of the British Aristocracy*, New Haven, 1990.

Capra, Carlo, "Nobili, notabili, elites: dal 'modello' francese al caso italiano," *Quaderni Storici*, 13:1 (1978).

Cardoza, Anthony L., "Elites patrimoniali e proprietà urbana a Torino: 1856–1914" *Storia Urbana*, n. 68 (1996).

"Ennoblement in Liberal Italy" in *Les noblesses européennes au XIX siècle*, Rome, 1988.

"An Officer and a Gentleman: The Piedmontese Nobility and the Military in Liberal Italy" in *Esercito e città dall'Unità agli anni trenta*, Perugia, 1989.

"La ricchezza e i ricchi a Torino 1862–1912," *Società e Storia*, 58 (1995).

Carew Hunt, R. N., "Cavour e Francois Marce (1859)" in *Miscellanea cavouriana*, Turin, 1964.

Carpi, Leandro, *L'Italia vivente. Aristocrazia di nascita e del denaro, borghesia, clero, burocrazia*, Milan, 1878.

Carutti, Domenico, *Storia della diplomazia della corte di Savoia*, vol. IV, Turin, 1880.

Storia della Corte di Savoia durante la Rivoluzione e l'Impero francese, Turin, 1892.

Cassa di Risparmio di Torino nel suo primo centenario, 1827–1927, Turin, 1927.

Castronovo, Valerio, "Formazione e sviluppo del ceto imprenditoriale laniero e cotoniero piemontese," *Rivista Storica Italiana*, 78 (1966).

Giovanni Agnelli, Turin, 1977.

Storia del Piemonte, Turin, 1977.

Grandi e piccoli borghesi. La via italiana al capitalismo, Bari, 1988.

Castronovo, Valerio, and d'Orsi, Angelo, *Torino*, Bari, 1987.

Ceva, Lucio, "Forze armate e società civile dal 1861 al 1887" in *Atti del L Congresso di storia del Risorgimento italiano*, Rome, 1982.

Charle, Christophe, *Les élites de la république (1880–1900)*, Paris, 1987.

"Noblesse et élites en France au début du XX-siècle" in *Les noblesses européennes aux XIXe siècle*, Rome, 1988.

Chaussinand-Nogaret, G., *Une histoire des élites, 1700–1848*, Paris, 1975.

Chevallard, Carlo and Frova, Pietro, *Cronaca di Torino. 2000 anni di date, avvenimenti e curiosità*, Turin, 1972.

Chiaramonte, Umberto, *Economia e società in provincia di Novara (1919–1943)*, Milan, 1987.

Cian, Vittorio, "Vita e coltura nel periodo albertino. Dal carteggio edito ed inedito di P.A. Paravia," *Atti della R. Accademia delle Scienze di Torino*, 65 (1929–30).

Cibrario, Luigi, *Notizie genealogiche di famiglie nobili degli antichi stati della monarchia di Savoia*, Turin, 1866.

Cobban, Alfred, *The Social Interpretation of the French Revolution*, Cambridge, 1964.

Cognasso, Franceso, *Storia di Torino*, Turin, 1934.

"Nobiltà e borghesia a Torino nel Risorgimento," *Bollettino Storico-bibliografico Subalpino*, 60:1–2 (1962).

Life and Culture in Piedmont, Turin, 1970.

Cohen, Abner, *Two-Dimensional Man: An Essay on the Anthropology of Power and Symbolism in Complex Society*, Berkeley, 1974.

Confederazione Nazionale Agraria, *Atti del II Congresso Agrario*, Bologna, 1911.

Coppini, P. R., "Aristocrazia e finanza in Toscana nel XIX secolo" in *Les noblesses européennes au XIXe siècle*, Rome, 1988.

Costa di Beauregard, C. A., *Un uomo d'altri tempi*, Turin, 1897.

Covato, Carmela, "Educata ad educare: Ruolo materno ed itinerari formativi" in Soldani (ed.), *L'educazione delle donne. Scuole e modelli di vita femminile nell'Italia dell'Ottocento*, Milan, 1989.

Cronistoria dell'Accademia Filarmonica di Torino nel primo centenario della sua fondazione, Turin, 1915.

Dagna, Paola, "Un diplomatico ed economista del Settecento: Carlo Baldassarre Perrone di San Martino (1718–1802)" in *Figure e gruppi della classe dirigente piemontese nel Risorgimento*, Turin, 1968.

Daumard, A., "Wealth and Affluence in France" in W. D. Rubinstein (ed.), *Wealth and the Wealthy in the Modern World*, London, 1980.

Davico, Rosalba, *"Peuple" et notables (1750–1816). Essai sur l'Ancien Régime et la Révolution en Piemont*, Turin, 1981.

Davis, James C., "The Decline of the Venetian Nobility as a Ruling Class," *The Johns Hopkins University Studies in Historical and Political Science*, series 80, n. 2 (1962).

Davis, John, "The Napoleonic Era in Southern Italy: An Ambiguous Legacy?" in *Proceedings of the British Academy*, Oxford, 1993.

"Remapping Italy's Path to the Twentieth Century," *Journal of Modern History*, 66:2 (1994).

D'Aristo, Vico, *Quando ero in Collegio*, Milan, 1928.

D'Azeglio, Massimo, *Things I Remember (I miei ricordi)* translated by E. R. Vincent, London, 1966.

De Rosa, Gabriele, *Storia del movimento cattolico in Italia. Dalla Restaurazione all età giolittiana*, Bari, 1966.

Del Negro, Piero, *Esercito, stato, società. Saggi di storia militare*, Bologna, 1979.

Di Gregorio, P., "Nobiltà e nobilitazione in Sicilia nel lungo Ottocento," *Meridiana*, 16 (1994).

di Robilant, Luigi Nicolis, *Un prete di ieri: Il canonico Stanislao Gazelli di Rossana e S. Sebastiano*, Turin, 1901.

Donati, Claudio, *L'idea di nobiltà in Italia, secoli XIV-XVIII*, Bari, 1988.

Donna d'Oldenico, Giovanni, *L'Accademia di Agricoltura di Torino dal 1785 ad oggi*, Turin, 1978.

Elenco dei nobili caduti, decorati, Turin, 1918.

Ellero, Pietro, *La tirannide borghese*, Bologna, 1879.

Falco, Giancarlo, "L'organizzazione bancaria cattolica in Piemonte, 1909–1919. Contributo alla documentazione," *Bollettino Storico-bibliografico subalpino*, 68:3–4 (1969).

Falletti, Pio Carlo, *Saggi*, Palermo, 1885.

Farneti, Paolo, "La classe politica della Destra e della Sinistra" in Isabella Zanni Rosiello (ed.), *Gli apparati statali dall'Unità al fascismo*, Bologna, 1976.

Ferrero, Guglielmo, *The Gamble: Bonaparte in Italy 1796–1797*, London, 1961.

Ferrone, Vincenzo, "L'apparato militare sabaudo tra l'antico regime e l'età na-
poleonica," *La nuova atlante e i lumi. Scienze e politica nel Piemonte di Vittorio
Amedeo III*, Turin, 1988.

Frassati, Luciana, *Torino come era: 1880–1915*, Losanna, 1958.

Frigo, Daniela, *Principe, ambasciatori e "jus gentium": l'amminstrazione della politica estera nel Piemonte del Settecento*, Rome, 1991.

Furet, François, *Interpreting the French Revolution*, Cambridge, 1981.

Gabaleone di Salmour, R., *Le riforme ed il patriziato*, Turin, 1847.

Gallenga, Antonio Carlo Napoleone, *Country Life in Piedmont*, London, 1858.

Genta, Enrico, "Il concetto di nobiltà: problemi ricorrenti," *Rivista Araldica*,
74:2–30 (1976).

Senato e senatori di Piemonte nel secolo XVIII, Turin, 1983.

"Eclettismo giuridico della Restaurazione" in *Studi in memoria di Mario E.
Viora*, Rome, 1990.

Gerth, H. H. and Mills, C. Wright, *From Max Weber: Essays in Sociology*, New
York, 1958.

Gerbore, Pietro, *Dame e cavalieri del Re*, Milan, 1955.

Giacomelli, Alfeo, "La dinamica della nobiltà bolognese nel XVIII secolo" in
Famiglie senatorie e istituzioni cittadine a Bologna nel Settecento, Bologna, 1980.

Girelli, Angela Maria, *Le terre dei Chigi ad Ariccia (secolo XIX)*, Milan, 1983.

Guasco, M., *Fascisti e cattolici. I cattolici alessandrini di fronte al fascismo*, Milan,
1978.

Hamburg, G. M., *Politics of the Russian Nobility, 1881–1905*, New Brunswick,
1984.

Hansen, Edward C. and Parrish, Timothy C., "Elites versus the State: Towards
an Anthropological Contribution to the Study of Hegemonic Power in
Capitalist Society" in George E. Marcus (ed.), *Elites: Ethnographic Issues*,
Albuquerque, NM, 1983.

Harris, Jose and Thane, Pat, "British and European Bankers, 1880–1914: an
'aristocratic bourgeoisie'" in P. Thane, Roderick Floud, and Geoffrey
Crossick (eds.), *The Power of the Past: Essays for Eric Hobsbawm*, Cambridge,
1984.

Istituto Centrale di Statistica, *Il valore della lira dal 1861 al 1965*, Rome, 1966.

Istituto Nazionale dell'Economia Agraria, *Inchiesta sulla piccola proprietà coltiva-
trice formatasi nel dopoguerra*, vol. X, Eugenio, Turbati, *Piemonte*, Rome,
1934.

Istituto Sociale di Torino, *L'Istituto Sociale nel suo settantennio, 1881–1951*,
Turin, 1951.

Jocteau, Gian Carlo, "Un censimento della nobiltà italiana," *Meridiana*, 16
(1994).

Kaelble, Hartmut "Borghesia francese e borghesia tedesca. 1870–1914" in
J. Kocka (ed.), *Borghesie europee dell'Ottocento* (Italian translation, A. Banti
ed.), Venice, 1989.

Lamont, Michèle, *Money, Morals, and Manners*, Chicago, 1992.

Lebrun, Richard A., *Joseph de Maistre: An Intellectual Militant*, Montreal, 1988.

Levi, Fabio, *L'idea del buon padre. Il lento declino di un'industria familiare*, Turin, 1984.

Levi, Giovanni, "Strutture famigliari e rapporti sociali in una comunità piemontese fra Sette e Ottocento" in *Storia d'Italia, Annali*, vol. 1, *Dal feudalismo al capitalismo*, Turin, 1978.

Levra, Umberto, "Torino tra primazia risorgimentale e apologia dinnastica" in his *Fare gli italiani. Memoria e celebrazione del Risorgimento*, Turin, 1992.

Licini, Stefania, *Milano nell'800: élites e patrimoni*, Bologna, 1994.

Lieven, Dominic, *The Aristocracy in Europe, 1815–1914*, London, 1992.

Loriga, S., "L'identità militare come aspirazione sociale: nobili di provincia e nobili di corte nel Piemonte della seconda metà del Settecento," *Quaderni Storici*, 2 (August 1990).

Lovera, C and Rinieri, I., *Clemente Solaro della Margarita*, 3 vols., Turin, 1931.

Lucas, Colin, "Nobles, Bourgeois, and the Origins of the French Revolution," *Past and Present*, 60 (August 1973).

Lyttelton, Adrian, "Landlords, Peasants, and the Limits of Liberalism" in John Davis (ed.), *Gramsci and Italy's Passive Revolution*, London, 1979.
"The middle classes in Liberal Italy" in J. Davis and P. Ginsborg (eds.), *Society and Politics in the Age of the Risorgimento. Essays in Honor of Denis Mack Smith*, Cambridge, 1991.

Mack Smith, Dennis, *Cavour*, London, 1985.
Italy and its Monarchy, New Haven, 1989.

Macry, Paolo, *Ottocento: Famiglia, élites e patrimoni a Napoli*, Turin, 1988.

Maggia, G., *Lotte sociali e lotte politiche nel Canavese nel primo dopoguerra*, Turin, 1973.

Malafakis, Edward E., *Agrarian Reform and Peasant Revolution in Spain*, New Haven, 1970.

Malatesta, Alberto (ed.), *Enciclopedia biografica e bibliografica italiana*, series 43, *Ministri, deputati e senatori dal 1848 al 1922*, 3 vols., Milan, 1930.

Maldini Chiarito, Daniela, "Trasmissione di valori e educazione familiare: le lettere al figlio di Costanza D'Azeglio," *Passato e Presente*, 13 (1987).

Manning, Roberta Thompson, *The Crisis of the Old Order in Russia: Gentry and Government*, Princeton, 1982.

Manno, Antonio, *Il patriziato subalpino. Notizie di fatto storiche, genealogiche, feudali ed araldiche*, 2 vols., Florence, 1895.

Mantegazza, N., *Guida alle case della città e sobborghi di Torino*, Turin, 1856.

Manzone, Beniamo, *Il Conte Moffa di Lisio*, Turin, 1882.

Marazzi, Alessandro, *1700 anniversario dell'Accademia Filarmonica. Notizie storico-artistiche sul palazzo*, Turin, 1984.

Marchisio, Silvia, "Ideologia e problemi dell'economia familiare nelle lettere della nobiltà piemontese (XVII–XVIII)," *Bollettino Storico-bibliografico Subalpino*, 83:1 (1985).

Masi, E., *Asti e gli Alfieri nei ricordi della Villa di San Martino*, Florence, 1903.

Massa Piergiovanni, Paola, "Eredità, acquisti e rendite: genesi e gestione del patrimonio dei Duchi di Galliera (1828–1888)" in *I Duchi di Galliera. Alta finanza, arte e filantropia tra Genova e l'Europa nell'Ottocento*, vol. 1, Genoa, 1992.

Mayer, Arno J., *The Persistence of the Old Regime: Europe to the Great War*, New York, 1981.

Mazzonis, Filippo, "Usi della buona società e questioni d'onore. Etichetta e vertenze cavalleresche nei manuali per ufficiali" in *Esercito e città dall'Unità agli anni trenta*, Perugia, 1989.

McDonogh, Gary Wray, *Good Families of Barcelona*, Princeton, 1986.

Mension-Rigau, Eric, *Aristocrates et grands bourgeois. Education, traditions, valeurs*, Paris, 1994.

Meriggi, Marco, "La borghesia italiana" in Jurgen Kocka (ed.), *Borghese europee dell'Ottocento* (Italian translation, A. Banti, ed.), Venice, 1989.

"Lo 'spirito di associazione' nella Milano dell'Ottocento (1815–1890)," *Quaderni Storici*, 77: 26:2 (1991).

Milano borghese: Circoli ed élites nell'Ottocento, Venice, 1992.

Missori, Mario, *Governi, alte cariche dello stato e prefetti del Regno d'Italia*, Rome, 1973.

Gerarchie e statuti del P.N.F. Gran consiglio, Direttorio nazionale, Federazioni provinciali: quadri e biografie, Rome, 1986.

Mola, Alessandro, *Storia dell'amministrazione provinciale di Cuneo dall'unità al fascismo*, Turin, 1971.

Monaco, Michèle, *Clemente Solaro della Margarita. Pensiero ed azione di un cattolico di fronte al Risorgimento italiano*, Turin, 1955.

Monale, Bianca, "Lineamenti generali per la storia dell'*Armonia* dal 1848 al 1857," *Rassegna Storica del Risorgimento*, 43 (1956).

Montroni, Giovanni, *Gli uomini del Re: la nobiltà napoletana nell'Ottocento*, Catanzaro, 1996.

Moroni, Andrea, "Le ricchezze dei Corsini. Struttura patrimoniale e vicende familiari tra sette e ottocento," *Società e Storia*, 32 (1986).

Nada, Narcisio, *Roberto D'Azeglio*, vol. I, Rome, 1965.

Nitti, Francesco Saverio, *Scritti di economia e finanza*, vol. 1, *La ricchezza dell'Italia*, Bari, 1966.

Notario, Paola, *La vendita dei beni nazionali in Piemonte nel periodo napoleonico (1800–1814)*, Milan, 1980.

Ottolenghi, Leone, *La vita e i tempi di Giacinto Provana di Collegno*, Turin, 1882.

Passerin d'Entreves, Ettore, *La giovinezza di Cesare Balbo*, Florence, 1940.

Pedlow, Gregory W., *The Survival of the Hessian Nobility, 1770–1870*, Princeton, 1988.

Perrero, Domenico, *I Reali di Savoia nell'esiglio*, Turin, 1898.

Perticone, Giacomo, "Il regime costituzionale nel primo decennio dello Statuto," *Rassegna Storica del Risorgimento*, 39 (1952).

Pescosolido, Guido, *Terra e nobiltà. I Borghese, secoli XVIII e XIX*, Rome, 1979.

Petersen, Jens, "Der italienische Adel von 1861 bis 1946" in H. U. Wehler (ed.), *Europaischer Adel, 1750–1950*, Gottingen, 1990.

Petitti di Roreto, Carlo Ilarione, *Opere scelte* (ed.) G. M. Bravo, Turin, 1969.

Petrusewicz, Marta, *Latifondo. Economia morale e vita materiale in una periferia dell'Ottocento*, Venice, 1989.

Piergiovanni, Paola Massa, "Eredità, acquisti e rendite: genesi e gestione del patrimonio dei Duchi di Galliera (1828–1888)" in G. Assereto (ed.), *I Duchi di Galliera, alta finanza, arte e filantropia tra Genova e l'Europa nell'Ottocento*, Genoa, 1991.

Pinelli, Ferdinando, *Storia militare del Piemonte in continuazione di quella del Saluzzo, cioè dalla pace d'Acuisgrana sino ai di nostri*, Turin, 1854.

Prato, Giuseppe, *La vita economica in Piemonte a mezzo il secolo XVIII*, Turin, 1908.

L'evoluzione agricola nel secolo XVIII e le cause economiche dei moti del 1792–1798 in Piemonte, Turin, 1909.

Fatte e dottrine economiche alla vigilia del 1848. L'Associazione agraria subalpina e Camillo Cavour, Turin, 1920.

Predari, Francesco, *I primi vagiti della libertà italiana in Piemonte*, Milan, 1861.

Primi quindici anni della Fiat. Verbali dei Consigli di amministrazione, 1899–1915, Milan, 1987.

Pugliese, S., *Due secoli di vita agricola. Produzione e valore dei terreni, contratti agrari, salari e prezzi nel Vercellese dei secoli XVIII e XIX*, Turin, 1908.

"Produzione, salari e redditi in una regione risicola italiana," *Annali di Economia*, vol. III, 1926–27, Milan, 1927.

Quazza, Guido, *Le riforme in Piemonte nella prima metà del Settecento*, 2 vols., Modena, 1957.

Raumer, Frederic von, *Italy and the Italians*, London, 1840.

Real Collegio Carlo Alberto di Moncalieri. Nel LXXV anno della fondazione, 1838–1913, Turin, 1913.

Real Collegio Carlo Alberto di Moncalieri, 1838–1938, Turin, 1938.

Retallack, James, *Notables of the Right: The Conservative Party and Political Mobilization in Germany 1876–1918*, London, 1988.

Ricci, Raffaello, ed., *Memorie della Baronessa Olimpia Savio*, 2 vols., Milan, 1911.

Ricuperati, Giuseppe, *I volti della pubblica felicità. Storiografia e politica nel Piemonte settecentesco*, Turin, 1989.

Ricuperati, Giuseppe and Carpinetti, Dino, *Italy in the Age of Reason, 1685–1789*, London and New York, 1987.

Roberts, J. M., "Lombardy" in Albert Goodwin, ed., *The European Nobility in the Eighteenth Century*, London, 1953.

Robinson, Michael, *Naples and the Neapolitan Opera*, Oxford, 1972.

Rodolico, Niccolò, *Carlo Alberto. Negli anni di regno, 1831–1843*, Florence, 1936.

Carlo Alberto negli anni 1843–1849, Florence, 1943.

Storia del parlamento italiano, Palermo, 1963.

Rogier, F. L., *La R. Accademia Militare di Torino. Note storiche, 1816–1870*, 2 vols., Turin, 1916.

Romanelli, Raffaele, "Political Debate, Social History, and the Italian *Borghesia*: Changing Perspectives in Historical Research," *Journal of Modern History*, 63:4 (1991)

"Famiglia e patrimonio nei comportamenti della nobiltà borghese dell'Ottocento" in Lucia Frattarelli Fischer and Maria Teresa Lazzarini (eds.), *Palazzo De Larderel a Livorno*, Milan, 1992..

"La nobiltà nella costituzione dell'Italia contemporanea," *Storia Amministrazione Costituzione*, 3 (1995).

"Urban patricians and 'bourgeois' society: a study of wealthy elites in Florence, 1862–1914," *Journal of Modern Italian Studies*, 1:1 (1995).

Romano, Roberto, *L'industria cotoniera lombarda dall'Unità al 1914*, Milan, 1992.

Romano, Sergio, "Le nobiltà, lo stato, e le relazioni internazionali" in *Les noblesses européennes au XIXe siècle*, Rome, 1988.

Romeo, Rosario, *Cavour e il suo tempo (1810–1842)*, vol. I, Bari, 1977.

Dal Piemonte sabaudo all'Italia liberale, Turin, 1963.

"Una iniziativa costituzionale del maresciallo La Tour nel novembre 1847" in *Civiltà del Piemonte. Studi in onore di Renzo Gandolfo nel suo settantacinquesimo compleanno*, Turin, 1975.

Rosso, Claudio, *Una burocrazia di antico regime: I segretari di stato dei Duchi di Savoia*, Turin, 1992.

Rumi, Giorgio, "La politica nobiliare del Regno d'Italia" in *Les noblesses européennes aux XIXe siècle*, Rome, 1988.

Salvadori, Massimo L. , *Il movimento cattolico a Torino 1911–1915*, Turin, 1969.

Sauli d'Igliano, Ludovico, *Reminiscenze della propria vita*, edited by G. Ottolenghi, 2 vols., Rome, 1908.

Segretariato Generale del Senato, *Elenchi storici e statistici dei senatori del Regno, 1848 al 1 gennaio 1937*, Rome, 1937.

Sereni, Emilio, *La questione agraria nella rinascita nazionale italiana*, Turin, 1946.

Il capitalismo nelle campagne (1860–1900), Turin, 1947.

Serpieri, Arrigo, *La guerra e le classi rurali italiane*, Bari, 1930.

Simmel, Georg, "The Nobility (1908)" in *On Individuality and Social Forms: Selected Writings*, Chicago, 1971.

Snowden, Frank M., "The City of the Sun: Red Cerignola, 1900–15" in Ralph Gibson and Martin Blinkhorn (eds.), *Landownership and Power in Modern Europe*, London, 1991.

Soave, Sergio, "Las nascita della Democrazia Cristiana" in Beppe Manfredi, (ed.), *Il partito cristiano. D.C. e mondo cattolico in Piemonte 1900–1975*, Turin, 1978.

Società Camillo di Cavour, *Un secolo di vita del Whist. Annali della nostra società dal 1841 al 1940*, Turin, 1941.

Solaro della Margarita, Clemente, *Memorandum storico-politico*, Turin, 1852.

Gli avvedimenti politici, Turin, 1853.

Questioni di Stato, Turin, 1854.

L'uomo di Stato, indirizzato al governo della cosa pubblica, Turin, 1863—64.

Souvenirs historiques de la marquise Constance d'Azeglio née Alfieri tirés de sa correspondance avec son fils Emmanuel, avec l'additon de quelques lettres de son mari le marquis Roberto d'Azeglio de 1835 à 1861, Turin, 1884.

Spring, David (ed.), *European Landed Elites in the Nineteenth Century*, Baltimore, 1977.

Stone, Lawrence and Fawtier Stone, Jean C., *An Open Elite? England 1540—1880*, Oxford, 1986.

Stumpo, Enrico, *Finanza e stato moderno nel Piemonte del Seicento*, Rome, 1979.

"I ceti dirigenti in Italia nell'età moderna. Due modelli diversi: nobiltà piemontese e patriziato toscano" in Amelio Tagliaferri (ed.), *I ceti dirigenti in Italia in età moderna e contemporanea*, Udine, 1984.

Symcox, Geoffrey, *Victor Amadeus II: Absolutism in the Savoyard State 1675—1730*, Berkeley, 1983.

Tabboni, Simonetta, *Il Real Collegio Carlo Alberto di Moncalieri. Un caso di socializzazione della classe dirigente italiana dell'800*, Milan, 1984.

Testa, Gian Albino, "La strategie di una famiglia imprenditoriale fra otto e novecento," *Bollettino Storico-bibliografico Subalpino*, 79:2 (1981).

Thayer, John, A., *Italy and the Great War: Politics and Culture, 1870—1915*, Madison, 1964.

Thayer, William Roscoe, *The Life and Times of Cavour*, 2 vols., Boston, 1911.

Thompson, F. M. L. , *English Landed Society in the Nineteenth Century*, London, 1963.

Torino, Turin, 1881.

Traniello, Francesco, "Le origini del movimento cattolico in Piemonte" in Beppe Manfredi (ed.), *Il partito cristiano. D.C. e mondo cattolico in Piemonte 1900—1975*, Turin, 1978.

Tuninetti, Dante Maria, *Squadrismo, squadristi piemontesi*, Rome, 1942.

Vaccarino, Giuseppe, "La classe politica piemontese dopo Marengo nelle note segrete di Augusto Hus," *Bollettino Storico-bibliografico Subalpino*, 51 (1953).

Villani, Pasquale, "Ricerche sulla proprietà fondiaria e sul regime fondiario nel Lazio" in *Annuario dell'Istituto storico italiano per l'età moderna e contemporanea*, vol. XII, Rome, 1960.

Villari, Luigi, *Italian Life in Town and Country*, London, 1912.

Visceglia, Maria A, *Il bisogno di eternità: I comportamenti aristocratici a Napoli in età moderna*, Naples, 1988.

Visceglia, Maria A. (ed.), *Signori, patrizi, cavalieri nell'età moderna*, Bari, 1992.

von Raumer, Frederic, *Italy and the Italians*, London, 1840.

Whittam, John, *The Politics of the Italian Army, 1861—1918*, London, 1977.

Woolf, S. J., *A History of Italy, 1700—1860*, London, 1979.

"Some notes on the cost of palace building in Turin in the 18th century," *Atti e Rassegna tecnica della Società Ingegneri e Architetti in Torino*, 15:9 (1961).

"Studi sulla nobiltà piemontese nell'epoca dell'assolutismo," *Memorie dell'Accademia delle scienze di Torino*, series 4a, n. 5, Turin, 1963.

"Economic Problems of the Nobility in the Early Modern Period: the Example of Piedmont," *Economic History Review*, 17 (1964).

Zamagni, Vera, "The Rich in a Late Industrialiser" in W. D. Rubinstein (ed.), *Wealth and the Wealthy in the Modern World*, London, 1980.

Zanetti, D. E., *La demografia del patriziato milanese nei secoli XVII, XVIII, XIX*, Pavia, 1972.

"The Patriziato of Milan from the domination of Spain to the unification of Italy: an outline of the social and demographic history," *Social History*, 2 (1977).

Zangheri, Renato, "La proprietà in Italia durante gli anni francesi," *Studi Storici*, 20:1 (1979).

Zucchi, M., "I moti del 1821 nelle memorie inedite di Alessandro Saluzzo" in *La Rivoluzione del 1821, Studi e documenti raccolti da T. Rosi e C. P. Demagistris*, Turin, 1927.

Zussini, Alessandro, *Luigi Caissotti di Chiusano e il movimento cattolico dal 1896 al 1915*, Turin, 1965.

INDEX

CAMBRIDGE STUDIES IN ITALIAN HISTORY AND CULTURE

Printed in the United States
131840LV00005B/25/A